EXPERIMENTAL WRITING IN COMPOSITION

PITTSBURGH SERIES IN COMPOSITION, LITERACY, AND CULTURE

David Bartholomae and Jean Ferguson Carr, Editors

EXPERIMENTAL WRITING
IN COMPOSITION

AESTHETICS AND PEDAGOGIES

PATRICIA SUZANNE SULLIVAN

University of Pittsburgh Press

Published by the University of Pittsburgh Press, Pittsburgh, Pa., 15260
Copyright © 2012, University of Pittsburgh Press
All rights reserved
Manufactured in the United States of America
Printed on acid-free paper
10 9 8 7 6 5 4 3 2 1

Library of Congress Cataloging-in-Publication Data

Sullivan, Patricia Suzanne.
  Experimental writing in composition : aesthetics and pedagogies / Patricia
Suzanne Sullivan.
    p. cm. — (Pittsburgh series in composition, literacy, and culture)
  ISBN 978-0-8229-6208-3 (pbk.)
  1. English language—Rhetoric—Study and teaching (Higher) 2. Literature,
Experimental. I. Title.
  PE1404.S857 2012
  808'.0420711—dc23   2012022371

To my sister, Catherine, who shared her writing with
me and wanted to know what I really thought.

CONTENTS

ACKNOWLEDGMENTS

It isn't possible to thank everyone I need and want to thank, but I will attempt to do so. I would like to thank some of my colleagues and friends who first explicitly welcomed me into the field of composition when they invited me to contribute to proposals for a panel for the Conference on College Composition and Communication: Angie Farkas, Jean Grace, and Linda Huff. Keely Bowers, Juli Parrish, Lisa Schwartz, Chris Warnick, Mari Pena-Jordan Xenakes, and many others provided smart conversation and friendly, often humorous support.

Jonathan Arac, Dave Bartholomae, Kathryn Flannery, Catherine Gammon, Joseph Harris, Paul Kameen, John Poulakos, and Mariolina Salvatore were models for me as thoughtful teachers, curious intellectuals, rigorous readers, and kind colleagues. I especially would like to thank Jim Seitz for being an amazing teacher, administrator, reader, writer, mentor, colleague, and friend and for holding hands with me and chanting the alphabet when it was about the most awkward thing for the both of us to do in a roomful of K–12 teachers. In other words, thanks to Jim for being game.

Other colleagues and friends who talked with me, read my work, listened as I discussed a student text, shared ideas, or otherwise made my professional life immeasurably richer include Nicole Aljoe, Beth Britt, Kimberly Brown, Chris Gallagher, Laura Green, Stephanie Jirard, Kathleen Kelly, Marina Leslie, Guy Rotella, Kim Van Alkemade, and Susan Wall. Susan and Chris especially pushed my thinking and my writing in ways I always wanted to live up to (even when I didn't know how). Numerous graduate students at Northeastern University kept me on my toes while I thought through the arguments in this book. Special thanks in particular to Emily Artiano, Michael Dedek, and Stephanie Loomis Pappas.

My professional life has been wonderfully full of excellent friends, colleagues, and graduate students, but I have a particular fondness for undergraduates, especially the first-year writing students I've taught almost every year since I first started teaching. There are so many of them, but the three writers whose work I engage in this book—Cecelia Rodriguez, Anthony Portis, and Bernadette Loftus—helped me to realize the crucial role that humility and listening play in my teaching.

Thanks also to Dave Bartholomae, Jean Ferguson Carr, and Joshua Shanholtzer at the University of Pittsburgh Press. The Pittsburgh Series in Composition, Literacy, and Culture rocks. Thanks also to the two anonymous reviewers at the University of Pittsburgh Press for smart, incisive, and extensive comments.

Finally, very few things happen in my life without the rest of the Sullivans finding out and offering their two cents. I am grateful to Joseph, Thom, and Stephen, who gave me books, places to stay, fishing (and guitar) lessons, and who generally helped toughen me up for Writing Program Administration (WPA) work in ways they never could have anticipated. And for my parents, Joseph and Patricia, who let me read whatever I wanted, stay up as late as I wanted, and kept me well supplied with notebooks, pens, typewriters, and unconditional love, thank you with all my heart. Not least, thank you to my sister, Catherine, to whom this book is dedicated, for showing me at a very young age what a "real" writer does.

EXPERIMENTAL WRITING IN COMPOSITION

INTRODUCTION

AESTHETICS AND PEDAGOGIES

In *Experimental Writing in Composition: Aesthetics and Pedagogies,* I critically examine the role that theories of "aesthetics" (variously defined) play in major composition pedagogies. Scholars in composition and rhetoric such as Peter Elbow, Wendy Bishop, Winston Weathers, Lillian Bridwell-Bowles, Patricia Bizzell, Geoffrey Sirc, Gregory Ulmer, Cynthia Selfe, and Jeffrey Rice (among others) argue for the importance of teaching experimental and alternative styles of writing—including mixed genres, fragmented texts, collages, experiments in grammar, and various multimedia texts—alongside or instead of the traditional forms and genres employed in college composition classes, such as five-paragraph themes, personal essays, literary essays, argument essays, and research papers. Arguments for experimental writing, whatever pedagogical project they serve (for example, expressivist, multicultural, postmodern), claim to critique the limits of normative forms of writing associated with academic discourse by invoking the liberating and critical power of art. Though the lines dividing different pedagogical projects can be blurry and shifting, in general these arguments claim that through the "freer" aesthetic space created by experimental and alternative discourses, students may be allowed to express their unique individualities, articulate marginal or underrepresented social realities, and/or critique the limits of dominant sociopolitical discourses and the institutions that perpetuate these discourses.

Historically, scholarship that addresses innovative or alternative forms, styles, or discourses has tended to argue why and how such innovative or alternative texts should be taught in undergraduate writing classrooms. These arguments and the pedagogies that follow from them suggest explicitly or implicitly not only that our pedagogical practices should be changed, but also that the values and goals of the field of composition and rhetoric need to be revised. In addressing these claims about practices and goals, I do not argue for teaching experimental writing in composition classrooms; nor do I aim to explain how to teach such texts (though I do reflect on how my experiences teaching such texts have come to inform my current thinking about composition pedagogy). Instead, I use aesthetic theories, particularly those of various avant-gardes, to critically examine those arguments in composition and rhetoric in order to reflect on how the field articulates the dialectics that shape it: between individual autonomy and alienation, the individual and the social (whether represented by social groups or institutions), freedom and social determinism, knowledge and art, determinate and indeterminate judgment, tradition and innovation, and between school and the "real world." I also share lessons learned from histories of the avant-garde: the current viability of concepts of avant-garde art; the story of its successes and failures in its attempt to bring together art and everyday praxis; its claims (and the historical limits of those claims) to employ innovation for sociopolitical critique and transformation; and finally, the ways in which avant-garde art has challenged, or significantly altered or been absorbed by, art institutions and commodity culture.

While the discourses of aesthetics underlying pedagogies of experimental writing may generate new possibilities, they also generate new problems (and refigure old ones) for the field of composition and rhetoric and the teaching of writing. These problems involve the way we construct and position our students, the forms and modes we teach, the ways in which we evaluate the work of student writers, the roles that we imagine writing might play in relation to other media, and how we construct the field's ongoing struggle with its institutional and disciplinary locations. Thus, *Experimental Writing in Composition* is as much an investigation of conventional composition as it is an investigation of unconventional composition.

When I suggest that we reflect on the dialectics that shape the field of composition and rhetoric, I mean by "dialectic" the rhetorical structure created by the construction of a hierarchical relationship of mutually defining terms understood to be oppositional. In the classical tradition, the point of reference here is the sophistical concept of *dissoi logoi:* two (contrasting) words. The rhetorical technique of *dissoi logoi* entailed producing contrary arguments on an issue, with the victor often demonstrating his or her rhetorical prowess by proving the weaker term or argument to be the stronger. Thus, one might argue, for example, that when art is opposed to knowledge in the context of education, art should be the goal, not knowledge. In this rhetorical opposition, knowledge is more commonly understood as the dominant term; therefore, an argument for art takes up the challenge of making the weaker term appear stronger. In composition, for example, academic writing, defined in opposition to creative writing, assumes the dominant position; therefore, an argument that would call for the teaching of creative texts in required composition classes would attempt to make the weaker argument appear to be the stronger. Or, for a broader example, advocates of experimental writing give precedence to innovation over tradition in the dialectical relationship of the two terms. Historically, rhetorical education has preferred tradition over innovation, continuity over discontinuity, dominant discourses over emerging discourses.[1]

In my brief list of dialectics relevant to arguments for experimental writing in composition, those who advocate changing pedagogical practices and goals in classrooms variously claim that innovative texts can help students reclaim their individuality in the face of deterministic social discourses, free them from socially oppressive genres, help them create art as a way of thinking differentiated from epistemic rhetorics, and help them give meaning and expression to their experiences and knowledge outside of academic concerns.

Conventional Composition	Experimental Composition
Traditional/conventional writing	Innovative/unconventional writing
Social	Individual
Constraint	Freedom
Determined (textual production)	Free (textual production)
Alienation	Autonomy
Knowledge/epistemic	Art/aesthetic
School	Real world/everyday life

Of course, the dialectical relationships of the above list are not rigid or natural. Indeed, as I will show later, arguments for experimental writing will variously make the case for the individual over the social or the social over the individual. Additionally, such arguments often attempt to redefine apparent dialectical relationships, reject them (often by proving the falsity of the opposition), or transcend them. Indeed, it is both a rhetorical and historical effect that constructs a dialectical relationship. For example, in the dialectic that opposes academic writing to personal writing—giving preference to one over the other—several compositionists (such as Patricia Bizzell) argue that the opposition is false and suggest a third position made possible by the synthesis of the two types of writing into a hybrid or mixed academic discourse. Similarly, vis-à-vis arguments for teaching the production of multimedia texts in composition classrooms, in the dialectic that opposes traditional writing to innovative or unconventional writing, some compositionists resolve the dialectic by giving preference to tradition; whereas others resolve the dialectic by giving preference to innovation. Furthermore, some of the arguments for multimedia composition refuse the academic/personal discourse dialectic and instead situate themselves in opposition to the dominance of print or alphabetic literacy.

Most arguments for experimental writing in composition, however, rather than transcend or synthesize, employ these dialectics in the service of a range of broad projects that include reclaiming the writer as an autonomous creative and expressive subject; using experimental writing as a means of sociopolitical critique in the context of ideologically conservative and constraining academic discourses (or alphabetic literacy); reflecting literacy in the context of postmodernity; or effecting a direct challenge to, or significant revision of, composition's institutionality (both its institutional location and its institutional identity as a field). While these various goals may not coincide obviously, the advocates of experimental writing share common dissatisfactions, which they locate in particular forms or discourses, usually called "traditional" or "academic."[2] The idea of academic discourse functions as the space in which to place much that is wrong with composition: academic discourse, it is said, prevents students from producing writing that is relevant to their lives; it inhibits personal expression; it prevents the articulation of knowledges or experiences outside of the dominant culture; and, finally, under its limited economy, it inhibits sociopolitical critique. Arguments for experimental writing, therefore, point to a space we fill with our dreams and desires for composition to be "otherwise" than what it is or has been, an alternate space in composition that, I would suggest, has been created by aesthetics.

Initially, it might seem that "poetics" is a more apt term than "aesthetics" in composition since both "poetics" and composition underscore "production" or "making" (see, for example, the work of Derek Owens or James Berlin, both of whom often emphasize "poetics" rather than "aesthetics"). Similarly, it might seem that "alternative" and "style" or "mode" might be more appropriate terms to use in composition than "experimental" and "writing," particularly in the context of composition (e.g., Weathers, *Alternate Style*). And clearly, as Kathryn Flannery demonstrates in *The Emperor's New Clothes,* one can manage a substantial critique of broader ideological issues by working with "style" as a key term. Indeed, there is a resurgent interest in style as a key term (see particularly Butler, *Out of Style*). However, in what follows, "experimental," "writing," and "aesthetics" represent most broadly and accurately a nexus of interests in the field. This does not mean that I am unaware of the connotations for "alternative."[3] Nor does it mean that I am unaware of the ways in which "innovative" and "experimental" may imply different pedagogical projects, writing processes, or textual characteristics (see also my discussion of the politics of innovation vis-à-vis scholarship in the field of composition in chapter 2).

While I will sometimes refer to arguments in the field by the terms other authors use ("unconventional," "innovative," "alternative"), I have settled generally on the word "experimental" partly because it denotes the risk-taking in the field that I think most arguments for such pedagogies suggest and partly because underlying many of the arguments for pedagogical changes in composition are some of the experimental, avant-garde impulses of the sort Sirc, Rice, and Ulmer address. Similarly, though this book is framed by arguments in the field of composition about multimedia texts, the book began with an interest in writing and maintains its focus on writing, albeit while also considering how multimedia literacies affect what writing is and the ways in we teach writing in composition classrooms.

Finally, in what follows, "aesthetics" is the most appropriate key term for my purposes because it allows me to address not only a wide range of arguments in composition for experimental writing, but also the claims those arguments are making about the social functions and values of such writings. In other words, aesthetics broadly understood includes not just styles and poetics, and references to perceptions, but also the function and value (and ideologies) of art and the role of aesthetic judgment. Though I have endeavored here to provide some initial explanation of my terminological choices, the question of which terms composition scholars use in the field will continue to be a source of investigation throughout the book.

AESTHETICS IN ENGLISH STUDIES, COMPOSITION, AND RHETORIC

My choice of "aesthetics" as a key term, rather than "poetics," also points to the historical moment in English studies from which this book emerges. As in composition, where art or aesthetics seems to be a space of freedom and possibility, which we fill with our desires for the future to be different, so too in English studies, "aesthetics" has been often posited as a term that might give purpose and structure to a field struggling for relevance and identity. Many books and articles from the last ten or fifteen years have attempted to reclaim aesthetics for literary studies, or for the humanities more broadly. The goals of those reclamation attempts and the ways in which various issues in the study of aesthetics get figured are revealing. For example, George Levine's *Aesthetics and Ideology* (1994) countered what he perceived as an overemphasis on ideological critique by suggesting a return to a more formalist criticism of the art object. Similarly, Elaine Scarry's *On Beauty and Being Just* (1999) tried to think through the value of beauty in contemporary critical contexts. Still other books address the problems of objects and methods of study, as well as question what might constitute the defining limits of a field, by offering readings of key texts in aesthetic theory—for example, Wlad Godzich's *The Culture of Literacy* (1994), particularly his discussion of theory and aesthetics in the chapter "The Tiger on the Paper Mat"; and Sam Weber's reading of Immanuel Kant in "The Foundering of Aesthetics." And books such as Barbara Herrnstein Smith's *Contingencies of Value* (1991), John Guillory's *Cultural Capital* (1995), and *Aesthetics in a Multicultural Age*, edited by Emory Elliott, Louis Freitas Caton, and Jeffrey Rhyne (2002), have tried to help the field of literary studies think through what it might mean to hold onto aesthetics as a key concept.

Similarly, some books that theoretically situate composition pedagogy within English studies also participate in the revision, recuperation, or reinvigoration of aesthetics. Joe Marshall Hardin's *Opening Spaces* (2001), for example, devotes an entire chapter, "English Studies, Aestheticism, and the Art-Culture System," to tracing the author-critic structure of literary studies and its impact on composition pedagogy, as well as analyzing how English studies and composition participate in broad discussions of cultural value. Tim Mayers's *(Re)Writing Craft* (2005) invokes the powers of art, craft, and poetry to shift attention in English studies from literary interpretation to a focus on the productive aspects of writing. In this shift, he argues, lies the future of English studies, a future best ensured by an alliance between creative writing and composition.[4]

This is not an exhaustive list. I offer this sampling as a way to suggest that after cultural studies and critical theory had risen to dominance (and were therefore increasingly seen as constraining and limiting) in English departments, there was in many instances a strong but varied response, particularly during the middle and late 1990s. Some wanted a return to humanist ideals of beauty; some wanted to use popular culture or multimedia (e.g., film, television, the Internet) to challenge traditional literary aesthetics; some took an interest in formalism; others wanted to challenge the reign of rational epistemology or intellectual critique. Scott Heller's 1998 "Wearying of Cultural Studies" spoke of a general malaise and burnout in the field of literary studies by those who felt that cultural studies had led them to a dead end.[5]

I tell this story about aesthetics in the field of English studies not because I think it led directly to the movement for teaching experimental writing in composition; rather, I offer it for two reasons. First, as I suggested above, in English studies references to aesthetics can represent what we most want or most fear when it comes to our disciplinary identity, and these desires and fears are often shared by compositionists within the larger field, even if they manifest themselves differently. Second, I offer this snapshot because in late 1990s and turn of the century, when I began formulating the ideas that led to this book, I was situated in an English department, which at the time allowed me to engage this resurgent interest in aesthetics and to think deeply about how I saw it paralleled in the field of composition and rhetoric. On a good day, I was at the exciting intersection of creative writing, composition and rhetoric, and literary and cultural studies. On a bad day, I was somewhere in the cracks between (though being in the cracks has some serious advantages and allows for some unconventional thinking when no one is policing the boundaries). So, as English studies as a whole put aesthetics on the table for discussion, with all its hopes and dreams and fears and nightmares for what it might do for the field, particularly for the study of literature, I thought about the hopes and dreams and fears and nightmares that composition was having at the time for its own field. I began to think about how composition was starting to see its commitment to academic discourse and to analytical cultural studies as constraining and limiting. I also read the calls to change or reform composition pedagogy through the lens of English studies' larger concerns with the role that aesthetics might play in constituting a field and object of study. What I found in composition scholarship were several trends that seemed to speak to a larger set of tensions in the field.

First, I noticed arguments for teaching more literature in writing classes and for doing so not just as an occasion for critical analysis. Though there have been many such arguments over the years, the set of texts that best offers a glimpse of this historical moment is the series of exchanges and responses sparked in 1993 by Lindemann and Tate's articles in *College English* about the use of literature in composition (Lindemann, "Freshman Composition"; Tate, "A Place for Literature"). While Lindemann and Tate argue for and against the role of literature in the composition classroom, other scholars also explored the intersections of literary studies and composition and rhetoric, not just for the role of reading (and theories of reading or interpretation) in writing classes, but also for the production or rhetorical aspects of literature.[6] The other trend I noticed was an increasingly loud call to think about the relationship between creative writing and composition. Important figures for me at that time were Wendy Bishop, Katherine Haake, and, to some extent, Lynn Bloom. My institutional and disciplinary location encouraged me to notice these trends, scholars, and arguments.

As I delved deeper into these calls to use creative, experimental, or innovative texts in composition, I came to see them not so much as an attempt to heal disciplinary conflicts and divides (though there was a fair amount of that) but as an attempt to reclaim writing as an art form, or to borrow from Scott Heller's summary of the situation in the humanities, particularly English studies, as an attempt to reclaim the aesthetic dimensions of writing: "Maxed out on political analysis and cultural studies, scholars in the humanities have begun to talk again about the joys and pleasures of good, powerful—even beautiful—writing" (A15). Compositionists were also "maxed out," but on conventional personal essays, research papers, and impersonal, thesis-driven essays, and on academic writing more generally. Even those critical essays informed by cultural studies were beginning to show some signs of pedagogical strain. One of the ways dissatisfaction with conventional composition manifested itself was in the arguments for experimental or innovative writing in composition classrooms, whose power, I was coming to see, derived from (often) implicit aesthetics that valued writing as art and students as artists.

As I began to focus my attention on these arguments, I realized that this desire in composition studies to reclaim the power of writing as art ebbs and flows in different historical and social contexts. I will be tracking some of the ebb and flow in this book, noticing how art as a category was called into service in composition in every decade from the 1960s through the 1990s for a variety of literacy projects. But, more importantly for my concerns in this book, I realized that this desire in composition to tap into the power of writing as an art form was, and is, often done without any critical self-consciousness of the aesthetic theories that were being invoked and marshaled for the cause of changing the way we teach writing. There was, in other words, a kind of tacit, commonsense assumption about what writing as art does or could do. This fact more than anything else motivated the work that follows. What, I wanted to know, could we learn about composition as a field and about our theories and pedagogies for teaching writing if, instead of treating them as tacit common sense, we brought the language and concepts of aesthetics to the surface for further examination?

In some instances, of course, compositionists have been explicit (though not particularly self-critical) about the aesthetics they were invoking in their attempt to reform composition. Sheri Gradin, for example, in *Romancing Rhetorics* traces the impact of romantic aesthetics on the field of composition, attempts to counter James Berlin's critique of the ideology of romantic aesthetics and expressive rhetoric, and demonstrates the complexity of the romantic legacy in order to reclaim certain values for contemporary composition. Similarly, in the work of Geoffrey Sirc, Ulmer, and Rice, which I discuss in greater detail in later chapters, avant-garde aesthetics (borrowed from the likes of Marcel Duchamp, Joseph Beuys, Joseph Cornell, William Burroughs, and Amiri Baraka) are advanced as a resource for reimagining the work of teaching writing in what Ulmer has called variously "an experimentalist electronic paradigm" or the age of "electracy" ("Textshop for Post(e)pedagogy" 39, and *Internet Invention* xii). However, as I will show, if composition and the avant-garde share many of the same goals, they also confront similar obstacles and problems. Therefore, in this work, I aim to lay bare implied aesthetics and put critical pressure on certain overt aesthetic investments in order to see what other lessons composition might learn from aesthetic theories—whether romantic, modernist, avant-garde, or postmodern.

DIALECTICS OF COMPOSITION AND OF THE AVANT-GARDE

The history of writing instruction and its relationship to aesthetics is a long one. At least in Western cultural history, one could go as far back as the Sophists to think more about the tensions and complementarities among knowledge, rhetoric, and art. A thoughtful study of texts by Gorgias or Plato or Aristotle would be one place to start, and then the study would continue on through the ages. As Richard Lanham demonstrates, the Renaissance would be a particularly fruitful period to examine for the relationship between rhetorical or literacy education and aesthetics (*Style* and *Literacy and the Survival of Humanism*). Or, as Sharon Crowley, among others, demonstrates, nineteenth-century belletristic rhetoric is a rich field to plow (*Composition in the University*). But what I concluded from studying the history of aesthetics and composition scholarship was that the version of the field of composition I most wanted to speak to was the late twentieth-century (and early twenty-first-century) institutionalization of composition, which emerged as a field in the United States beginning in the 1960s. Then I began to see the arguments in composition for experimental and innovative writing as representative of significant challenges to the ways scholars and teachers in composition had imagined the role that students and their writing might play in the field and in college classrooms.

Arguments for experimental writing in composition, especially as they invoke art and the power and value of art in service of pedagogical projects, share many of the values and goals of various historical avant-garde movements. I am not saying that avant-garde movements of the twentieth century led to experimental writing in composition, or that there is in any way a causal relationship. Of course, there are cases (which I discuss in later chapters) of overt importation, such as in the work of Ulmer, Sirc, and Rice, whereby the techniques and values of avant-garde artists are brought into the scene of the writing classroom. However, what I argue is that experimental writing in composition participates in the larger set of dialectics that have animated both twentieth-century art and education. Composition participates in the larger scene of these dialectics for a variety of reasons. Since composition is often institutionally situated in English departments and often situated intellectually within English studies, it sets itself in relation to the larger issues and concerns of English studies. One might tell an interesting story of composition in which some of the figures who shaped it as a field began as students and scholars of literary studies and brought those interests and concerns to the teaching of writing. Similarly, one might also tell a story in which composition courses are prerequisites to more advanced courses in literature. Finally, one might tell a story in which the recent interest in experimental multimedia texts brings to the fore the repressed fourth C, communication, or returns the rhetoric half of composition and rhetoric to dominance. As I will discuss in more detail later, Rice and Selfe, with very different agendas, both see the increasing interest in multimodal or multimedia literacy as just such a return of the repressed.[7]

The historical avant-garde (of the early twentieth century in Europe and of the 1960s in the United States) represents a response to various social conflicts and crises and institutional dynamics. Experimental writing in composition from the 1960s through to the present is a response to similar social conflicts, crises, and institutional dynamics. Both avant-garde artists and writing teachers have struggled with the role of art in society and with negotiating certain key dialectics as I described them earlier: tradition/innovation, social/individual, constraint or determinism/freedom, alienation/autonomy, knowledge/art, institutional life/everyday life. In positioning the student writer as an artist and his or her writing as an art form, arguments for experimental writing in composition first aimed to alleviate students' presumed alienation from school literacies, as well as to reunite school and everyday life for students by emphasizing the freedom and agency of the individual student. Second, such arguments worked to conceive of composition as that which teaches students to use writing as sociopolitical critique via innovative forms. And finally, arguments for experimental writing in composition claimed to reform, challenge, or even destroy the institution of composition itself. The goals articulated by these arguments for experimental writing find their echoes in the goals of various historical avant-garde movements since, generally, avant-garde art has attempted three broad projects. It has attempted to unite art with everyday praxis by finding ways of expressing realities or experiences outside those of the dominant aesthetics or culture. It has worked to produce art that is politically critical and/or socially transformative. And finally, it has sought to resist institutionalization and absorption by challenging or attempting to destroy traditional aesthetics, often employing innovative forms in the service of this project.

Historically, there are many avant-gardes, their projects are often irreconcilable, and one might even argue that avant-garde art is no longer viable. These assertions can make it difficult to speak authoritatively or comprehensively about an "avant-garde aesthetic." Even so, I suggest that compositionists can benefit from exploring some of the discussions about avant-garde art. As the field of composition negotiates these dialectical tensions, it behooves us to examine historically and theoretically the successes and failures of the avant-garde as a way to shed some light not only on the possibilities but also on the problems of using experimental writing to reform composition.

As Charles Russell notes in his preface to *Poets, Prophets, and Revolutionaries,* the term "avant-garde" has seeped into our everyday vocabulary and can describe not only art, but also fashion, politics, business practices, and so on—indeed, the term "avant-garde" as an adjective is often applied to ideas, objects, practices, or people that are new, innovative, cutting edge, or experimental (v–vi). Even in these loose senses of the term, there is something about it that suggests that the criteria for evaluating the new dress, business practice, writing, music have not yet caught up with the object or practice. There is still, in other words, something futuristic or "avant" about these new things, ideas, practices, people. The "avant-garde" suggests, then, a significant break with the current practices or traditions. For example, avant-garde art can be seen as opposing classical and modernist aesthetics, including such values as organic unity, coherence, beauty, order, transcendence, representation, the autonomous role of art, and aestheticist attitudes. Additionally, avant-garde art is said to be futuristic if not prophetic, innovative, nonrepresentational (or at least challenging representational stability), fragmented, sublime, aware of its contingent and social nature, a process, a performance, or happening (not an art object), irrational, critically negative (nihilistic), anti–status quo, self-critical and self-reflexive (meta-aesthetical), anti-institutional, and intent on reintegrating art and everyday praxis.

Yet, these characterizations and distinctions are tenuous at best, given the vast amounts of modernist and avant-garde literature and the variety of critical interpretations of their significance.[8] When critics and theorists address the topic of avant-garde art, they are faced with the problem of making distinctions: formal, political, historical. For example, modernist writers and artists are preoccupied with "making it new" (to quote Pound).

But if avant-garde writers are merely formally innovative, then what is the difference between modernism and the avant-garde? Additionally, proponents of the viability of a contemporary avant-garde often assume that such art implies a progressive (or "leftist") politics. As we will see in chapter 2, the assumption that avant-garde art is politically progressive becomes complicated once one looks more closely at the historical contexts for specific avant-garde movements (e.g., Italian futurism) as well as when one begins to look at histories of the avant-garde in American culture from the 1950s onward.

Finally, periodization is equally problematic since modernism and the avant-garde coexist, by and large, historically. In fact, the confusion between modernism and the avant-garde can extend to analyses of individual writers. Depending on which critic you are reading, T. S. Eliot is a modernist (see Russell) or T. S. Eliot is an avant-gardist (see Perloff, *21st-Century Modernism*). Additionally, once one tries to take postmodern writing into account, the confusion triples and the conflation shifts wildly from modern/avant-garde to modern/postmodern to avant-garde/post-modern. Indeed, when one reads arguments for the viability of a contemporary avant-garde that situates itself within the context of postmodernity —arguing that the avant-garde anticipated postmodernity—one begins to wonder if the differences in terms even matter anymore or if history has become one proleptic mess. It is no wonder, then, that composition-ists who argue for experimental or unconventional writing in composition pedagogies demonstrate such vacillating aesthetics, bumping around higgledy-piggledy among romantic, modern, avant-garde, and postmodern aesthetics. Indeed, this polysemous nature of avant-garde aesthetics is what often lends arguments for experimental writing in composition such power. In other words, many compositionists can argue for change and reform in composition pedagogy, while at the same time minimizing the sense of radical rupture by letting avant-garde aesthetics echo their historical precedents.

For example, contemporary arguments for experimental writing in composition, with their emphasis on the individual student, echo many of the concerns of expressivist composition of the 1960s and 1970s. Thus, if we want to understand the calls for experimental writing in our time, we need to consider some history of composition, particularly the aesthetics asserted and implied by expressivism as well as its legacy in contemporary composition. After all, expressivism in the 1960s and 1970s helped to forge and hold a place in composition for writing as art and for the student writer as artist. But this historical understanding of the aesthetic and pedagogical legacies of expressivism requires more than a mere reiteration of critiques of expressivism in composition. Many of the claims made about the value of experimental writing in composition echo, either explicitly or implicitly, claims made about the significance of avant-garde art. This is particularly true in regard to the avant-garde's conception of the individual artist. For this reason, histories, theories, and critiques of avant-garde art can help us to think through such issues as the dialectic of individual autonomy and alienation, the relationship of the individual to the social collective, as well as our assumptions about the relative freedom provided (or not provided) by aesthetic discourses. While many of the arguments for experimental writing in composition borrow their enthusiasm for the power of the innovative and experimental forms from the history of avant-garde art, my retracing in chapter 1 of the parallels between the individual artist in avant-garde theories and the individual student writer in composition aims to help us think more critically about the politics of innovative style as a locus of individual freedom.

While expressivists who argue for the teaching of experimental writing often critique academic discourse (not only the forms advanced by current traditionalism but also the newer cultural studies or rhetorical versions), they are more concerned with the student as individual, his or her honest or authentic writing/self, and therefore relegate social or ideological concerns to the background. Compositionists who advocate experimental writing in service of multicultural, social constructionist, or postmodern pedagogies similarly challenge the hegemonic ideologies associated with academic writing. But they tend to foreground the ways in which alternative forms of writing represent social groups and situate individual students within larger social structures and discourses. In doing so, they attempt not only to help the individual student, but also to change larger social, political, and institutional structures, including the field of composition.

In chapter 2 I examine some key arguments for teaching experimental writing by this second group of compositionists. Many of these arguments claim that experimental writing (reading it, teaching it, writing it) is inherently political both in the context of the classroom and in the context of larger institutions (for example, the field of composition). To address these claims, I examine historical and theoretical debates about the politics of the avant-garde as a way to shed some light on, and problematize, assumptions made by this second group of compositionists about the progressive politics of experimental writing, the category of innovation, and the degree to which experimental writing is an attempt to critique, reform, or destroy the field of composition, particularly as it identifies itself with the teaching of academic writing. In particular, I argue that successful avant-garde approaches and aesthetic values have been either co-opted by late capitalism's marketing culture or accommodated by discourses of power (including those of governmental, educational, and mass media institutions). I examine the ways that experimental and alternative writings in composition are already in the process of being absorbed, accommodated, and managed by various apparatuses of authorization and dissemination, thus appearing to limit significant critique and perpetuate business as usual in composition.

Continuing to focus on the ways in which experimental writing challenges the field of composition and rhetoric, its goals and pedagogies, in chapter 3 I argue that the field's interest in experimental writing is both a response to various crises in judgment in composition and a catalyst for provoking such crises. Drawing upon the work of theorists of aesthetic judgment, such as Barbara Herrnstein Smith, Immanuel Kant, and Jean-François Lyotard, and examining recent scholarship in composition on evaluation and assessment of student writing, I argue that many compositionists have neglected to address the ways in which the teaching of unconventional or experimental writings demands a reconsideration and revision of the criteria by which student writing is judged. Such an examination of our evaluative criteria would challenge the dominant pedagogies and conceptions of literacy education by which the field of composition constitutes itself and its goals. In particular, I use Lyotard's argument that truly experimental writing produces an entirely new pragmatic situation, paired with Aristotle's notion of prudence, to refigure the composition teacher as a prudent judge who must evaluate experimental student writing in the absence of previously established criteria.

If, in the preceding chapters, I address the issues of experimental writing pedagogies, aesthetics, and judgment in broad terms, then in chapter 4 I address these issues through a case study of the collage. Indeed, this chapter serves as a kind of companion chapter to earlier ones, primarily chapter 3 on the crisis of judgment in composition. The collage is by far the most dominant experimental form taught in composition classrooms, yet very little work has been done that investigates, in more depth, theories and histories of the collage. Claims for its value to writing instruction variously argue for the collage as part of the writing process, point to its significance as a postmodern form, and even appeal to its history as popular arts and crafts technique. Bringing together some histories and theories of the collage as an art form with arguments for its efficacy in the teaching of writing, I examine the collage as an instance that exemplifies the multiple and often contradicting claims made for experimental writing in composition. Here, I argue that the dialectical tensions inherent in historical and theoretical debates about the values of the collage are inherited by arguments for the collage in composition pedagogy. Furthermore, in chapter 4, I closely read several textual collages written by undergraduates in one of my freshman writing classes. I not only test claims I advanced in chapter 3 about the necessity of revising our criteria and processes of judgment vis-à-vis experimental student writing, but I also show in detail how my evaluative abilities as a teacher are affected by specific collages written by individual students. I demonstrate how, in the act of reading experimental student writing, one might pedagogically use reflections on the act of judgment as a way to keep in play what both conventional and experimental writing have to offer composition students and teachers.

Arguments to expand the composition curriculum include not only print texts generated by the resources of alphabetic literacy but also other media such digital video, Web pages, social networking tools, mobile applications, audio texts, and even, in some cases, sculptural and performative products and productions. For example, some compositionists suggest that teaching the production of multimedia texts in composition courses is merely an updating of the means of persuasion, since traditional rhetorical principles abide (see Selfe, *Multimodal Composition*), a position reminiscent of Winston Weathers's attitude about Grammar B. This is the new project for the old business of composition. Yet other compositionists such as Sirc, Rice, and Ulmer—not coincidentally relying on the cultural legacy of avant-garde art (with a healthy dose of poststructuralist theory often in the form of references to Jacques Derrida)—argue that composition as we know it is over, its goals, values, and principles thoroughly destabilized as multimedia texts (often digital, but not always) mark a radical break with older pedagogical projects. In my last chapter, I point out the ways in which multimedia composition is and isn't changing composition pedagogies. As with previous arguments about experimental writing and mixed genres, more contemporary arguments suggest that only (or especially) through the use of new technologies and media, students may be allowed to express their unique individualities, articulate marginal or underrepresented social realities, and/or critique the limits of dominant sociopolitical discourses and the institutions that perpetuate these discourses. In addition, I try to shed some light on and provide some insights into the possibilities for resolving, or even living productively with, tensions created by these dialectics.

EXPERIMENTAL EXPRESSIVISM

AUTONOMY AND ALIENATION

Contemporary arguments for experimental writing in composition, with their emphasis on the individual student, echo many of the concerns of expressivist composition of the 1960s and 1970s. Thus, if we want to understand the calls for experimental writing in our time, we need to consider some history of composition, particularly the legacy of expressivism in contemporary composition, as well as the aesthetics asserted and implied by its legacy. After all, expressivism in the 1960s and 1970s helped forge and hold a place in composition for writing as art and for the student writer as artist. This historical understanding of the aesthetic and pedagogical legacies of expressivism requires more than a mere reiteration of critiques of expressivism in composition. Many of the claims made about the value of experimental writing in composition echo, either explicitly or implicitly, claims made about the significance of avant-garde art. This is particularly true in regard to the avant-garde's conception of the individual artist. For this reason, I argue that histories, theories, and critiques of avant-garde art can help us think through such issues as the dialectic of individual autonomy and alienation, the relationship of the individual to the social collective, as well as our assumptions about the relative freedom provided (or not provided) by aesthetic media. While many of the arguments for experimental writing in composition borrow their enthusiasm for the power of the innovative and experimental forms from the history of avant-garde art, my retracing of the parallels between the individual artist in avant-garde theories and the individual student writer in composition pedagogies aims to help us also think more critically about the politics of innovative style as a locus of individual freedom.

EXPRESSIVISM AND INDIVIDUAL FREEDOM: THEN AND NOW

Historically, arguments for experimental, innovative, and unconventional writing in composition have their roots in the projects of composition teachers and scholars of the 1960s and 1970s. A lot happened pedagogically in these decades in the teaching of writing: sentence combining, tagmemics, current-traditionalism, classical rhetoric for the modern writer, and radical textbooks and curricula. Yet what histories of composition tend to make clear is the formative role expressivist pedagogies played in the field of composition. That this legacy of expressivism would find itself bolstering an increasing number of arguments for experimental writing in composition in the 1980s and 1990s will come as no surprise when one analyzes composition scholars' understanding of the aesthetics underlying such experimental texts.

Arguments of the 1980s and 1990s for experimental writing in composition echo earlier expressivist arguments of the 1960s and 1970s about the right and need of the individual to express her own experiences in the context of a dehumanizing educational system and society. Students are alienated, teachers are alienated, the old ways of writing don't seem to capture the spirit of the times, so let's throw them out, let's burn incense and listen to rock music, burn down the rhetoric building[1] and try to find forms and language that help us express where we are right now.[2] To put it into somewhat clichéd images, the 1960s and 1970s in composition (or at least the liberating projects of many expressivist and process folk) represented the Woodstock of composition: it was (or wanted to be) wild and unrestrained and beautiful and muddy, a little out of control, a big mess, and something that composition in the 1980s and 1990s would have a hard time recovering from. Writing instruction up until then was assumed, more or less, to reproduce the values of the dominant social ideology, and teachers of the 1960s and 1970s (obviously not all, but some who helped to create and define the field of composition) wanted to make writing matter to students, personally *and* politically.

Lad Tobin captures both the argument and spirit of these times. While questioning the assumed link between expressivism and the writing process movement (6), he does not deny that the "writing process movement," as the name of a historical moment in composition, has come to represent some of the same projects and values of expressivism: "But in the composition world, the term has come to mean something else [other than just a generalized process]: an emphasis on the process, student choice and voice, revision, self-expression. But most of all it has come to mean a critique (or even outright rejection) of traditional, product-driven, rules-based, correctness-obsessed writing" (5). He goes on further to describe the position that writing process folk could imagine themselves in, even as late as the 1980s: "And while we advocated radical change, we were comforted by the knowledge that we occupied the higher moral ground. After all, we were speaking up against rigidity, legalism, authoritarianism, fuddy-duddyism. We were speaking up for students, freedom, innovation, creativity, and change" (5).

The writing process movement and expressivism seem to have been critiqued, overwhelmed, or just overshadowed by the rise of critical cultural theory in the field of composition in the 1980s and 1990s, which had a different set of political and epistemological projects. Yet it is also true that the position Tobin describes—the higher moral ground from which compositionists speak "against rigidity, legalism, authoritarianism, [and] fuddy-duddyism" and speak "up for students, freedom, innovation, creativity, and change"—would assert itself again and again in the arguments for experimental writing in composition classrooms, arguments put forth in a kind of second-wave expressivism by compositionists such as Winston Weathers, Wendy Bishop, Lillian Bridwell-Bowles, Derek Owens, and Geoffrey Sirc, among others.

I begin with this hint at histories of 1960s and 1970s expresssivist experimental composition pedagogy not because I want to write a history of experimental writing in composition from the 1960s onward, but as a way of framing my discussion of what I see as a hinge text, a text that looks backward to the sixties and seventies while looking forward to the eighties and nineties: Weathers's *An Alternate Style: Options in Composition*. In his text I find the traces of both earlier composition projects and avant-garde aesthetics, many of which animate more contemporary arguments for teaching experimental writing in composition. Broadly speaking, Weathers's book captures the desire to combine the freedom of expression of the sixties and seventies with the more measured intellectual and political restraint characteristic of the eighties. Don't burn down the rhetoric building, redecorate it; experiment with forms, but only in the context of established precedents; learn the rules before you break them; have your wild hippie weekend, but come back to the suburbs to clean up and show up for your middle-class day job on Monday. It is a sophisticated mass marketing of the sixties and seventies radical impulse to blow open forms of writing for a more savvy consumer of the eighties.[3]

Generally, Weathers identifies what he sees as the inadequacy of traditional modes of writing in composition, offering an argument for expanding our "repertoire" and providing alternative models for student writing. He does not mount an impassioned attack on academic writing or traditional prose forms; on the contrary, he reminds his readers that alternate styles, what he calls "Grammar B," in no way threaten traditional styles, what he calls "Grammar A" (*Alternate Style* 3). Weathers's description of the characteristics of Grammar A represents the traditional values and conventions of composition. We will see this list repeated in later arguments in composition:

> [Grammar A] has the characteristics of continuity, order, reasonable progression and sequence, consistency, unity, etc. . . . Our assumption—regardless of liberality so far as diversity of styles is concerned—is that every composition must be well organized and unified, must demonstrate logic, must contain well-developed paragraphs; that its structure will manifest a beginning, middle, and end; that the composition will reveal identifiable types of order; that so far as the composition deals with time it will reveal a general diachronicity, etc. Our teaching and texts will be concerned, almost without exception, with "subject and thesis," "classification and order," "beginning and ending," "expansion," "continuity," "emphasis," and the like. (*Alternate Style* 6)

While Weathers grants that traditional prose forms and values associated with those forms have their uses and places, he argues that they are also limited: "What I've been taught to construct is: the well-made box. I have been taught to put 'what I have to say' into a container that is always remarkably the same. . . . I may be free to put 'what I have to say' in the plain box or in the ornate box, in the large box or the small box, in the fragile box or in the sturdy box. But always the box—squarish or rectangular" (*Alternate Style* 1–2). Different kinds of containers, Weathers suggests, allow writers more freedom in regard to content, offer them the means to say new things, are more suitable to some writers' mental processes, and, finally, can provide writers more rhetorical flexibility (2). The heart of Weathers's argument, then, does not lie in the use of alternate styles to reject traditional modes of writing or the ideologies associated with them. Rather, it lies in what these styles offer, that is, the freedom to choose one's way of writing. Adopting the imagined voice of a generic student, Weathers writes,

> I'm asking simply to be exposed to, and informed about, the full range of composition possibilities. That I be introduced to all the tools, right now, and not be asked to wait for years and years until I have mastered right-handed affairs before I learn anything about left-handed affairs. That, rather, I be introduced to all the grammars/vehicles/tools/compositional possibilities *now* so that even as I "learn to write" I will have before me as many resources as possible. I'm asking: that all the "ways" of writing be spread out before me and that my education be devoted to learning how to use them. (2)

The emphasis is not so much on the implications of the forms chosen as on offering students a range of possible forms or styles and, therefore, on enabling the individual writer's freedom of choice.

Some sense of the importance of these choices is actually offered in more political terms in one of Weathers's earlier essays, "Teaching Style: A Possible Anatomy": "we can tell students that style is a gesture of personal freedom against inflexible states of mind, that in a very real way—because it is the art of choice and option—style has something to do with freedom; that as systems—rhetorical or political—become rigid and dictatorial, style is reduced, unable as it is to exist in totalitarian environments. We can reveal to students the connection between democracy and style, saying that the study of style is a part of our democratic and free experience" (369). Here, democracy is the right of the individual to resist totalitarianism, and style is a means by which an individual ensures that right. Despite the power of this kind of rhetoric, the emphasis in the above argument, as well as in *Alternate Style,* is on the connection between style and the individual, not on the connection between style and democracy. The agonistic relationship of the individual to the collective is obscured by a conception of democracy in which political or social freedom is conflated with the freedom of the individual as consumer. Furthermore, the larger political significance of stylistic contestation (i.e., the attempt to oppose a rigid or dictatorial rhetorical system) is similarly obscured by positing an autonomous individual who has the freedom to choose willfully and consciously a particular style. Finally, style (and by extension, the individual) will appear to reside in the aesthetic realm, and therefore may potentially be relevant to, but not determined by, social conditions.

In his preface to *Alternate Style,* Weathers claims that different styles can represent different mentalities, realities, and voices (3). There are no specific social realities mentioned, just "certain thought processes, certain world views, certain notions about the nature of man and society" (12). Students are denied freedom to experiment or to take on the responsibility of more mature writers; they must choose from acceptable techniques and forms. "[Grammar B] is a mature and alternate (*not* experimental) style used by competent writers and offering students a well-tested set of options" (8).[4] Indeed, Weathers's book primarily offers itself as a resource, a veritable catalog of definitions and examples of "well-tested" options, such as collage/montage, pastiche, playful (wordplay) texts, as well as repetitious and fragmented texts. All of these alternate styles, however, have been removed from their historical or social contexts and therefore appear transhistorical and ideologically neutral.

If a reader didn't know under what circumstances these "options" were produced or received, after reading Weathers's book, she or he would still not know. Weathers merely offers a list of forms and authors. For instance, though he mentions William Burroughs (as an example of collage), he does not confront the actual text of Burroughs, with its junkies, homosexuals, and sadistic violence; nor does he mention what it might be like for students to imitate *Naked Lunch.* The one example that Weathers does discuss in some detail is Tom Wolfe's *The Kandy-Kolored Tangerine-Flake Streamline Baby.* Though Weathers draws our attention to the influence of rock-and-roll music, "television, and movies on the evolution of Grammar B" (*Alternate Style* 10)—particularly on the "new journalism"—the bulk of his discussion is devoted to narrating Wolfe's process of writing the "memo" that would eventually become part of *The Kandy-Kolored Tangerine-Flake Streamline Baby:* "Finally, up against a deadline, the only thing Wolf [*sic*] could do was to 'type up my notes' with the understanding that the *Esquire* editor 'will get someone else to write' the story. . . . 'I just started recording it all, and inside a couple of hours, typing along like a madman, I could tell that something was beginning to happen'" (10).

While students must choose acceptable models of Grammar B and employ them consciously and carefully, it seems to be the case that experimental or innovative styles just happen to "real writers." "Real" writers are receptive to the rhythms of the contemporary scene; inspired (tortured?)

by a kind of divine madness, they merely "record it all." The kind of analysis Weathers offers here makes the story of innovative or experimental literature read less like a series of agonistic attempts (sometimes failures) to represent different social realities in the face of dominant styles than a narrative of individual creativity. It seems, then, that the force of Weathers's argument relies upon a romantic aesthetics rooted in the autonomy of the individual artist/writer as free (or freeing himself or herself) from determinate social discourses and aesthetics and at the same time open to channeling the powerful experience of the everyday person in the contemporary moment.

While Weathers is different from many expressivists whose commitment to the unmediated expression of an existing self sometimes seems to ignore or obscure the medium (e.g., the style of actual words on the page), his arguments give precedence to the individual over any conception of the social. In *Alternate Style,* the emphasis on the individual over the social collective or political aggregate simultaneously empowers and disempowers the student writer. In Weathers's argument, individual choice relies upon a conception of the aesthetic as the source of freedom. Yet at the same time, Weathers's argument moves access to this kind of productive and active artistic (and political) freedom further out of the reach of students, relegating them once again to acts of reception and consumption. Because students are only allowed to choose from "well-tested" models, they merely imitate the artist's autonomy by making a kind of consumer choice about the styles they will adopt (hopefully finding something "off the rack" that will fit their individual reality, identity, "voice," or "mentality"). Students get the freedom of art as a source of variety without any of the risks that art usually entails, for example, irrelevance, misunderstanding, censorship, suppression, and the like. But if they aren't allowed to take risks by experimentation, then students do not quite get the critical power that kind of freedom can afford. They are ill prepared to see the extent to which alternative styles can truly function as challenges to dictatorial or totalitarian rhetorical or political systems if they cannot begin to consider the ways in which those systems—even democratic ones—attempt to thwart or absorb such challenges.

Democracy as Weathers conceives it, then, is less the negotiation of power between individuals and groups than it is a conception of democracy shot through capitalist ideology. Students get autonomy, but it is an autonomy that can't quite make their choices anything more than a matter of personal preference or personal taste. For example, in an interview with Wendy Bishop for an introduction to her *Elements of Alternate Style,*

Weathers comments on one of the essays in the collection: "I much enjoyed the fast-food metaphor that Darrell Fike and Devan Cook present in the opening essay ["'Would You Like Fries with That?': Ordering Up Some Writing: Fast Food for Thought"]. I agree. Who wants the same hamburger served the same way every time we eat out? Most of us enjoy switching to pizza and even tacos, now and then. Nor do we need to stop there. A really sophisticated 'eater' may reach out for something beyond fast food itself, maybe something gourmet, perhaps even champagne or caviar on occasion" (Bishop, "Alternate Styles" 5). Though no one (Fike, Cook, or Weathers) seems to reflect on this metaphor, one is left to wonder if most of the writing done in composition classes should be considered fast food while the kinds of more literary, experimental writing should be considered more sophisticated, or gourmet fare. Do alternate styles in composition contribute to the project of changing students' class tastes (a project traditionally the province of literature classes) from the rather working-class or middle-class (a McDonald's burger?) to those of the upper class, by giving them a "taste" for the gourmet, for champagne and caviar? What is ostensibly an argument for variety is actually inflected with class tensions. But if an alternate style cannot exactly bear the burden of changing students' tastes, it can at least offer bored students consumption as diversion: "Other justifications for the alternate style can perhaps be found. (Perhaps it is justifiable on the ground of novelty or welcome relief if nothing else)" (Weathers, *Alternate Style* 13).

Weathers's text touches on many of the issues we will see again in subsequent arguments for experimental writing: approximating the freedom and autonomy of creative artists by offering students options; alleviating the boredom and alienation of students (and teachers) by providing them with the diversion of innovative or alternate styles; providing students the opportunity to "express" their individual experiences (as long as they fit into some well-tested model) against the dehumanizing politics and circumstances of modern society. In these kinds of arguments, style as art may be offered as an expression of individual experiences or individual realities without posing any major challenge to dominant discourses or to the institutional mandate of composition to teach normative or academic discourses. Alternate style could function in its freer space as social critique, yet it merely ends up presenting itself as a commodity to be consumed by the individual, a distraction that is ultimately irrelevant and ineffective.

In the late 1990s, Wendy Bishop and David Starkey both edited collections that reclaim the spirit of Weathers's original project, though Bishop's project is not so much a reclamation as it is a reassertion of what she sees as Weathers's emphasis on form and his pluralist project:

> A group of writers who are also writing teachers gathers together and decides to teach compositions, plural, to teach unrelated and related forms, to seek out distant cousins, black sheep and adopted relatives, and to valorize form as process, form as experience, form as many shapes, form as the activity that enlarges the options of our minds. What they produce are the fifteen essays in this collection that seek not to replace what you know about writing, what you've learned so far, but to augment, complicate, tease, challenge, and extend what you do as a writer. . . . For a teacher, I hope these essays and the spirit of the book provide you with support for teaching writing the way you know it should be taught. (Bishop, "Alternate Styles" 4)

Many of the fifteen essays in Bishop's collection, *Elements of Alternate Style: Essays on Writing and Revision,* repeat or continue Weathers's project from *An Alternate Style.* Thus, there are essays on how to experiment with crots (a kind of paragraph fragment), lists, labyrinthine sentences, sentence fragments, collage, montage, repetition of words and phrases, double-voice styles (in the form of writing in columns or juxtaposed as paragraphs), paragraphs of only one-syllable words, fractured narratives, and alternative or creative research projects, as well as other writing assignments and exercises that emphasize wordplay, improvisation, rhythm, playing with perspective and point of view shifts, electronic chats, and so on. In other words, if Weathers's book was an argument for teaching alternate styles, the collection Bishop edited is less a new argument per se than an updated demonstration of the teaching of alternate style in action, including assignments, descriptions of classrooms, and some excerpts of student texts with occasional commentary and reflection.

In the introduction to his collection, *Teaching Writing Creatively,* David Starkey, unlike Bishop, attempts to reframe the value of alternate or experimental styles for more modern students and for a more multicultural and theoretical composition field. He tries to remarket a predominantly expressivist pedagogy through the concept of "polyculturalism." That his project echoes earlier expressivist projects is clear from the claims he makes about how experimental writings can alleviate teacher and student boredom and alienation: "Increasingly, composition teachers resist being characterized by their counterparts in literature as dull, inconsequential thinkers and writers—the drudges of the English Department. Instead, they realized that teaching writing need not be a workaday pursuit. They are likely to share the conviction of contributors to this volume that students should have a stake in the writing they do, and that student and teacher writing problems are often very similar. Teachers like these value playful, passionate writing as much as writing that claims to be objective. They admire innovative form and alternate style. They cherish honesty" (Starkey xv). His introduction and many of the essays collected in the book stress formal experimentation with little or no discussion of political or ideological implications, invoking instead the importance of individual self-expression.

As in the case of Winston Weathers, any potentially radical disruption of the composition classroom is contained by self-discipline and by the goals of an expressivist pedagogy: "Writing assignments seem dangerously 'fun,' yet despite all this freedom, students are continually evaluating their own motivation for writing and questioning the honesty with which they write" (Starkey xvii).[5] Establishing a genealogy for the work of *Teaching Writing Creatively,* Starkey invokes the figures of Peter Elbow and Donald Murray and the significant part that expressivist pedagogies have played in the project of expanding the variety of texts composition teachers teach: "Both men have transgressed against conventional notions of style, voice, and genre. Both believe that in an important sense, as Murray (1995) . . . argues, 'all effective writing is autobiographical' (11). Both have 'dared to experiment'" (Starkey xiv). It remains unclear, however, why innovative styles are needed to generate autobiographical writing in composition classes. If a teacher wanted students to write autobiography, he or she could do that without introducing the complexities of innovative styles.

As if multiculturalism had not already been a problematically pluralist project, continually challenged throughout the 1980s and 1990s by political and ideological conflicts and power differentials, Starkey's replacement of "multi-" with "poly-" highlights even more so the pluralist goals of experimental writing in composition, meanwhile conflating social diversity, individualism, and formal variety in often problematic and confusing ways. Space prevents me from addressing all of the arguments in *Elements of Alternate Style* and in *Teaching Writing Creatively.* In both collections, however, students write collages, fractured narratives, and multivoiced texts; experiment with revision; employ alternative research strategies; and produce language poetry, fragmented texts, and fractured narratives; and other experimental writings as described above. Yet despite this variety, the students' writing overwhelmingly represents students' experiences in the form of variations on the genre of the personal narrative: my day as a lifeguard, my parents' divorce, my experiences growing up, I was an ugly duckling, why I hate red lights, my parents, my family, my friends, what I do for fun, and the like. Broadly construed, the self can be considered social, but there is very little evidence that students or teachers are reflecting critically (if at all) on the social selves represented in students' personal writings. In other words, neither students nor the teacher-scholars who cite student work are commenting on how a student's individual experience relates to larger social categories or structures such as race, class, gender, and so on. Neither is the student's writing an occasion for examining the ways in which social discourses inhibit, contain, or prevent these innovative writings from functioning as social critique. Accordingly, the individual student's writing cannot seem to intervene in, or even evidence an awareness of, the politics of normative social discourses because there is no sense of the ways in which discourses compete for dominance.

In these two anthologies, we see the same set of gestures toward the politics of innovative forms that Weathers makes. Yet, here too, the value of personal expression remains unquestioned, ahistorical, and asocial. The evaluation of these personal writings completes the circle of expressivist pedagogy as teachers evaluate them either for the emotional responses they arouse in the teachers or for how these writings have helped students find entertaining and enjoyable ways to express their experiences. In sum, a pedagogy of self-expression is enabled by an aesthetic that links the uniqueness of innovative forms with the uniqueness of students as individuals.

ACADEMIC LITERACY, ALIENATION, AND STUDENT AS ARTIST: THEN AND NOW

The historical context from which expressivist pedagogies emerged helps us to see why and how it might be that the expressivists in composition are drawn to experimental writing as a way to fulfill the goals of teaching writing. Though any specific teacher or compositionist may prove the exception to the label, generally expressivism refers to a writing pedagogy that gives priority to the individual student, to his or her experiences, and to the expression of those experiences over and above other work in the writing classroom, work such as the interpretation and analysis of texts, the construction of logical (thesis-driven) arguments for some real or imagined audience, or the construction of research papers and the like. Of course, a given pedagogy can combine any or all of the above or other practices. Expressivist teachers will often include readings; social-constructionist reading-based writing classes will often ask students to articulate (construct) their experiences in writing; and most contemporary composition pedagogies, whether they are self-conscious about it or not, employ many of the pedagogical values and strategies of the writing process movement with which much expressivist pedagogy is entwined. Yet despite revisions of expressivist pedagogies to make them more explicitly compatible with a more recent theoretically or rhetorically informed field of composition,[6] it remains true that in the ways they construct and position students, in the ways they imagine the goals of a writing class, and in the ways they construct their courses and classrooms (including the role of the teacher), there are tendencies that may identify certain compositionists and pedagogies as "expressivist."

James Berlin reminds us that there is a range of expressivists: "At one extreme can be found the anarchists, arguing for complete and uninhibited freedom in writing, including the intentional flouting of all convention. At the other extreme are the few that are close to the transactional category—especially to epistemic rhetoric" (*Rhetoric and Reality* 146). He also proposes a list of some characteristics of expressivism, particularly as it functioned in 1960s composition: "a common epistemology: the conviction that reality is a personal and private construct," "truth is always discovered within, through an internal glimpse, an examination of private inner world"; and the "social world is . . . suspect because it attempts to coerce individuals in thoughtless conformity" (145). Already we can see why experimental writing might be attractive in a pedagogy that embraced such values: experimental writing enables the expression of unique individual experiences, flouts convention, and provides ways for students to avoid that coercive social conformity represented by conventional academic prose. But there's more. Berlin and others tell the story of the emergence of expressivism from a key text in composition history's process movement: Rohman and Wlecke's *Pre-Writing: The Construction and Application of Models for Concept Formation in Writers* (1964). From their study, Rohman and Wlecke make the case for a process-pedagogy of self-discovery through such practices, at the time unconventional, as journal-keeping, meditation, and the use of analogies. Additionally, as Berlin and others also point out, they call on M. H. Abrams's canonical text on romanticism, *The Mirror and the Lamp,* to "underscore the organic, creative features of composing" (Berlin 146–47). The result, as Berlin succinctly puts it, is that "writing is seen as art, an art that arises from within the writer" (147).

All of this emphasis in expressivist (and process) pedagogy on the individual, on experience, freedom from convention, and creativity can be read in histories of composition as a critique of and opposition to the then dominance of current-traditional rhetoric in writing classrooms.[7] Current-traditional rhetoric, no more the homogeneous monolith than expressivism, has been characterized, again by Berlin, in the following ways with the following emphases:

> The writing class is to focus on discourse that deals with the rational faculties: description and narration . . . exposition . . . and argument. . . . Current traditional rhetoric thus teaches the modes of discourse with a special emphasis on exposition and its forms—analysis, classification, cause-effect and so forth. . . . The writer must take pains that language not distort what is to be communicated. Language must be precise. . . . Finally, since language is to demonstrate the individual's qualifications as a reputable observer worthy of attention, it must conform to certain standards of usage, thereby demonstrating appropriate class affiliation. (*Rhetoric and Reality* 8–9)[8]

Expressivism opposed such current-traditional approaches and other versions of school writing, or "Engfish" (Macrorie), or theme-writing (Coles), by advancing a writer-and-process–oriented pedagogy. Though many in composition will recognize what "Engfish" or "theme-writing" signals, it is worth quoting part of Macrorie's opening chapter to *Telling Writing* in order to recall his articulation of the general situation for both teachers and students of writing and his hope for what expressivist approaches to writing offered:

> In the Engfish paragraphs of the student themes the words almost never speak to each other, and when they do, they say only "Blah." . . . They [students] spent too many hours in school mastering Engfish and reading cues from teacher and textbook that suggested it is the official language of the school. In it the student cannot express truths that count for him. He learns a language that prevents him from working towards truths, and then he tells lies. In this empty circle teacher and student wander around boring each other. But there is a way out. . . . The way out and the way to good writing is to tell the truth about one's experience. (3–4, 5)

Similarly arguments for experimental writing tend to aver that the personal expression of the individual student is inhibited by the wrong kind of language (e.g., "a language that prevents him from working towards truths"), limited by the general "rules" of school writing, and that more normative or conventional genres of academic writing produce or exacerbate students' alienation. For example, the authors in Wendy Bishop's collection *Elements of Alternate Style* tend to frame their essays around both the teachers' desires and their perception of the students' desires to "break the rules." Here are a couple of explicit moments from the collection *Elements of Alternate Style:* "Sometimes you want to break the rules. Write the way that sounds best to you. A way that makes your writing fun and different" (Fike and Cook 12); "In fact, alternative styles—which can be indirect, which can violate certain rules of grammar and usage, which can allow for digression, play, and self-expression—may actually be more effective in certain writing situations" (Tobin, "The Case" 44). For some arguments, the breaking of rules appears to allow for self-expression without challenging the ideologies of conventional writings.

Many of the arguments I have examined suggest that alternative or experimental styles will allow for self-expression, which academic writing constrains; other arguments for experimental writing in composition more vehemently oppose and critique the ideologies associated with academic discourse as well as challenge commonsensical assumptions about the value of school literacies. Lillian Bridwell-Bowles succinctly puts it this way in "Freedom, Form, Function: Varieties of Academic Prose": "But the main insight I have about my own literacy history is that none of the important or meaningful writing I have ever produced happened as a result of a writing assignment given in a classroom" (50). The assertion that the kinds of writing taught in composition classrooms are irrelevant to students is similarly echoed by Derek Owens in *Resisting Writings (and the Boundaries of Composition).* He argues that students don't care about the writing they produce in composition classrooms since they rarely bother to retrieve their writing at the end of the semester—it sits around like so much "rubbish" in English departments (25). Furthermore, Owens suggests that this student alienation is due to the lack of opportunities for students to write in innovative or experimental ways: "it's no wonder that students often view writing as a chore conceived by teachers to produce anxiety, and not as an aesthetic medium capable of being orchestrated (literally, *composed*) into a pastiche of exciting, critical forms" (24). By reconceiving writing as an "aesthetic medium," he claims that students will no longer see writing as a chore or work that they must do for a given class or teacher, but as something more exciting and relevant, something that they do for themselves.

As of yet, these arguments—represented thus far mostly by Weathers,

Bishop and Starkey and their contributors, Bridwell-Bowles, and Owens —call mainly for a more inclusive, pluralist pedagogy in composition. Though they may be hard on academic writing or on the rules of school writing in general, none has quite gone the route of wanting to get rid of academic writing altogether. Mostly they want experimental writing alongside, as an option or alternative, more conventional forms of writing. Sirc, however, seems to suggest that these compromises proffered by composition (of the 1980s, 1990s, and early 2000s) are watered-down versions of the truly revolutionary pedagogies and aesthetics of what he calls the "Happening Composition" of the 1960s.

In his *English Composition as Happening*, Sirc tells several allegorical stories of avant-garde art (mostly of the 1960s, but some from earlier in the century, and mostly American, though some European) and retraces the innovative work of such compositionists as Ernece B. Kelly, Ken Macrorie, Charles Deemer, William Lutz, and William Coles. Though many of Sirc's points of reference from 1960s composition would be considered expressivist, he does not take the label for himself, he does not quote or praise more contemporary expressivists or advocates of experimental writing, and in a move I find intriguing, he more or less ignores the work of Elbow. I find this absence intriguing because Sirc's argument echoes Elbow's, but with more references to avant-garde art. (Perhaps Sirc's texts foreground the anarchist strains in Elbow's earlier writings?) Both Sirc and Elbow want a classroom without teachers, a space or "happening" that a teacher might initiate and set in motion but then sit back and enjoy what their students produce, whether notes or e-mail messages or chatroom discussions or other informal writings.[9] Elbow, too, wants writing with heart, writing that speaks in an original voice with emotion, writing that renders experience. The following passage by Sirc could have been written by an edgier Elbow: "For some reason, expressionism has become an outré term in Composition Studies (though certainly not in any other field of art). The thought of students mining the refuse lot of their own lives to trace moments of becoming, of passages, has become laughable if not downright worrisome in post-Happenings Composition, a solipsistic exercise that takes time away from the crucial interrogation of power and knowledge. But what more revolutionary content can there be?" (*English Composition as Happening* 176–77). And Sirc and Elbow have a straw man in common: David Bartholomae. Sirc attacks academic writing and its relation to the educational institutions and the field of composition as an institution particularly as it is represented in the field of composition by *Ways of Reading* and the scholarship of Bartholomae. According to Sirc, academic writing is at the very least inadequate to the needs and experi-ences of contemporary college students, so much so that repeatedly he makes statements about student writing such as these: "Composition as Happening means the displacement of such texts [e.g., the kind of texts students might produce in response to assignments from *Ways of Reading*] from the writing class, substituting a basic awareness of how to use lan-guage and information, a cool project, a sense of poetry" (277); "They will write nothing, of course, this lively in their formal essays" (199); "There's a reality in these [electronic] discussions that I seldom see in their stan-dard papers" (200). At the very worst, Sirc claims, academic writing is part and parcel of the oppressive educational-military-industrial war machine: "What [students are] . . . trying on, really, is irremovable, the straight jack-ets of formalist grammar and essayist prose, the grammar of the monu-ment that will crush them and bury them. . . . I can witness the guillotine-rhythm of Bartholomae's gerunds—knowing, selecting, evaluating, re-porting, concluding, and arguing—every day in the academy" (230–31). It is worth quoting Sirc at length more on this issue to get the full flavor of the revolutionary enthusiasm he musters, with echoes of the sixties in the year 2002: "What would empower students more—teaching them how to accommodate to the rules of academic discourse; or teaching them that if they organized they could demand that they be allowed to write any way they wanted, that they would not have to waste so much time learning to speak like us (their own language being almost all right)? What if they gave a war and nobody came? What if they had an academic discourse and nobody used it?" (222).

Sirc seems to resist a politics of form, rejecting the kind of arguments advanced by compositionists discussed above: "Happenings Composition prizes the stuff left behind, the otherwise-discarded, because it reveals a particular life. If the class is in any way a Happening, then the ad hoc— the prewriting, quizzes, exercises, notes, journals, email, false starts— is sometimes the most permanently satisfying text of all" (177). Indeed, though he prefers allegorical forms and forms that highlight juxtaposition —since he agrees with Craig Owens that allegorical forms such as mon-tage and collage are the major postmodern art forms—he asserts that he is not interested in making claims for the value of certain forms over oth-ers: "Students working in whatever medium, trying to do something that sends someone to heaven" (*English Composition as Happening* 292).

However, if there is no argument for particular forms per se (e.g., collage or hypertext), there are plenty of arguments against forms and genres, particularly academic, as those which further alienate students, which prevent them from getting in touch with their experiences, which inhibit what Sirc sees as the most valuable project of the avant-garde and its potential gift to composition—the approaches by which students can bring together art and everyday life: "Real-life situations, then, as the ultimate text. This falling back on the basics of situation, of baseline experience, this text-as-passage, allows not only a blurring of art and life, but a blurring of genres as well, every compositional form/genre indistinct, subsumed by the rhythm of temporal movement," and "informal writings are central to a Happenings curriculum because students learn more about their personal style and statement in those open forms" (*English Composition as Happening* 151, 282).

Ultimately, what Sirc wants is, in many ways, more expressivist than what even earlier expressivist compositionists such as Macrorie and Coles wanted. Sirc wants writing in any form (except academic) that invokes an emotional response, that speaks of a less alienated, less exhausted individual (*English Composition as Happening* 209); writing that is sweet, joyous, intelligent, exciting, available to all, exhilarating (230); writing that articulates "deeply felt truths" (269), that conveys a "sense of enchantment" or "magic" (289), of "discovery and wonder" (281), that represents a "life lived in mental and spiritual splendor" (291). Ultimately, Sirc suggests that what we need is a "rhetoric of the heart," which "instead of tracing cultural tradition . . . penetrate[s] to the core of human emotion" (288). Though occasionally he rejects expressivism[10] as well as the social constructionism of contemporary advocates of the teaching of academic discourse, in the end Sirc stands up for students' spirituality and heart by arguing for a vision of composition in which students are artists and their writing art: "Late Sixties Composition staked this social transformation on an aesthetics, based in an embodied spirituality; currently Composition's more ideological theorists and practitioners stake it on a (often mean-spirited) thought-and-language based textual politics. . . . A politics without wonder and poetry, without a deep sense of sublime joy, will never be enlightening, will never be anything more than a scolding complaint" (291–92).

It is hard to say in Sirc's argument, and in the arguments of other neoexpressivist experimental compositionists, whether conventional academic genres and discourses (and all the rules that accompany them) produce or merely augment students' alienation, but it is clear that academic writing, or school writing, is understood as alienated labor, that is, something that students produce for someone else, for someone else's reasons, purposes, and enjoyment. This is generally speaking what alienated labor is. Whether academic essays broadly understood across decades of the teaching of writing are, or must be, inherently alienated labor is debatable. But the production of these personal and artistic student writings, compared to academic prose, is understood as nonalienated labor since students are free to choose their own styles, topics, and voices and often write from their own experiences. Therefore, the arguments claim, these writings are more significant and more valuable for students. This is a key assumption in many arguments for experimental writing in composition: innovative writings as "aesthetic mediums" or art are understood as noncommodities, separate and free from any market relations of the academy. Yet, even if the appeal to the aesthetic seeks to escape the overdetermined space of the writing classroom and its production of academic prose, Fredric Jameson cautions us against such broad appeals to the production of art as nonalienated labor: "For one thing, the very experience of art itself is alienated and made 'other' and inaccessible to too many people to serve as a useful vehicle for their imaginative experience. This is so whether it is a question of high art or mass culture; in both cases, for very different reasons, the experience of production of such art forms is inaccessible to most people (including critics and intellectuals), who thereby find themselves thrown back on an experience of both kinds of art as sheer receptions (whence the attractiveness of those categories for contemporary theory)" (*Postmodernism* 146).

Jameson describes what I see as two serious obstacles in pedagogies for experimental or innovative writing informed by aesthetic concerns: first, students may well be alienated from experimental works of literature, if not more generally alienated from the acts of reading and writing; and second, many students think that they do not have access to the modes of production that might make their writing significant beyond the classroom. Jameson further suggests that part of the alienation from the modes of production comes from understanding these modes as too huge and complex for anyone to consider mastering: "they inspire very little optimism about the potential control or mastery over processes, oneself, and nature and collective destiny, which nonalienated labor necessarily includes and projects" (147). Although Jameson is here referring to other media such as television, he might as well be describing the situation that the student writer faces when encountering the sheer variety of writing in our society, the demands upon students within the institution of education, and the mystification of judgment on the effectiveness of any given mode of writing.

I have been critiquing expressivist arguments in composition for experimental writing on a range of issues. These problems have precedence in the various ways in which the individual is posited vis-à-vis society in the context of aesthetic theory: the right of the individual to express his or her own unique reality or experience in the context of democracy as counter to totalitarianism; the need of the individual to express his or her own reality, especially emotions, creativity, imagination, and experience, in the face of normative or traditional discourses and versions of society that oppress and constrain the individual. In other words, experimental writing as an "aesthetic medium" (in the words of Derek Owens) is said to provide the individual student with a measure of freedom and relief from alienation. Furthermore, experimental writing posited as nonalienated labor is claimed to be more relevant to a student's life.

The irony of these arguments is that they want to contextualize experimental writing, defining it in terms of its relevance to lived experience and to the freedom it offers from an oppressive society, yet they fail to acknowledge that the avant-garde aesthetics implied by experimental writing already have a historical context that complicates their arguments or even calls them into question. That is, in focusing on students as individuals who can overcome their own alienation through artistic means, expressivist proponents of experimental writing seem unaware that, historically, artists have struggled with both their autonomy and alienation in terms of a competing desire to maintain or obtain individual freedom and a desire to perceive themselves as participating in a social collective. The story of the individuality and autonomy of the individual artist is caught up in stories of the autonomy of art. Such stories illuminate and complicate claims made for the role that experimental or alternate styles might play in ensuring the individual freedom of the student writer.

AVANT-GARDE: THE PROBLEM OF AUTONOMY

In *Theory of the Avant-Garde,* Peter Bürger suggests that history can inform our understanding of both the autonomy of the individual artist and the autonomy of art. To be sure, Bürger does not construct a cause-and-effect relationship between the emergence of a concept of autonomous art and such historical occurrences as the French Revolution or other attempts by the bourgeoisie to liberate itself from monarchial or regressive feudal tendencies in society. Clearly, as he argues, both the artist and art had achieved a degree of autonomy prior to the revolutions of the late eighteenth century (24). Indeed, while art's autonomy is significant to the development of the avant-garde, it is actually the establishment of the institution of art that makes possible the avant-garde's attack on art *as* institution.

Yet even the establishment of the institution of art is not an adequate explanation for emergence of the avant-garde. As Bürger notes, the institution of art had been firmly established at the end of the eighteenth century with the emancipation of the bourgeoisie, yet the avant-garde's project of self-criticism does not begin until the beginning of the twentieth century. This is because though art had been established as an institution, there was still some residual political content to works of art, thus implying that art maintained some connection to sociopolitical context: "The self-criticism of the social subsystem that is art can become possible only when the contents also lose their political character, and art wants to be nothing other than art. This stage is reached at the end of the nineteenth century, in Aestheticism" (Bürger 26–27). Though we will return to Bürger's argument about the avant-garde's attack on aestheticism and the institution of art in the next chapter, Bürger's broad history of the historical emergence of the avant-garde begins to highlight the dialectic of autonomy and alienation latent in avant-garde responses to the institution of art.

To describe this dialectic briefly, the other side of the autonomy of the individual artist and the autonomy of art is the artist's alienation and the social irrelevance of art. Bürger, ever careful to avoid nondialectical histories, is wary of telling stories about the relationship between the art market and the emergence of autonomous artists and art.[11] However, these stories are told and retold by various theorists of the avant-garde and are worth briefly reiterating here. With the emancipation of the bourgeoisie and the rise of market culture, the artist found himself cut loose from his usual patrons, the court and the church. As art now had no ostensible obligations to any institution or group, the artist and art were both "freed" from their places in the social schema. The freedom of the artist, however, had its other side, alienation. Indeed, romanticism, modernism, and avant-gardism all posit an artist who is alienated from society. How artists responded to their autonomous/alienated positions varied within each historical movement. Generally speaking, socially progressive romantics, such as William Wordsworth and Friedrich Schiller, attempted to embrace their autonomy in order to critique bourgeois society, imagine a better future, and reclaim a sense of individual and social wholeness. Schiller, in particular, relied upon the autonomy of the aesthetic to unite individuals and a society fragmented by the emergence of modern conditions such as the division of labor. The modernists, apparently despairing over ever alleviating their alienation, doubtful about the future, and skeptical regarding the possibility of collective social action, retreated into the hermetic space of art's autonomy. But the avant-gardists, simultaneously relying on and criticizing art's autonomy, tried to destroy the institution of art in an attempt to reintegrate art and everyday praxis, thus attempting to both unalienate themselves and others and, simultaneously, recover a sense of the future, a future that unlike the one imagined by the romantics, tended to embrace the advantages of modernity.

These stories can, of course, be contested by the details of specific historical movements, artists, and artworks, but they provide a broad outline of various reactions to the autonomy-alienation problematic. Whatever the various responses of the romantics, the moderns, and the avant-gardists, what remained a constant problem for artists in all these movements was the tension between the freedom of the individual and social determinism or social responsibility.

Indeed, Nicos Hadjinicolaou argues that the avant-garde is, in many important ways, a continuation, but also a revision, of the romantic emphasis on the individual. He reminds us that, in *The Theory of the Avant-Garde*, Renato Poggioli acknowledges the "kinship" between the avant-garde and the romantics via their shared interests in the strange and the novel. He argues that if the avant-garde is critical of the modernists, it is also true that "the anti-traditionalist and anti-academic attitude so typical of avant-gardism was at the heart of the debate between the 'classics' and the 'romantics,'" and that "the key image [of the avant-garde artist] (predominant at least until the end of World War II) is essentially romantic: the solitary artist who is misunderstood by his contemporaries but who will be discovered and appreciated by posterity, when future generations have reached the stage he now occupies" (Hadjinicolaou 55). In fact, Hadjinicolaou also points out that the "opposition between the artist and the bourgeois, which is characteristic of avant-gardism, effectively began with romanticism" (55).

Similarly, Charles Russell traces the modernists' romantic legacy: "Modernist writers on the whole have reacted against the individualist, expressionist, and socially active tendencies of the romantic movement. However, these modernist aesthetic strategies are direct legacies of literary romanticism, for even if the modernist vision is decidedly more private and self-contained than the romantic, these strategies sustain the romantic belief in the unique attributes of the literary work and the special capabilities of the poet to apprehend and articulate a realm of significant value and meaning, freed from the debasing contingency of modern bourgeois life" (13).

In fact, both modernism and avant-gardism can be said to share these traces of romantic concepts of the individual artist who not only opposes the bourgeois order, but who also, as poet, has "special capabilities" and as a result has an important role to play vis-à-vis society: "The myth of the poet as a prophet had been revived and developed since the early days of romanticism. . . . It will suffice to say that almost all the progressive minded romantics upheld the belief in the avant-garde role of poetry, even if they did not use the term 'avant-garde' and even if they did not embrace a didactic-utilitarian philosophy of art" (Calinescu 105). As Calinescu further points out, however, this idea of the poet as avant-garde is particularly romantic. It is not to be confused with the kinds of political projects of later avant-gardes signaled generally by the didactic purpose of much avant-garde art, or signaled below by specific references to the avant-garde's explicit commitment to particular political projects (e.g., Italian fascism, antiwar movements, or various versions of communism). The romantic poet—for instance, Shelley—is avant-garde as a result of his heightened imagination: "In other words, poetry has to play a great social role not because it can 'popularize' some idea or other, but simply because it stimulates the imagination" (Calinescu 105).

Poets may be, as Shelley argues in *A Defence of Poetry*, "heralds," their minds "mirrors of futurity." They may even be "the unacknowledged legislators of the world." But as Russell reminds us, "we may also read in these words, as has Raymond Williams, an implicit helplessness in the word 'unacknowledged' which severely qualifies the noble calling of 'legislator of the world'" (Russell 19).[12] In other words, even if ideally the poet is capable of communicating his vision of the future (thereby hoping to affect society), there is no guarantee that his audience will listen or heed his work. Indeed, the first avant-garde writer that Russell discusses is Rimbaud, who, like Shelley, figures the poet as a "seer." Russell suggests that part of what makes Rimbaud avant-garde and not just romantic or modernist is that Rimbaud is compelled to depersonalize the poetic process. In support of this claim, Russell quotes Rimbaud: "It is wrong to say: I think. One ought to say: People think me [*On me pense*] . . . I is someone else" (Russell 51). Yet, in the end, Russell argues that although Rimbaud, like many modernist and avant-garde writers, attempted to reject this "conception of the poet as privileged visionary," his inability or unwillingness to dismiss this conception "suggests that what Rimbaud desired was a version of Romantic inspiration" (51).

If, on the one hand, Rimbaud's attempt to depersonalize his poetry through derangement of his senses fails and results in his return (regression) to romantic images of the individual poet, then, on the other hand, experimental writing in composition in the context of postmodernity seems to move in the opposite direction. In the face of depersonalizing discourses, it attempts to relocate the individual self by invoking a rather romantic conception of the individual writer, who must, to quote Derek Owens, "rebel against the state's highly successful program of defining education as a process of rigid mechanization and self-effacement" (*Resisting Writings* 231). A significant tension in the history of the avant-garde is just this vacillation between personalization and depersonalization. Yet, most of the arguments in composition for experimental writing emphasize only the personal, thus in many ways returning to a romantic subject and denying or ignoring the attempts of the avant-garde to move the source of art away from individual creativity and relocate it in social praxis (see my discussion of Bürger, Jameson, and Russell below).

But moving the source of art away from individual creativity is difficult if we agree that the success of avant-garde art seems to require the positing of an autonomous individual. For example, Hadjinicolaou argues that the avant-garde continues, like romanticism, to emphasize the importance of the individual artist, even to the extent of perpetuating the cult of genius: "we can advance the thesis that elitism, inherent in the ideology of avant-gardism, is a sign of the permanence of the cult of the genius" (54). Yet, as I suggested above, avant-garde art, through its practices, seems to deny the importance of individual production. For example, Bürger argues that some avant-garde art is a radical negation of the individual: "In its most extreme manifestations, the avant-garde's reply to this is not the collective as the subject of production but the radical negation of the category of individual creation" (51). As evidence to support this claim, Bürger presents the example of Duchamp signing mass-produced objects and submitting them to art exhibits (51), thus mocking the emphasis on an artist's individual signature (e.g., "R. Mutt" instead of "Duchamp") for purposes of exhibition and calling into question the institution of art's need to imagine the work of art as the product of a individual creative artist. As Bürger notes, however, even if the avant-garde in its most extreme manifestations attempted to negate the category of individual production, it did not advance a concept of collective production.

Bürger also argues that the avant-garde attempted to move further in the direction of reintegrating art and everyday praxis. Specifically, instructions for making Dadaist poems can be read like simple "recipes" that the reader can follow (e.g., take a newspaper, cut it up, select words randomly, and paste together into a poem). Thus, the lines between producer and recipient are blurred since anyone can make a Dada poem. As Bürger notes, "All that remains is the individual who uses poetry as an instrument for living one's life as best as one can" (53). Yet, as Bürger acknowledges, the idea of everyone as an artist can lead to solipsism (53).

Indeed, solipsism is a problem not only for avant-garde conceptions of art, but also for related conceptions of experimental student writing. Taken to its radical conclusion, the argument that a student's individuality requires a corresponding unconventional form of writing would lead to idiosyncratic solipsistic writing that no one but the writer could understand. Indeed, we see this problem evidenced in Starkey's remarks when he discusses the problem of evaluating his students' attempts at language poetry: "So if a student claims that her work accomplishes its purpose—no matter how obscure and solipsistic that purpose might be—what right does an instructor promulgating the values of language poetry have to disparage that work?" (129). The problems of judging the unconventional, indeed idiosyncratic, language of experimental writing and the way those problems are managed (including requiring students to write reflective or explanatory essays) will be addressed in chapter 3, on judgment. However, the problematic of judgment is not the real issue here, but instead it is the possibility that an individual's experimental writing leads not to communication of some alternative reality but to noncommunication. Much avant-garde art risks noncommunication because of three aspects: its emphasis on extreme freedom, recipes and other nonlogical approaches to composition, and the fact that the art or writing produced can be so private as to be solipsistic. As Russell notes, it is difficult to tell when a poet, in his or her capacity as seer, is creating a new language for a new world and when he or she is solipsistic. Discussing the specific example of some poetry by Apollinaire, Russell gestures to this larger problem: "If 'Arbre' is an expression of a state of simultaneity that has achieved the 'fourth dimension,' that achievement is so private as to be impenetrable. Apollinaire might have achieved here such a totally lyrical moment that the unity of time, space, and the poet was the expression of a solipsistic projection, but in doing this, he undermined his role of the seer" (83). Despite running the risk of being misunderstood or ignored, individual freedom is of the utmost importance to many avant-garde artists and movements. Russell discusses Dada, particularly the work of Tristan Tzara:

> Thus, like Rimbaud, Tzara proposed a programmatic, if not rational, process of derangement in order to thrust the artist and the audience into a state of irrational reality. An ideal is stated: out of destruction ("without aim or design") comes purification, a goal in spite of itself. The newly cleansed individual will thus be free to live and create spontaneously. This new freedom represents an absolute condition for Tzara. In this purified state the individual will know no restriction, no necessity except maintaining the freedom. To a certain extent, this is a goal implicit in all avant-garde work. (104)

The avant-garde artist's upholding of the value of individual and artistic freedom creates problems for the politics of the avant-garde.

Though the varying politics of the avant-garde will be discussed at length later, it is worth addressing briefly here a second dialectic, that is, the dialectic between individual freedom and social commitment. The individual artist distances himself or herself from society so as to both critique it and imagine new futures, but this autonomy and alienation can make it difficult for the individual artist to align with a political program. Such an alignment can dismiss the autonomy of art and the artist, refiguring the first as subservient propaganda and the second as servant of some political party. Furthermore, the avant-garde artist's general desire for individual freedom is constrained not just by his or her relationships with political groups, but by the need to reconcile the individual/social dialectic by joining together with like-minded artists to establish a movement. Indeed, this is one of the aporias of the avant-garde that Hans Magnus Enzensberger identifies, particularly as it is manifested in the surrealist movement: "The new doctrine crystallizes, as always, around its yearning for absolute freedom. The word fanaticism [used by Breton in reference to freedom as the "old human fanaticism"] is already an indication that this freedom can be acquired only at the price of absolute discipline: within a few years, the surrealist guard spins itself into a cocoon of regulations" (39). The closest parallel in composition to this problem is articulated in the work of Winston Weathers. Students have the freedom to choose their alternate styles as long as they abide by the rules, set by their teachers and/ or by the model texts of literature they are imitating. Similarly, in the work of Wendy Bishop, students can experiment with their writing as long as they discipline themselves in reflective writings for the teacher.

We can also see from the history of the avant-garde that the avant-garde's emphasis on the freedom of the individual is further aggravated within the context of postmodernism. With postmodern theorization of the relationship between language and the individual subject, avant-garde claims about the importance of individual expression become problematic. Though many of the advocates of experimental writing in composition understand and acknowledge a social constructionist view of language and the individual subject, they continue to posit the individual as the locus of freedom. It is the individual, in other words, who opposes dominant normative discourses, chooses his or her style, opposes self-effacement, and operates as the site of local resistance in postmodern society. Yet, within the context of postmodernity, both the individual and art lose their autonomy. As Fredric Jameson puts it, "We must however add that the problem of expression is itself closely linked to some conception of the subject as a monadlike container, within which things felt are then expressed by projection outward. What we must now stress, however, is the degree to which the high-modernist conception of a unique style, along with the accompanying collective ideas of an artistic or political vanguard or avant-garde, themselves stand or fall along with that older notion (or experience) of the so-called centered subject" (15). Furthermore, this loss of the autonomous stable subject and its unique style of expression is accompanied by the loss of agency the artist might have as critic of dominant discourses: "Gone are the modernist and avant-garde premises of the privileged nature of the artist's perspective and language. No longer does the feeling of alienation suggest a compensating critical vantage point from which the artist can declare his or her independence from the dominant culture. . . . The concept of the integral self, struggling against the oppressive embrace of the social realm by falling back upon a cherished sense of personal authenticity, is swept aside as a delusive fiction which ensured the legitimacy of the social opposition against which it fought" (Russell 247). Thus, the desire of experimental expressivists to alleviate student alienation and free the individual student through the teaching of innovative styles by invoking the critical purchase of avant-garde art encounters several conflicting conceptions of subjectivity in aesthetics and pedagogies.

For example, it would appear that experimental expressivists' romantic and avant-garde aesthetics (with its romantic traces) would prove efficacious in a version of composition as still predicated on a humanist conception of the student as a coherent subject/agent. In "The Subject of Discourse," John Clifford highlights the ways in which this traditional humanist subject is understood: as creative individual, as locus of significance, as originator of meaning, as an autonomous being, as aware of ends and means, of authorial intentions and motivations (39). Though postmodern and Marxist critics have contested this kind of humanist rhetoric, it remains an informing discourse of composition pedagogy, particularly of expressivist experimental composition, with its emphasis on individuals and choice: "Encouraging writers to develop prose styles that reflect their individuality, for example, is one technique among hundreds that ensures our positions, as teachers and grade givers, the writer's position as student and supplicant, and both as unequal subjects in a constructed hierarchy. At the same time, such rituals foster the illusion of individuality and choice, as if the student writers created the possible styles of a given discourse genre" (46). To try to use unique personal styles as a way to resist the overdetermined nature of the genres and discourses students face in writing classrooms is, in Clifford's argument, to mask and thus perpetuate the powerlessness of student writers.

If, on the one hand, the loss of a stable, unified subject position inhibits the individual freedom necessary for the production of avant-garde art, on the other hand, compositionists who advocate experimental writing might see in the multiplicity of subject positions for their students a reason to teach multiple forms: as Bridwell-Bowles says, "Multiple identities, multiple languages, multiple rhetorics" ("Freedom, Form, Function" 54). A dominant discourse (and ideology) is posited—such as rational, linear, objective academic discourse—which can be opposed by the individual who chooses an alternate style or creates an experimental text. This is still the avant-garde position. But the paradox in various arguments in composition for the freedom of the individual alongside the multiplicity of postmodern subjectivities, as, for example, expressed by Bridwell-Bowles, is that in the context of postmodern subjectivities, the traditional humanist subject (or as Jameson describes it above, the modernist or avant-garde artist-subject) no longer has the kind of autonomous freedom that might allow students to choose from their multiple identities.

In a poststructuralist and postmodern framework, the individual is already the subject of multiple social discourses. Writing and the self are both decentered, both seen "not only as the effect of language patterns but as the result of multiple discourses already in place, already overdetermined by historical and social meanings in constant internal struggle" (Clifford 40). If there is any hope for intervention in this scene of constraint on the individual, it is found in the idea that "the inevitable contradictions within subject positions can be a catalyst for resistant and counterhegemonic thinking" and that when "we finally perceive how hegemonic rituals construct us in ways we would like to oppose, we want to be agents instead of subjects" (Clifford 41, 50). What Clifford is teasing out here is the powerlessness and passivity associated with subjectivity (subject equals subjection, even though in other contexts a subject is the source of activity/verbness), compared to the conscious action of an agent, as in an agent for change. Additionally, while Clifford does not continue his discussion of agency, one can imagine that agency need not reside in an individual, but may reside in a group of people, with or without the concept of subjectivity. That is to say, though teachers of writing imagine agency as individual, inhuman forces or anonymous or depersonalized actions or texts can, in fact, also act as agents. One might imagine, for example, that student texts might act as agents by highlighting for readers (intentionally or not) the contradictions of subject positions.

The tension between empowering the individual and fostering collective action abides and remains unresolved in literacy education generally and composition pedagogy specifically. Writing is both a solitary act and a social act; we both teach individual students and participate in a social process. Expressivist arguments for experimental writing tend to elide or evade discussions—detailed historical material discussions—of the larger social relations of students' experiments. Yet other arguments for experimental writing in composition, as we shall see, attempt to address them head-on by highlighting the dialectic between the individual and the social, particularly in terms of cultural or postmodern pedagogies, by arguing for the teaching of experimental and innovative academic discourses, and by calling into question composition in its institutional contexts.

EXPERIMENTAL WRITING AND THE POLITICS OF ACADEMIC DISCOURSE

COMPOSITION'S INSTITUTIONS

As I showed in the previous chapter, while expressivists who argue for the teaching of experimental writing often critique academic discourse (not only in the forms of current traditionalism but also in the newer cultural studies or rhetorical versions), they are more concerned with the student as individual, his or her honest or authentic writing/self, and therefore relegate social or ideological concerns to the background. Compositionists who advocate experimental writing in service of multicultural, social constructionist, or postmodern pedagogies similarly challenge the hegemonic ideologies associated with academic writing. But they tend to foreground the ways in which alternative forms of writing represent social groups and situate individual students within larger social structures and discourses. In doing so, they attempt not only to help the individual student, but also to change larger social, political, and institutional structures, including the field of composition.

In this chapter, I examine some key arguments for teaching experimental writing by this second group of compositionists. Many of these arguments claim that experimental writing (reading it, teaching it, writing it) is inherently political, both in the context of the classroom and in the context of larger institutions (for example, the field of composition). To address these claims, I examine historical and theoretical debates about the politics of the avant-garde as a way to shed some light on, and problematize, assumptions made by this second group of compositionists about the progressive politics of experimental writing, the category of innovation, and the degree to which experimental writing is an attempt to critique, reform, or destroy the field of composition, particularly as it identifies itself with the teaching of academic writing.

DIVERSITY, CRITIQUE, AND TRANSFORMATION

Critics of traditional academic discourse link it with objectivity, rationality, and the conventions of academic prose most in evidence in the characteristics of the essay form as listed by Derek Owens: "Introductions and conclusions, primary theses, repeated premises, linear progression, obligatory citation, orderly and incremental dialectic, supportive anecdotes, professional vocabulary, 'standard' usage, footnotes and endnotes, bibliographies and appendices: these are the capital ingredients of our academic language, all spun together with the interrelated rhythms of the sentence and the paragraph" (*Resisting Writings* 29).[1] While Owens here helps us see many of the formal and structural aspects of academic prose, other proponents of alternative academic discourses help us identify academic values or ideologies more broadly. Patricia Bizzell, for example, describes the dominant worldview of those in power in academic communities:

> This worldview speaks through an academic persona who is objective, trying to prevent any emotions or prejudices from influencing the ideas in the writing. The persona is skeptical, responding with doubt and questions to any claim that something is true or good or beautiful. Not surprisingly, the persona is argumentative, favoring debate, believing that if we are going to find out whether something is true or good or beautiful, the only way we do that is by arguing for opposing views of it, to see who wins. In this view, only debate can produce knowledge. Knowledge is not something immediately available to experience, nor is it revealed from transcendent sources. Additionally, the persona is precise, exacting, rigorous—if debate is going to generate knowledge, all participants must use language carefully, demonstrate their knowledge of earlier scholarly work, argue logically and fairly, use sound evidence, and so on. ("Intellectual Work of 'Mixed' Forms" 2)

Chris Thaiss and Terry Myers Zawacki take a slightly different approach in their study of academic and alternative discourses, *Engaged Writers, Dynamic Disciplines: Research on the Academic Writing Life*. They acknowledge that descriptions and definitions of academic writing are often abstract, and understandably there is no one definition. Yet, as they studied actual academics and their writing, as well as actual students and their writing, they came up with three broad categories of characteristics of academic discourse, "regardless of differences among disciplines and individual teachers" (5):

> 1. Clear evidence in writing that the writer(s) have been persistent, open-minded, and disciplined in study.

> 2. The dominance of reason over emotion or sensual perception.

> 3. An imagined reader who is coolly rational, reading for information, and intending to formulate a reasoned response. (Thaiss and Zawacki 5–7)

Thaiss and Zawacki go on to elaborate, qualify, complicate, and discuss examples and exceptions to these three characteristics. Indeed, it is part of the general argument of alternative discourses that academic discourse is not as monolithic as it might be described or as it might seem. I have quoted these three formulations of academic writing not to point out their gaps or contradictions (of which there are many), but to show how arguments for experimental writing and alternative discourses characterize academic prose, its features, its values and implied limitations (e.g., its exclusion or backgrounding of emotion or personal experience, its dominance by reason and discipline, and the like).

Proponents of experimental writing tend to associate academic discourse and its features and values negatively with the project of literacy education as the reproduction of the status quo or dominant cultural ideologies. In "Freedom, Form, Function," Bridwell-Bowles links academic prose with "rational thought and clear exposition" (56), "uniformity, order, clarity, rules and principles" (58).[2] Invoking postmodernism, the explosion of the literary canon, and multiculturalism, she argues that "we have to encourage many different types of writing, and not just a variety of academic discourse, but experimental writing as well" (56). According to Bridwell-Bowles, the older forms are no longer adequate in the face of contemporary social issues: "What could possibly be written in a 5,000 word essay on abortion that would change anyone's mind? On complex matters such as these [e.g., El Salvador, Bosnia-Herzegovina, Israel/Palestine,

AIDS], we need a wide variety of forms of writing, produced from multiple perspectives, alongside a variety of other media. If form follows function, and the functions of most written language are multiple, then we need to investigate new forms" ("Freedom, Form, Function" 55). Not only are the older forms inadequate, academic discourse often reproduces specific ideologies: "In this address, I have argued for diversity because I believe that calls for standardization often mask white, middle-class, male-dominated traditions" (58). New forms, in Bridwell-Bowles's argument, allow writers to "express ways of thinking that have been outside of the dominant culture" and can teach students to "critique not only their material and their potential readers' needs, but also the rhetorical conventions that they are expected to employ within the academy" ("Discourse and Diversity" 349). Although students in composition classes are clearly situated within the university and interpellated by the ideology of academic discourse, Bridwell-Bowles's argument attempts to buy them some freedom and distance from dominant discourses as well as to allow for them some "ways of thinking" outside of the dominant culture.

The claim that through experimental writing students can get distance from and step outside of the dominant culture is ironically similar to the claim made by advocates of the teaching of academic discourse. For example, in several of her earlier essays in *Academic Discourse and Critical Consciousness,* Patricia Bizzell argues that academic writing affords students some critical distance from their own experience. From this distance, she maintains, students can not only critique the subjectivities they bring to their educational experience but also revise the academic community and by extension the larger social community as well, since, as Bizzell claims, academic discourses and public discourses are contiguous.[3] In other words, teaching students the academic discourse of power is one way to authorize them to participate in critical conversation both academically and sociopolitically. However, advocates of innovative or experimental writing, while acknowledging that academic discourses can be empowering and diverse, argue that they are not diverse enough, and that, in fact, their power is achieved by excluding alternative forms and the neglected realities, experiences, knowledges, and ideologies these forms represent. Although it could be argued that one might write a rather radical and critical text in the most conventional academic form (with radical content, for example), advocates of experimental and innovative forms in composition generally adopt the line of argument expressed by Jonathan Monroe in "Poetry, the University, and the Culture of Distraction": "recent antigeneric texts share an understanding that innovations at the level of formal syntactics may have an antinormative force at least equal to if not greater than that of texts that count on having their effects through even the most polemical contentual stances articulated in more normative modes" (4). In effect, critical and political differences in composition might be represented through both radical content and radical form, but apparently formally innovative texts, regardless of content, have potentially "greater" force than conventional texts with radical content.[4]

Seeing innovative and experimental writings as a way to diversify academic prose even further, Bridwell-Bowles offers not just examples of formal experimentation—language play, fragmentation, nonlinear arguments, or nonargumentative writings—but examples of ways of writing (from Adrienne Rich, Virginia Woolf, Hélène Cixous, Gloria Anzaldúa, Patricia Williams, Countee Cullen, and Keith Gilyard, to name a few) that represent different cultural experiences of race, class, sexuality, and gender ("Discourse and Diversity" 356–60). The teaching of these innovative discourses in composition classes is meant to ensure students' freedom. For example, the "freedom" in the title of Bridwell-Bowles's "Freedom, Form, Function: Varieties of Academic Discourse" refers not only to the freedom to critique academic rhetorical conventions, but also to the freedom to "dream" of different social realities and to "transform" current social realities (47). Though Bridwell-Bowles does not put her argument in these terms, it seems clear that social transformation depends upon dreaming the future, which in turn depends upon positing a space free from determining social discourses.

In a similar vein, Derek Owens argues in *Resisting Writings (and the Boundaries of Composition)* that innovative writings allow for the inclusion and representation of more and various social and individual voices (49, 168), provide access to new modes of critical thought (178), and make visible, by negation, the rules of academic writing (66), though, unlike Bridwell-Bowles, who situates her argument within the context of postmodernity, Owens dismisses poststructuralism and postmodernity as nothing more than a breakdown of genres (155). Owens's book is valuable for the sheer amount and variety of formal options, texts, and authors that he addresses. It is a veritable cornucopia of experimental and innovative writings. Owens roughly divides his examples into alternatives to the essay form, alternatives to "Eurocentric discourse," and alternatives to masculinist discourse. Examples include Charles Olson, Gertrude Stein, Ezra Pound, William Carlos Williams, H. D., Virginia Woolf, Ntozake Shange, Geneva Smitherman, Leslie Marmon Silko, Ishmael Reed, Nicole Brossard, Rachel DuPlessis, Hélène Cixous, Michelle Cliff, and Charles

Bernstein, just to name a few. Additionally, his book is admirable for the ways in which it tries to claim sociopolitical and historical significance for many of these forms of writing. The aesthetic variations that Owens lists include feminist writings, African American writings, and samples from modernist and avant-garde literature. These examples provide alternatives to the more familiar academic essays, which predominate in composition courses. As with many arguments for experimental writing, Owens associates conventional texts with the reproduction of a problematic status quo. Indeed, Owens argues that opposing the oppressive aspects of education depends upon "how imaginatively we search for ways of spending time with our students that help us rebel against the state's highly successful program of defining education as a process of rigid mechanization and self-effacement, how imaginatively we withstand the insidious, institutional drive to erase any and all creative ruptures as we advocate pedagogies of imaginative, constructive resistance" (*Resisting Writings* 231).

Whereas Bridwell-Bowles speaks mostly of innovation and experimentation as the "other" of academic or rational writing, Owens explicitly names the other of academic writing as art, claiming that art, in its capacity to change or transform social realities and resist the institutional erasure of the self, is necessary to writing instruction as a mode of "survival" (*Resisting Writings* 227). But as innovative or experimental writing, art is also a kind of resistance to the dehumanization of education and dominant discourses through "guerilla warfare" (85). Owens's language seems both romantic (opposing "rigid mechanization" and "self-effacement") and vaguely militaristic and violent: "rebel" "withstand," "erase," "resistance," "survival," and "guerilla warfare." This is powerful language. Yet Owens's vision of experimental writing in composition classes leaves out just the kind of violent, aggressive, hard-to-read, hard-to-contain art that exploits most effectively the very ruptures he mentions. Just to show the internal conflicts in Owens's text, I want to examine how difficult it is to make these kinds of claims for experimental or innovative writing as art and art as a kind of resistance in composition.

By reading and imitating various texts, students in Owens's classroom will learn to understand and value the different writing conventions, as well as the experiences, values, and views of a variety of groups in society, for example, feminists or African Americans, that these texts represent: "During each section students read essays that reflect in some way the compositional orientation currently under investigation, discuss the techniques and assumptions housed within [within?] those texts, and finally write texts that are evaluated to some extent on how well they adhere to similar writerly objectives" (Owens, *Resisting Writings* 186). As easily as Owens has read the examples of experimental writing in his book, the students will also successfully read the experimental texts in the writing classroom. There is one instance in which Owens admits his failure to make sense of an innovative or experimental text. Apparently, he was a little mystified by some poetry of H. D. (53). However, since Owens does not comment at length on the effect of his inability to interpret or understand what are, for a lot of readers, difficult modernist or avant-garde texts, I cannot conclude much more from this exception than that Owens is suggesting that sometimes incomprehensibility happens but that it is not an obstacle to either students' appreciation of these texts nor is it an obstacle to their attempts to imitate these texts.

Because a large part of the work of his class is to ask students to analyze the texts they read, he admits that "rhetorical analysis was what students consistently found most difficult" (188). The kind of rhetorical analysis he asks for is mostly formal: "the writer's use of terse sentences, colorful vocabulary, staccato paragraphs, parenthetical asides, etc." (188). A problem with such an approach is that it dismisses other rhetorical concerns such as the elusive audience, a text's content, or its context. If I agree with Owens that being able to recognize and name certain formal moves is some of the most difficult work for students even when they read the most familiar of texts (e.g., the five-paragraph essay), then it seems to me that Owens would discuss in more detail the difficulty of asking students to read what would be not only formally, but perhaps ideologically, difficult texts.

There is no indication, in other words, that Owens has anticipated any possibly adverse student reactions to feminist, African American, gay or lesbian, working-class, non-American, or politically "different" texts. In Owens's multicultural classroom, no one freaks out at having his or her values questioned, challenged, or dismissed. If these experimental or innovative writings were to be understood as "resistant," one would assume that they manifest or generate some kind of conflict with dominant forms and ideologies, not just in the culture at large, but also within writing classrooms. Yet despite political claims couched in military language of resistance and warfare, Owens does not seem to have anticipated or prepared for probable ideological conflicts because his pedagogical project leans more towards multicultural pluralism.

For example, Owens quotes at length from Ishmael Reed's description of the violence in education and his notion that critiques should be leveled at those people responsible for the "national mind . . . [who have] done some very bad things with their propaganda and racism" (*Resisting Writings* 85). Reed describes the conflict as one "between the barbarians and the Christians. And you know, I'm glad I'm on the side of the barbarians. So this is what we want: to sabotage history" (qtd. in *Resisting Writings* 85). However, when Owens chooses examples of rap music as representative of the conflict between dominant and more emergent discourses, he is careful to avoid "rappers who are blatantly misogynist and homophobic, of which there are quite a few" (200). He also intentionally chooses only those texts that have not been made "ugly" by commodity culture. In fact, he argues that like "any commercially profitable medium, the artistry of 'black culture' has its ugly side—Ice Cube's malt liquor ads, Ray Charles' odious Pepsi commercials—rap certainly has its share of crap" (200). Rap is the only "aesthetic medium" that gets singled out for such censorship by Owens.

I have to resist his easy dismissal of Ice Cube's malt liquor ads or Ray Charles's "odious" Pepsi commercials. Students are much more attuned and savvy about commodity culture than Owens appears to be. Why not start there? What do those Ice Cube malt liquor ads look like anyway? How do those ads work with and against constructions of African Americans? Owens walks a thin line between wanting the forms he chooses to be less socially determined while at the same time wanting them to be socially important and relevant. Though he acknowledges that new art forms can become commodified and deployed in advertising, his denial of the specific and ideological ways in which consumer culture can co-opt innovative or new art forms problematically undermines his claims about art as resistance.

Additionally, Owens's clear preference for literary texts prevents him from acknowledging that it is not just that innovative art forms get co-opted by commodity culture (e.g., advertising), but that in fact, many of the most innovative and experimental texts and art forms are generated by advertisers.[5] Therefore, he must, as a teacher, carefully select examples of rap music which don't represent that confusion between art as resistance and art as commodity (in service of selling products). Nor does he imagine advertising, even though obviously selling something, might be a site for political commentary or social critique. In general, Owens suggests that teaching writing as an art and encouraging students to use their imaginations are all ways to locate freer spaces—figured as "ruptures"— from which students and teachers can resist dominant discourses and structures, particularly institutional ones. Yet the problematic ideologies of these texts have been sanitized and erased. The chosen rap song will be a kind of innovative and radical text compared to the traditional five-paragraph theme, and so it might challenge a student reader's notions of acceptable writing conventions, and it might or might not call into question a student's values or ideology. But bringing into a classroom texts that are blatantly homophobic, misogynistic, or racist would require finding a way to negotiate a discussion of the controversial aspects of these texts.

Given such dramatic examples as the outcry in response to the University of Texas at Austin's proposed freshman writing curriculum entitled "Writing about Difference," it is not surprising that Owens or anyone else would be reluctant to bring such controversial texts into the freshman writing class (see Brodkey, "Making a Federal Case"). Owens's argument, however, rests on the claim that a variety of forms speaks the silent, makes visible the invisible, and invites the excluded into the circle of inclusiveness. Although he invokes the trope of survival (a pedagogy of variety allows for the survival of marginal discourses and groups) and quotes Reed's idea of sabotaging history, one is led to conclude that the amount of anger, violence, censure, and oppression—not to mention students' own ideological positions and reactions, or the very real possibility of having one's class shut down—might be more than a reader or teacher can handle.

Yet many students are often very well aware of the racism, homophobia, misogyny, classism, and so on that is perpetuated in society on a daily basis. Just because Owens is careful to screen and censor his choice of experimental texts does not in any way preclude the possibility (or inevitability) that students will, despite his best intentions, have to confront such texts; nor does it preclude the possibility that they will produce their own versions of such misogynistic, homophobic, racist, and classist texts, albeit now in the spirit of experimentation. There is little sense in Owens's argument that he is willing to acknowledge these possibilities, or that, having encouraged students to express their experiences of society in innovative forms, he has prepared himself or his students not only for the complexity of formal resistance but also for the complexity of ideological resistance, whether figured as politically "progressive" or "conservative."[6] In other words, a progressive politics for innovative forms seems to come at any expense, even if it means censoring texts and ignoring the social realities of students.

Claims for the politics of experimental writing in composition tend to follow Owens's trajectory, yet histories and theories of the avant-garde caution us against assuming that innovation has such a progressively political force. Additionally, arguments for experimental writing in composition invoke the socially transformative and futuristic impulses of the avant-garde. This last position is most explicitly summarized by Bridwell-Bowles: "our language and our writing should be adequate enough to make our dreams, visions, our stories, our thinking, and our actions not just revolutionary but transformative. . . . We need to encourage them [students] to dream, to think in new cycles and to have visions for the future that are hopeful" ("Freedom, Form, and Function" 46–47). Exploring historical and theoretical accounts about the politics (socially transformative or prophetic) of the avant-garde and claims about the value of innovation as a category can help us reflect more critically on arguments for the politics of experimental writing in composition, particularly as they situate themselves in relation to the presumably conservative pedagogical project of teaching academic writing.

POLITICS OF THE AVANT-GARDE

Histories of the emergence of the term "avant-garde" show that initially the term was linked with broader political projects. The idea of avant-garde art is generally attributed to the utopian socialist Saint-Simon in his 1825 work *Opinions littéraires, philosophiques et industrielles*. There, in the process of constructing a political philosophy, Saint-Simon posits an alliance between artists, scientists, and industrialists for a better society. The role of art in general (not just that of particular artists) is to prepare the people for the emergence of new ideas and new sensibilities: "What destiny more beautiful for the arts than to exercise a positive influence on society, a true ministry, and to project themselves ahead of all the intellectual faculties, in the era of their greatest development" (Saint-Simon, qtd. in Hadjinicolaou 41).[7] There is no sense here, or in the later work of the Fourierist Gabriel-Désiré Laverdant, that the artists will be responsible for *producing* or *generating* these new ideas.

In a true sense of the military avant-garde, they merely prepare the way (and the people) for reception of these new ideas by expressing the most advanced social tendencies of a society: "Art, the expression of society, manifests, in its highest soaring, the most advanced social tendencies: It is the forerunner and the revealer. Therefore, to know whether art worthily fulfills its proper mission as initiator, whether the artist is truly of the avant-garde, one must know where Humanity is going, what the destiny of the human race is" (Laverdant, qtd. in Hadjinicolaou 41). Even given these early appearances of references to the avant-garde function of art, Nicos Hadjinicolaou argues that the term "avant-garde" was predominantly used in political discourse during the nineteenth century and only later borrowed by artists at the beginning of the twentieth century, just before World War I (43).

Undoubtedly early twentieth-century avant-garde artists and movements saw themselves as both politically and artistically the avant-garde of society. Sometimes, as is the case with Italian futurism, the artists seemed to suggest that they did indeed "know where Humanity is going," and saw their art as a way to get it there faster.[8] Other individual artists, allying themselves with political projects such as communism—for example, Vladimir Mayakovsy in Russia and Bertolt Brecht in Germany—demonstrated the often agonistic relationship of art to politics.[9] These artists were alternately embraced and rejected by their respective communist parties while simultaneously embracing and rejecting their propagandistic roles and accepting or criticizing the parties' attempts to constrain artistic freedom. Other times, however, as Charles Russell notes, avant-garde artists, while seeing themselves at the forefront of society, could only gesture hopefully to a vague future that was yet unknown to them and which had no specific content: "Apollinaire's emphasis here on the dynamics of discovery, rather than on the nature of the '*univers encore vierge,*' illustrates a general avant-garde tendency to focus on the primacy and intensity of the moment of creation; moreover, it exemplifies what proves to be the blind faith of most avant-garde writers in a future about which they are rarely specific" (Russell 73). And finally, some avant-garde movements, such as Dada, in its apparently ruthlessly nihilistic attitude, seem to offer little hope for the future.[10]

Despite the idea that much avant-garde art criticized the dominant bourgeois aesthetics and values of its time and therefore seems politically progressive, it is not the case that the politics or future vision of society that avant-garde art posited is necessarily positively progressive, egalitarian, leftist, or even liberal. In other words, avant-garde artists might have seen or described themselves as "progressive," but "progress" did not necessarily suggest the kind of contemporary American leftist or liberal politics implied in many arguments for experimental writing in composition. Additionally, the inherent elitism of the avant-garde creates problems for artistic movements. Even as they claim to reintegrate art and everyday life, by their very avant-garde nature, they create art that very few can appreciate or understand. This elitism has a way of reducing to an ignorant mass the very people whom avant-garde art ostensibly serves and to whom their art is supposed to appeal or inspire politically.

For example, while the Italian futurists began with democratic overtones in their original attack on institutions, the movement came to argue for a necessary elitism and over time became associated with dominant power structures of Italian society:

> Although the futurists at first attacked two institutions of substantial power, the monarchy and the church, and though they initially scorned the participation of industrialists, bankers, and fascists in their revitalization of society, they came to accept the permanence of the church and even to exalt the real powers that emerged by the end of the world war: the military, the industrialists, the bankers, and the businessmen. As early as 1913, in "The Futurist Manifesto of Lust," these men were depicted as modern conquerors who embodied a life force capable of manipulating great masses of people and sweeping the entire society to higher states of energy. Marinetti also expressed great faith in the working class and in the petite bourgeoisie, but revealed his fascist mentality when he argued that these men would have to be led by their natural superiors within each group, as well as by other men of vision and the artists of their society—whom he called, amazingly, the "proletariat of gifted men." Even before the fascist victory in 1922, then, the futurists, far from feeling alienated from their society, glorified the de facto powers in it. After 1922, futurism tended to become the new academy and continued to sing the praises of these institutional powers. (Russell 90)

One might argue that Italian futurism is the exception to the rule of progressive political avant-gardes, but I offer it here as a significant example for at least two reasons. First, though I agree with Andrew Hewitt that one cannot quite establish a cause-and-effect relationship between Italian futurism and Italian fascism, one can recognize the parallel trajectories between avant-garde art and various right-wing political movements: "Moreover, the fact that the emergence of the avant-garde as the dominant group within the cultural sphere broadly coincides with the emergence of fascism as a political movement, and that the waning of the avant-garde is marked by the emergence of National Socialism as a world political force, is taken as being of central importance" (Hewitt 38). Furthermore, Hewitt suggests that it is possible to see both fascism and the avant-garde as feeding from similar "ideological sources," for example, the "powers of science and technology" (52–53), both as emerging from an "anarchic form of socialism" (54), and both as responses to the problem of "cultural literacy and political oligarchy" (55). The point here is not to reductively equate the avant-garde with fascism but to recover a sense of the specificity of historical contexts to which various avant-garde movements responded and with which they were engaged.

Another reason that Italian futurism is key to a discussion of the politics of the avant-garde is that many of the avant-garde techniques initiated, developed, and explored by Italian futurist artists were borrowed and extended by other and later European avant-garde artists: "Their aggressive self-flaunting, declamatory manifestos, public proclamations, attacks on their audiences, occasionally absurd dress and behavior, nonsensical or outrageous poetry, theater, and music, all became models for twentieth-century avant-garde activities" (Russell 88). Again, the fact that Italian futurists would use these techniques to augment fascist political tendencies within Italian society whereas other avant-garde artists would use these same techniques in support of communism or democracy (for example, in late twentieth-century American art movements) shows that the politics of avant-garde formal practices are neither inherently conservative nor progressive but specific to their historical and social contexts.

Similarly, if the politics of the avant-garde are not inherently politically progressive, then neither are the politics of innovation or experimentation. While most of the arguments in composition I have discussed share an interest in availing themselves and students of established innovative writings (e.g., Weathers's "well-tested models"), it is also the case that most of the arguments make claims for the importance of innovation (beyond imitation) or experimentation (e.g., Bridwell-Bowles, Owens, Ulmer, Sirc). Though some theorists of avant-garde art dismiss innovation (or novelty) as a defining characteristic, without doubt avant-garde writing is understood as innovative.

The problem with innovation in terms of the contemporary avant-garde, by and large, is that it has been co-opted by the market economy of late capitalism. As Han Magnus Enzensberger puts it rather bluntly, "What is steadily being offered for sale is, as in other industries, next year's model" (25). It is not just that art works are subject to the market economy for buying and selling, but that, as both Jean-François Lyotard and Fredric Jameson also argue, avant-garde art and capitalism are locked into a reciprocal relationship. Lyotard claims, "In this way [necessarily combining innovation with the known], one thinks that one is expressing the spirit of the times, whereas one is merely reflecting the spirit of the market" ("The Sublime and the Avant-Garde" 106). For Jameson, avant-garde art has become even more completely integrated into capitalism: "What has happened is that aesthetic production today has become integrated into commodity production generally: the frantic economy of producing fresh new waves of ever more novel-seeming goods (from clothing to airplanes), at even greater rates of turnover now assigns an increasingly essential structural function and position to aesthetic innovation and ex-perimentation" (Jameson 4–5). Or, as Hadjinicolaou puts it, "The ideology of avant-gardism . . . is part of the capitalist market in general, for which innovation, the launching of new products, is a matter of survival" (56). According to this logic, new dish detergents and new artistic practices or techniques are one and the same: marketing strategies for consumer ob-jects already on the fast road to obsolescence.

A cynical reading, therefore, of arguments for innovative writing in composition, which denies the critical import of such writings, is that they are not only a way to give bored students something ostensibly fun and interesting to do in their required writing courses, but that these writings also constitute a new scholarly product for compositionists (including, obviously, the writer of this text) to latch onto and produce scholarly ar-ticles, conference papers, books, and dissertations, and a new package for the work of composition, a field imagined as seeking desperately to avoid belatedness in a rapidly changing educational landscape, one in which it seems knowledge has become increasingly intertwined with aesthetics and market value. In an educational market filled with bored consumers or clients (students), innovative writing is merely another "choice" offered by the teachers become salespeople.

Even if we bracket for a moment this argument about innovation and the market economy of late capitalism, the claim, made often by avant-garde artists or movements, that their art is actually a kind of negative political critique—that is, the very act of wreaking havoc on traditions and conventional forms is in itself a political act, regardless of content—is sub-ject to the same kind of pressures one can put on the claim that all avant-garde or innovative art is inherently politically progressive. Furthermore, a counterargument to this position would suggest that the lack of political commitment and content for much avant-garde art gives one merely the illusion of political or social critique via experimental form, while in actu-ality posing absolutely no threat or significant challenge to real material social conditions.

This is a rather complicated problem as Marcuse sets it out in "The Affirmative Character of Culture." On the one hand, autonomous art, freed from social determinism, can console us in our general suffering of material conditions, and yet this consolation can make us complacent and make it difficult to actually work to change those conditions. On the other hand, Marcuse will not deny that art might potentially also inspire us with visions of possibilities and better futures to change our condi-tions. It is distinctly possible that arguments for experimental writing in composition can function in both ways, either as illusion and consolation or as inspiration toward social change. In the context of composition, teachers of writing feel perhaps some consolation about what we are doing since, by giving students assignments for innovative or experimental writing, we are ostensibly bucking the system and challenging the status quo (which would have our students busy learning the modes of discourse, or argument, or more traditional academic prose, and the like). Students can't complain of their oppression or disciplining since we assign writings that allow them to break the rules and/or express their uniqueness and/or grant them opportunities to represent their particular social realities. In this way, innovative or experimental writing in composition might actually act to prevent larger social changes in the material conditions of the teaching of writing for both teachers and students. Is experimental writing a consolation, an illusion of freedom, while the business of composition goes on as usual? Or is experimental writing in composition an attempt to destroy or significantly reform the institution of composition, to change the real material conditions and practices of the teaching of writing?

AVANT-GARDE COMPOSITIONISTS

Both Ulmer and Sirc locate their agendas for composition explicitly in avant-garde aesthetics and practices in order to perform such negative critiques of the institutional location of composition and of composition as institution. They are less interested in offering alternatives to academic prose or revising academic discourses. Rather, Ulmer and Sirc resist disciplinary discourses in the name of art and in the service of students as artists. They both explicitly use avant-garde theories to break down the limits of disciplinary discourses, rejecting the critical impulse (and its attendant politics) in writing instruction, instead advocating the teaching of avant-garde techniques and aesthetics. Ultimately, they reject what they see as the centrality of modernist aesthetics to writing instruction. Sirc, in particular, not only performs a thoroughly negative critique of composition's "modernist" aesthetics, but also attempts to destroy the very institution of composition as it is shaped by those aesthetics.

In *Applied Grammatology* (and, with variation, in most of his work, including *Heuretics*), Ulmer suggests that avant-garde art—in its exploration of the cracks in institutions, aesthetics, and discourses—has forged the way for postmodern literacy: "Briefly put, the emergence of a postmodernized education (the entry of education into the contemporary paradigm) can be facilitated by a retracing of the paths (facilitations) already breached by the experimental arts of this century" (*Applied Grammatology* 168). Through such a historical tracing, the avant-garde can teach English studies how to close gaps between theory and pedagogy: "Keeping in mind the idea that a grammatological pedagogy is designed to close the gap between current theory and an outmoded practice, the new education will find in the arts a major reserve or resource for technique" (168). Using avant-garde techniques such as collage and mechanical writing, and emphasizing play and pleasure, Ulmer claims in "Textshop for Post(e)pedagogy" that the "point of the humanities laboratory is to take one step back from the information and skills relevant to the discipline in order to attend to the fundamental experience of creativity that motivates the production of literature in the first place" (56).[11] Ulmer does not mean by "creativity" any notion of the immediate expression of one's experience, or tapping into one's innate genius (59). Yet he argues that since the "pleasure of the creative process" is "why one writes in the first place," then allowing students to experience that pleasure is an important part of their literacy education.[12]

Students can take on the project of producing literature in Ulmer's "textshop" classroom because Ulmer challenges the kinds of implicit classroom aesthetics that often inhibit students' attempts to write creatively: "The advantage of beginning with the textualist assignment in the context of models drawn from the avant-garde is that the principle of 'everyone an artist' is explicitly part of the experimentalist aesthetics. Texts produced by students using 'mechanical' or automatic means have the same status of the tutor text. A student's ready-made is 'as good' as one by Duchamp. But the issue in the textshop is not the quality of the product, but the quality of the process, the goal being to simulate, if you like, the experience, the pleasure, of creativity" (58).

What is so inherently pleasurable about creativity is unclear. Is the pleasure to be had in putting things together, in thrilling to one's own knowledge of language, in enjoying the flexibility of one's imagination, or in anticipating the effect on a given set of readers? If students see the writing process (or the creative process) as torturous, how is a teacher to suggest the pleasures if the teacher can't begin to name them or even point to them? It seems that Ulmer is positing an almost "natural" pleasure in writing as creative process, a pleasure in the artistic process that is understood to work against some of its traditional opponents: analytic thinking (Ulmer, "Textshop for Post(e)pedagogy" 56), academic specialization (56), and reason (61).[13] Furthermore, he asserts that he is rejecting any understanding of creativity that involves "romantic theories of 'genius' and originality" (59–60) and instead proffering a version of creativity based on mechanical processes and invention (58). Writing is produced mechanically, yet still somehow is art.

Everyone—all students—can be artists as long as they "make something"[14] or at least "choose" some things to put together. It doesn't quite seem to matter *what* they make as long as they make something. Creativity might motivate the "writing" of literature (although as I have suggested even this premise is suspect), but the "production" of a text as literature involves more than Ulmer suggests, more than the creative process. The production of literature also includes complex networks of evaluations and judgments. Ulmer may assert that the "student's ready-made is 'as good' as one by Duchamp," but he undermines this claim by abandoning any notion of student writing as product (art) in favor of process: "But the issue in the textshop is not the quality of the product, but the quality of the process, the goal being to simulate, if you like, the experience, the pleasure, of creativity" ("Textshop for Post(e)pedagogy" 58). Ulmer doesn't discuss why his class is reading Blake's poem "Tyger" and doing mechanical and inventive things with it: "Transformation by antonymy (use a Thesaurus)"; and "Transformation by displacement (generated by looking up Blake's word in the dictionary, then replacing it with the first word above it of the same type [noun, verb, etc.]" (59). The lessons that Ulmer suggests his students will learn include the following: "the rhetorical effect from the commutation of a given poem into alternative versions (testing the romantic and formalist claims that a finished product is 'perfect'). The function and effect of diction, style, syntax, semantics, parts of speech, etc. in literature may be observed in the reworking of the poem" (58). As with Owens in his arguments in *Resisting Writings,* it is unclear what Ulmer might mean by the "rhetorical effect" since he does not explain; furthermore, as with Owens, the student's experimental writing seems to provide insight primarily into the formal qualities of the "tutor text."

As I see it, the unspoken lesson (unacknowledged by Ulmer) of such an assignment as described above is that despite his claim that everything is art and everyone is an artist, students could learn instead that actually only some things are art and only some people are artists. In Ulmer's essay, there is no discussion of how Blake's poem got to be art, why the class is not, in fact, looking at a fellow classmate's poem and "transforming *it* by antonymy" ("Textshop for Post(e)pedagogy" 59; emphasis mine). What students produce is on an equal level with Blake and Duchamp's work; or it really allows them to only "simulate . . . the experience, the pleasure, of creativity" (58). What are students lacking that they can only *simulate* the experience or the pleasure? The cultural authority of artists such as Blake and Duchamp?

Perhaps if the students were to ask why these works by Duchamp and Blake are considered art, then the category of art would need to be examined. Perhaps Ulmer could explain how Duchamp found a urinal, signed it "R. Mutt," and submitted it to an exhibition, attempting like a proper avant-garde artist to challenge the institution of art. Then perhaps Ulmer could explain how the institution eventually took Duchamp's work, as they took much avant-garde art, and appropriated it into the institution. Perhaps then, that class could have a very interesting discussion about their own institutional location, the ways in which even these experimental mechanical writings they've produced are already situated within institutional frameworks. Indeed, such an institutional framework seems to compel Ulmer to claim that the above kinds of formal lessons can be learned by working with Blake's poem while still maintaining the privileged position of literature. The appeal of experimental writing as radical is defused by the argument that experimental writing better teaches students how to understand the workings of canonical texts. The unconventional text often serves as a foil for teaching aspects of conventional texts, a move I will discuss in greater detail in chapter 4.

Yet, according to Ulmer, within the context of the disciplines of literature and composition, this kind of playful choosing or making, which destabilizes our notions of work/play, is useful to writing and literature instruction because it reveals the contingent nature of disciplinary discourses: "The textshop permits the student to by-pass initiation as a specialist (the 'specialist' is to modernism what the 'genius' was to romanticism), to confront simultaneously the provisional, permeable character of all knowledge, the creative 'ground' (*apeiron*) of the formation of the discipline" ("Textshop for Post(e)pedagogy" 62). One concludes that, rather than providing alternatives to disciplinary or academic discourse, Ulmer proposes that students bracket the conventional writing of criticism in order to tap into the source itself, that is, literature and the fundamental experience of creativity that motivates its production (56). Ulmer destabilizes the source or catalyst for the production of critical writing in English studies—literature—in order to show students that if literature is provisional and emerges from play, pleasure, and creativity, then disciplinary writings are similarly unstable and provisional, and therefore subject to negotiation. In other words, rather than academic writing giving students some distance from literature, the production of avant-garde writings gives students critical distance from disciplinary (academic) writing.

The desire to use the category of art, particularly avant-garde art, as a means of revealing the contingent nature of one's discipline and resisting the impulse to train students to be "specialists" or critics is also expressed in the work of Geoffrey Sirc. In much of Sirc's work, he looks for the excess that composition as a field cannot absorb, whether it be the happening aesthetic of the avant-garde, or the aggressive punk aesthetic of the 1970s, or postmodern literacies of hypertextual writing.[15] His essay "What Is Composition . . . ? After Duchamp" is an attempt to show the road we in composition can't seem to take because our aesthetics get in the way. Characterizing the work of contemporary composition as modernist, with Dave Bartholomae presented as a Clement Greenberg–like figure (holding up the modernist fort against kitsch and the avant-garde), and figuring the textbook *Ways of Reading* as the modernist museum par excellence, Sirc employs Marcel Duchamp in service of a full-scale attack on composition's modernist aesthetics. According to Sirc, this modernist version of composition values reproductions of masterpieces that result in the "literary hmmm," while devaluing the production of texts like Web sites, which result in the "wow" of *"l'art brut"* ("What Is Composition" 191).[16] Modernist composition is composition as "making" rather than "choosing" for the "readymade." Modernist composition is criticism (of one's writing, of oneself, of a discipline, and of culture) rather than the excess of unjuried (i.e., avant-garde) art.

There are several reasons Sirc will not compete with what he calls Bartholomae's "modernist composition." One key reason is that, according to Sirc, Bartholomae uses writing as criticism not to challenge the institution of composition but to bolster its institutional power:

> For [Clement] Greenberg, "The essence of Modern lies, as I see it, in the use of the characteristic methods of a discipline to criticize the discipline itself—not in order to subvert it, but to entrench it more firmly in its area of competence." For Bartholomae, the "goal is to call the discourse into question, to undo it in some fundamental way"; "an act of criticism would enable a writer to interrogate his or her own text in relationship to the problems of writing and the problems of disciplinary knowledge," not in order to subvert the discipline but to entrench it more firmly, determining "the way the text positions them [students] in relationship to a history of writing." (Sirc 183)

In "What Is Composition and (If You Know What that Is) Why Do We Teach It?" Bartholomae sees the work of composition as teaching students how to critically revise their "writing in schooling" (26). By emphasizing composition as critical revision, Bartholomae claims that he is altering "the same old routine"; he is not just "moving the furniture" but helping students learn how to change their writing (16). Taking an allegorical approach, wherein Bartholomae stands for modernist composition ("writing-in-schooling") and Marcel Duchamp stands for avant-garde composition ("writing-in-general"), Sirc implies that Bartholomae's concept of composition *is,* in fact, the same old routine. He argues that the modernist aesthetics in Bartholomae's version of composition value the progression (revision) of writing toward approved texts, "revision toward a *certain* style, toward a *certain* end" (Sirc, "What Is Composition" 190) and devalues the raw, unfinished writing that "circulates some interesting ideas" (196).

This is not an accurate representation of Bartholomae's project since he, too, is more than interested in raw, unfinished writing that "circulates some interesting ideas." In fact, Bartholomae acknowledges the difficulty of asking for and getting that kind of writing within the institutional location of composition: "As a faculty, we do not have a way of saying to a student, 'Make that essay a little worse, not quite so finished, a little more fragmented and confused,' and to say this in the name of learning. The institution is designed to produce and reward mastery, not to call it into question" (Bartholomae, "What Is Composition" 15). However, Sirc doesn't see Bartholomae's argument as any great threat to the regime of mastery, for in questioning the "good" essay and trying to open it up, Bartholomae is merely supplanting one form of mastery for another: not the possible but "no more than a personally-preferred version of official composition" (Sirc, "What Is Composition" 181), just "possible versions of the preferred" (194). Instead of the "good" paper, which tries to write an impersonal history of Taylorism, Bartholomae prefers the careful Mary Louise Pratt–like paper where the student would "interrogate" his or her "intellectual function within the regime of truth" ("What Is Composition" 17). This preferred version of composition still privileges the successful texts of master writers (e.g., Mary Louise Pratt).

Sirc tries to escape the institutional aesthetic, represented by canonical texts in composition, which encourages students to be forever trying (but inevitably failing) to imitate the masters: "I don't want to replace one canonical text with a new one (no matter how canonical I think Malcolm [X] should be in our culture). So lately my students have been reading an almost-anything-whatever like gangsta rap, along with a range of cultural responses to the material (from the media, the academy, Web-sites, and fellow-students), then writing their own. . . . Material is chosen not because it's a privileged text, a 'difficult' masterpiece from the 'history of writing,' but because it's around, on hand. It's whatever stands out from the endlessly-shifting screen before one" (Sirc, "What Is Composition" 186–87). Sirc rejects canonical texts, which are prized for their exhibition value, and embraces texts that have use-value. By use-value he does not mean writing as instrumental literacy in the context of schooling (e.g., academic writing). Rather, Sirc asserts the value of a text (any text) for the use-value (any use-value) it has for students (Sirc, "What Is Composition" 202). Furthermore, since the use-value is not prescribed, Sirc rejects the project of composition as that of "improving" students' writing: "I'm interested in failures that really aren't, in works barred from gaining the prize which end up changing the world. Brief, personal jottings that become the litany for posterity; the apparently impoverished composition that proves a rich text. . . . I'm interested in certain writing, writing done by anyone-whoever: useless, failed, nothing-writing by some nobody that turns out to be really something" (179).

Sirc doesn't want to have to make judgments about good or bad writing. Rather, "I want an aesthetic judgment, of course; but I want to judge a student's art as art, not as 'critical practice'" (Sirc, "What Is Composition" 203). In Sirc's argument, judgment is thrown out the front door only to come in the back door: the question of good or bad writing is transformed into the question of art or not-art. Since Sirc is sketchy at best regarding what art is, or even why it's important, one is left to conclude that art is anything that stands out. If that isn't helpful, then consider that all Sirc wants composition to be is "a field where language, thought and vision act upon one another" (Cabanne qtd in Sirc, "What Is Composition" 190). In the end, all that Sirc demands of writing "is that it have *writte,* that it expose itself, announce itself, appear as writing" ("What Is Composition" 204).

We have reached a paradox in Sirc's argument that echoes a paradox of the avant-garde. Sirc aims to collapse distinctions between art and everyday life, between academic writing and experimental writing (or any writing), but with such distinctions collapsed, it seems certain kinds of writing lose their edge in terms of significance. Similarly, as avant-garde art works to destroy the institution of art and its judgments and works to destroy art's autonomy, it loses both its special status and its critical purchase: "In the late capitalist society, intentions of the historical avant-garde are being realized but the result has been a disvalue. Given the experience of the false sublation of autonomy, one will need to ask whether a sublation of the autonomy status can be desirable at all, whether the distance between art and the praxis of life is not requisite for that free space within which alternatives to what exists become conceivable" (Bürger 54).

For Sirc to want to see composition as writing-in-general, by anyone without any more judgment than that the writing is art (and it's still unclear how or if he's making even this distinction), is an attempt to do away with teachers, students, classrooms, and composition as an institution. But, as Bürger reminds us, perhaps the distance between art and the praxis of life, or the distance between academic writing and nonacademic writing, is necessary to imagine alternatives to modernist composition.

Even Bartholomae's willingness to take student writing seriously does not persuade Sirc that Bartholomae is in any way challenging the institution of composition by disrupting high/low distinctions within composition: "Bartholomae's project uses 'student writing as a starting point'; it exists in relation to academic or 'high culture.' Ultimately, the modernist focus—in composition as in art—is institutional rather than conceptual. The institution is the aegis under which the project is carried out. Knowledge of the historical apparatus is a prerequisite in order to work within the discipline, learning the style and thinking which result in a Morris Louis or a Louise Pratt. Duchamp's conceptual has nothing to do with the institutional; of what use can be the institution's material reification?" (Sirc, "What Is Composition" 197).

To say that Duchamp's conceptual has nothing to do with the institutional is to overstate the case a bit. Much of Duchamp's work had quite a bit to do with the institution; in fact, in his attempts to negate the institution, Duchamp (like many avant-garde artists) was caught in a reactive relationship with the institution of art. And despite Duchamp's subversion of the juried exhibition and the institution of art as represented by the museum, eventually the institution of art (museums, art history, theory, and criticism) absorbed and accommodated, if not exalted, Duchamp. Sirc ignores the ways in which Duchamp and avant-garde artists in general are locked into these reactive relationships with art institutions. Similarly, he apparently ignores the ways in which institutions absorb, if not co-opt, avant-garde art.

Like Ulmer, Sirc wants everyone to be artists and all writing to be art. Additionally, he wants to put avant-garde practices in the service of having students produce writing that is more relevant to their lives (see my discussion of Sirc's expressivist tendencies in the previous chapter) and that is not only antidisciplinary and antimodernist, but also stridently anti-institutional. We have, then, in Sirc's arguments, a call to challenge all aspects of composition as the teaching of writing, its defining limits,

goals, and uses, as well as the aesthetics that inform and inflect its pedagogies. In this way, Sirc's arguments represent the extreme version of what
experimental writing can or should ultimately do: destroy composition as
we know it. This impulse, not to reform or revise traditional aesthetics or
the institution, but to perform a thoroughly negative critique, is a major
(and problematic) aspect of avant-garde aesthetics.

I hesitate to conclude as readily as Ulmer and Sirc that the lessons to
be learned from the avant-garde can be so successfully used in contemporary writing classrooms. Indeed, I retrace the paths of the avant-garde
more critically in order not only to discuss the avant-garde's successes,
but also to attend to the failures of the avant-garde, especially the ways in
which avant-garde art has challenged, resisted, and been accommodated
by art institutions. Such a retracing—different from Ulmer's and Sirc's in
my points of emphasis—will highlight the other kinds of lessons that we
in composition might learn from avant-garde art's historical relationship
to its institutions.

AVANT-GARDE ATTACKS ON THE INSTITUTION: SELF-CRITICISM

One of the defining characteristics of the avant-garde, according to
Peter Bürger, is its attack on the institution or the "productive and distrib-
utive apparatus and also . . . the ideas about art that prevail at a given time
and that determine the reception of the works" (22). Bürger also refers
to this attack on the institution of art as art's "self-critical" phase: "with
the historical avant-garde movements, the social subsystem that is art en-
ters the stage of self-criticism" (22). Self-criticism is differentiated from
criticism of the past and from system-immanent criticism. In criticism
of the past, artists focus on criticizing and rejecting prior art. In system-
immanent criticism, artists or art movements criticize each other but still
within the institution of art (21–22). The avant-garde is self-critical when
it takes on the very institution of art, rather than merely past art or other
present artists or schools. Despite this stage of self-criticism, however,
Bürger argues that the avant-garde failed in its attempt to destroy the institution of art. As I suggested in my earlier discussions, the attempt and
its failure are encapsulated in the example of the work of Duchamp:

> When Duchamp puts his signature on mass-produced, randomly chosen
> objects and sends them to art exhibits, this provocation of art presupposes
> a concept of what art is. The fact that he signs the Ready-Mades contains a
> clear allusion to the category of "work." The signature that attests that the

work is both individual and unique is here affixed to the mass-produced object. The idea of the nature of art as it has developed since the Renaissance—the individual creation of unique works—is thus provocatively called into question. The act of provocation itself takes the place of the work. But doesn't this make the category "work" redundant? Duchamp's provocation addresses itself to art as a social institution. Insofar as the work is part of that institution, the attack is also directed against it. But it is a historical fact that the avant-garde movements did not put an end to the production of works of art, and that the social institution that is art proved resistant to the avant-gardiste attack. (Bürger 56–57)

Indeed, what is interesting about the differences between the historical European avant-gardes and the American avant-gardes is how they come into being in reaction to their respective cultures' understandings of art as a "social institution" and how that social institution resists attacks by the avant-garde.

For example, the American avant-garde can seem only to repeat the techniques and strategies of the European avant-garde, which are increasingly ineffective in the context of late capitalism. Andreas Huyssen argues that postmodernism is, in fact, the endgame of the avant-garde. Huyssen claims that the United States did not really have an early twentieth-century avant-garde and that, in fact, it wasn't until the 1960s that the United States manifested significant avant-garde movements. As Huyssen argues, there needs to be at least two things in place for the successful emergence of an avant-garde: first, the establishment of bourgeois high culture; and second, political and social unrest. It wasn't until the 1950s in America that a high culture had been firmly established against which the avant-garde could position itself:

> The cultural politics of [early] 20th-century avantgardism would have been meaningless (if not regressive) in the United States where "high art" was still struggling hard to gain wider legitimacy and to be taken seriously by the public. . . . A European-style avantgardist revolt against tradition made eminent sense in the United States at a time when high art had become institutionalized in the burgeoning museum, concert, and paperback culture of the 1950s, when modernism itself had entered the mainstream via the culture industry, and later, during the Kennedy years when high culture began to take on the function of political representation (Robert Frost and Pablo Casals at the White House). (167–68)

Additionally, the 1960s were a time of social unrest in the United States—the civil rights movement, the Vietnam War, student protests, and the emergence of countercultures, among other factors. Granted, the 1960s were also a time of social unrest in Europe, yet Huyssen claims that since Europe had avant-garde movements in the early twentieth century and those movements had failed in their purposes (primarily to destroy the institution of art and reintegrate art with everyday praxis), for the Europeans the avant-garde during the 1960s was merely a case of ineffectual déjà vu.

For the Americans, however, the avant-garde of the 1960s was novel and exciting and still imbued with a sense of hope for the future (Huyssen 167). Additionally, the American avant-garde of the 1960s emerged into different historical circumstances than the historical European avant-garde of the early twentieth century, particularly vis-à-vis advanced technology and media apparatuses. In other words, the American avant-garde had to contend with mechanisms of late capitalism (e.g., mass media), which had already co-opted innovative strategies of both modernism and the avant-garde, rendering the American avant-garde ineffectual. As Huyssen concludes, American avant-garde art, in the context of postmodernism, becomes aestheticized rather than political.[17]

Huyssen's story of the differences between the historical European avant-garde and the American avant-garde are particularly helpful when considering the emergence of experimental writing in composition. Consider, for example, that composition begins to formulate itself as a field during the mid-1960s, and that soon after the solidification of the institution of composition come the critiques of the institution (e.g., "The Students' Right to Their Own Language"), and even calls to abolish composition as a required course.[18]

When I refer to the "attack" on the institution of composition, I mean both the institutional location of composition as a required undergraduate course and the institution of composition as a scholarly field. Although not necessarily identical (since not all of the scholarship in the field of composition addresses the required undergraduate writing course), I agree with Robert Connors's claim that the emergence of composition as a scholarly discipline has been, and continues to be, largely defined by attempts to reform required undergraduate writing courses: "[The 1960s were] an era in which reformism was immensely strengthened, becoming, indeed, the backbone of an ever-larger professional literature. Improving the freshman course (through New Rhetoric, or invention, or classical rhetoric, or Christensen paragraphing, or sentence combining) became the essential purpose of the books and essays that appeared in always-greater numbers" (56). Though Connors does not list the practices and goals of early expressivists and later writing process compositionists, they too might be seen as participating in both the reforming of writing pedagogies and the reformation of the field of composition (which came to be dominated by both expressivist and process practices and theories).

Perhaps one of the latest attempts to reform the freshman course is manifested in arguments for alternative, innovative, or experimental writing in composition. I call these arguments "attacks" on the institution of composition even if they don't call explicitly for abolishing composition because they challenge values and ideologies embedded in and perpetuated by dominant conventional practices of the teaching of writing. Indeed, one of the most explicit calls to change both the practices of teaching the required freshman writing course and the way we understand and construct the field of composition comes from Owens: "But if we say that constructions like these are 'just' the work of experimental writers and as such have little direct relevance to the business of composition theory, then we are saying that poeisis and experimentations have little if anything to do with composition studies. But if we admit that explorations implicit in these texts are indeed relevant to the nature of composition, and consequently to our discipline, then the assumptions upon which our field is built cry out for redefinition" (*Resisting Writings* 7). That's a big "if" embedded in Owens's argument. For those who see the purpose of the teaching of writing as primarily to prepare students for the writing they do in college (teaching the conventions of academic discourse), the "if" is beside the point. One need not "admit" that experimental writings have anything to do with the "nature of composition" as a field. Indeed, one could argue that the assumptions upon which our field has been built cannot withstand the teaching of experimental writing, that to include experimental writings into the mix would result not just in redefinition but in lack of definition.

It is just this lack of definitional limits for which Sirc seems to argue in "What Is Composition" and indeed throughout his book *English Composition as Happening*. Although Sirc does not call for abolishing required freshman writing courses, his arguments—about what kinds of writing should be taught and the ways in which writing should be taught—attempt to expand the definition of composition beyond the values implied by the teaching of academic prose. Thus, I consider Sirc's arguments attempts at "self-criticism" in the way Bürger means because Sirc is adamant that he is not interested in competing for dominance with other versions of composition, represented in his argument by the work of Bartholomae (that would be a system-immanent critique). Yet, if we stay within the logic of Sirc's "self-critical" institution-destroying argument, where composition is to be any writing by anybody, then there seems to be no point in having classes or teachers or students. And if those distinctions (writing in school, supermarket lists, essays, scrawled class notes) are destroyed, then how can the teaching of writing provide much help for students or teachers who must negotiate the dialectical relationship that continues to exist between individuals and institutions, or between social groups and institutions?

If one considers that the avant-garde's attempt to destroy the institution of art failed in that the institution accommodated and absorbed avant-garde through museums, art history, and art criticism, one could likewise say that the kind of negation and critique of the institution of composition posed by proponents of experimental writing is already in the process of being accommodated and absorbed by the institution of composition. Sirc's view that composition textbooks, such as *Ways of Reading,* "themselves are miniature museums, *boites-en-valises* without the irony, portable permanent collections or corporate-sponsored temporary exhibits of our Greatest Hits," points to the very predicament shared by composition and avant-garde art ("English Composition as Happening" 267).

Like art, composition, as I have been discussing it, is an institutional phenomenon. As such, it is maintained not only by literal institutions but also by all the discourses and material realities that maintain those institutions, for example, institutional missives, bureaucratic documents and policies, institutional procedures and resources, and extrainstitutional discourses and materials. Similarly, composition as an institutional phenomenon is a result of its understanding and presentation of general education requirements or curricular statements, the discourse that describes the goals of writing instruction as literacy education, the intellectual, disciplinary and political makeup of faculty and staff in given departments, and the time and resources available to such faculty.

Sirc's reference to *Ways of Reading* as a museum of sorts also points to the ways in which institutions—here both a textbook publisher and the universities that use such a textbook—appropriate and manage the radical potential of experimental writing in composition. For example, starting with the fifth edition and continuing in the sixth, seventh, and eighth editions, *Ways of Reading* has a specific packaged sequence entitled "Experimental Writing," so that students in composition classes (often required composition classes) can explore innovations in writing in just the methodical and critical way that Sirc rejects.[19] Similarly, a textbook by Robert Scholes, Nancy R. Comley, and Gregory Ulmer entitled *Text Book* offers students an opportunity to work with some more experimental and radical texts, such as those by André Breton, Roland Barthes, Susan Howe, Salvador Dali, and the like. Though *Text Book* originally billed itself as "an introduction to literary language," in its writing assignments, and in its new subtitle for the third edition, "Writing through Literature," it clearly offers students the opportunity to explore unconventional writing techniques, rather than engage primarily in analysis, interpretation, and criticism more characteristic of a literature textbook. Similarly, as I will discuss in more detail, textbooks such as Jeff Rice's *The Rhetoric of Cool*, Ulmer's *Internet Invention*, and Cynthia Selfe's *Multimodal Composition* have begun to market pedagogies for multimedia composition classrooms.

In addition to the above and to the scholarship (e.g., Sirc, Owens, Ulmer) that I have been addressing in more detail, a brief look at some programs from the Conference on College Composition and Communication and publications in the field suggests not just an increased interest in alternative writing by such noted scholars in the field of composition as Patricia Bizzell, Peter Elbow, Jacqueline Jones-Royster, and Victor Villanueva, but a desire to construct a new version of composition through alternative discourses. In fact, all four of the above compositionists spoke on a panel entitled "The Future of College Composition: Impacts of Alternative Discourses on Standard English." Bizzell, Elbow, and Jones-Royster later published versions of their papers in a collection of essays on alternative discourse, *Alt Dis: Alternative Discourses and the Academy* (Schroeder, Fox, and Bizzell). And in 2006, *Engaged Writers and Dynamic Disciplines: Research on the Academic Writing Life,* by Chris Thaiss and Terry Myers Zawacki, picked up where *Alt Dis* left off. Thaiss and Zawacki look at the employment of alternative academic discourse by scholars, teachers, and students across the disciplines.

It appears that experimental and alternative writings in composition are already in the process of being absorbed, accommodated, and managed by various apparatuses of authorization and dissemination. But if this is so, we need to ask: what is the relation of these arguments for experimental writing to attempts to reform the institution of composition? Have they produced material changes in theories, practices, and pedagogies? Do we have a significant critique at hand, or do these arguments for experimental writing merely maintain business as usual for composition?

Paul Mann's observations in *The Theory-Death of the Avant-Garde,* about the relationship between the avant-garde and bourgeois culture, are provocative when they serve as an analogy to the predicament of experimental writing in composition:

> It is typical of our discourse that not even the avant-garde's wildest disavowals could protect it from conscription into a tedious and dispiriting term of service as bourgeois conscience. All the histories reenact these indentures. The avant-garde was launched by the bourgeoisie and is locked into a decaying orbit around it; it was born with the bourgeoisie because the bourgeoisie had to externalize its opposition in order to better contain it. . . . Where will it find another agency to clear out its old cultural products and develop such striking new ones? How will the dialectic of modern culture survive without negation? (81)

If the experimental writing movement in composition acts as the "conscience" of composition and performs the service of clearing out its "old cultural products" and developing "such striking new ones," can it hope to be any more than the research and development department of the corporate university?

Following the logic of Mann's argument one might draw the following parallels: As with the avant-garde, so too with arguments for experimental writing or alternative discourses. No matter their "wildest disavowals," the liberatory or critical power of experimental or alternative discourses will be conscripted into a tedious and dispiriting term of service as academic discourse in required composition courses that reinforce or represent bourgeois conscience. Indeed, in "A Problem with Writing (about) 'Alternative Discourses,'" Sidney Dobrin makes a similar argument that the introduction of alternative discourses into the academy does not threaten the academic discourses so much as threaten the alternative discourses: "All discourse, labeled academic or any of the many other terms we use to delineate difference from academic discourse, such as 'home discourse,' 'parent discourse,' or 'personal discourse,' all identify discourses as non-academic discourse, mixed discourse, is to invoke academic discourse as the language through which, by which, and in which other discourses are codified. The very notion of hybrid discourses serves to fold all other 'parent' discourses into the hegemony and master narrative of academic discourse" (46).

To dovetail Mann's position and Dobrin's, arguments for experimental writing or alternative discourses thus "externalize" oppositions (otherwise internalized or implicit to the scene of teaching of writing or implicit in more traditional academic discourses) by objectifying ideology in the form of identifiable discourses. In other words, instead, of seeing the unconventional, experimental, or alternative as it is present in students' academic writing or even as it is in tension with pedagogies, curricula, and institutions, these arguments make a show of externalizing it; it is something outside of composition that must be brought in. Once dramatically brought in to the composition classroom, these other discourses can be better contained.

Compositionists think they are empowering students by valuing these alternative discourses, but I tend to agree with both Mann and Dobrin here: the net result is the reverse; the discourses that are brought into the composition classroom are devalued and disempowered, or disarmed, by being subjected to the dynamics of the institution. On the one hand, this could be viewed tragically: students may seek refuge in alternative discourses and that refuge is now subjected to the scrutiny and evaluation of the institution. Of course, the institution gets to "clear out the old cultural products and . . . [appear to have] striking new ones" (Mann 81). On the other hand, to read the scene in a more comedic frame, if one imagines that alternative discourses are infinitely generated, then by the time writing teachers bring rap music or YouTube (and the like) into the classroom, students will be in the process of moving on, or will have, in fact, already moved on to something else. Alternative or experimental texts outside the institution renew themselves and continually exceed the institutions' will to absorb, accommodate, or contain them.

It does seem that if experimental writing cannot quite resist being absorbed or accommodated by the institution, so that it cannot offer quite the freedom and liberation the rhetoric of such arguments in composition suggests, perhaps it can do more modest and local things. If experimental writing and traditional academic prose are locked into a dialectical relationship whereby even as experimental writing tries to critique and challenge academic prose, the teaching of experimental writing ensures the latter's perpetuation, perhaps it can at least constantly make clear the means by which academic prose maintains its dominance. Does experimental writing in composition offer a way to discuss the exclusionary tactics by which more conventional academic discourses remain dominant? Do these experimental and alternative discourses present our students with access to the excess (experiences, realities, ideologies, discourses) that cannot quite be contained by normative discourses of power (e.g., academic discourse)?

Or are we using experimental writing to teach surreptitiously rather familiar and traditional values about writing through juxtaposition? And if one way to see arguments for experimental writing is as an attempt to destroy or at least reform the institution of composition from the inside out through "self-criticism," it seems that we have yet to explore to what degree we have really allowed (or can really allow) experimental writing to disturb our material pedagogical and institutional practices. Will we be willing or able to revise in substantial ways the institutional discourses and practices that inform, if not dictate, how we evaluate student writings? If we are going to take seriously the significance of innovative or experimental writings, then our criteria and methods of evaluation need to change. However, this is easier said than done, as the criteria for evaluating student writing are informed by, if not dictated by, our understanding both of the institutional location of composition and the institution of composition as a field.

THE CRISIS OF JUDGMENT IN COMPOSITION

EVALUATING EXPERIMENTAL STUDENT WRITING

The presence of arguments in composition for experimental writing can be seen both as a response to a crisis of value and judgment in composition and as an attempt to bring about such a crisis. Some teachers of writing are uncertain about the value of teaching academic writing in an increasingly multicultural or postmodern educational environment. They might want to empower and liberate students from the constraints of conventional academic writing in order to better allow them to represent their social realities, or to critique the limits of dominant forms of writing, or to explore new perspectives and knowledges outside of those validated by educational institutions. However, how then do teachers situate the unconventional writings that students produce within the institutional discourses and practices that inform, if not dictate, teachers' judgments as composition teachers?

Conventional writing, by definition, implies agreed-upon stylistic or rhetorical conventions and more or less agreed-upon criteria for judgment. Of course, while many of the criteria are agreed upon, it goes without saying that within the range of conventional criteria, evaluations of student writing can vary from teacher to teacher, program to program, and institution to institution as a result of personal preferences, disciplinary and institutional formations and locations, pedagogical contexts, and so on. Thus, two teachers in the same department can grade the same essay differently, valuing certain conventions over others; conversely, two teachers from different universities might ostensibly give the same grade to an essay if they valued the same set of writing conventions.[1] Many criteria—clarity, unity, coherence, fluency, consistency, economy, logic, just to name a few—seem to function and circulate as objective universals or principles, though teachers are aware that they are neither objective nor universal.[2] Experimental writing, however, does not presuppose such preexisting or long-standing criteria. Indeed, experimental writing requires an explicit renegotiation of evaluative criteria. A teacher's ability to judge student writing can be paralyzed when traditional criteria fail to apply to a new form, or when traditional criteria and new criteria conflict irreconcilably, or when, simply, a teacher hasn't yet developed the criteria needed to evaluate what the student has produced. Confronted with a piece of unconventional student writing for which traditional principles or criteria seem inadequate, a teacher finds himself or herself in what Jean-François Lyotard, referring to the situation produced by experimental literature, calls a "pragmatic situation that did not exist before" (Lyotard and Thébaud, *Just Gaming* 11).

Most discussions of teaching experimental or other unconventional writing either gloss over or completely ignore the issue of evaluation. There are several reasons why teachers might not grade unconventional writing: they don't feel that it is fair to grade students on writing that students would not normally be expected to do in a conventional composition class (i.e., composition teachers know they are going out on a limb with weird writing assignments); teachers are asking students to take risks, and grading would inhibit students' willingness to take those chances; teachers consider unconventional writing as part of a larger writing process and submerge (or contain) any difficulties of grading unconventional writing in a portfolio context. However, even if a student's writing is not graded, teachers must be making some evaluative statements regarding such writing if they are responding to and claiming any value for unconventional student writing. Indeed, teachers respond to the pragmatic situations created by experimental writing in a variety of ways, including offering minimal evaluative response; applying previously established criteria to the new text that avert or contain any crisis of judgment; and displacing evaluation onto reflective essays that accompany experimental pieces.

Though I run the risk of invoking the alarmist tone of the "literacy crisis" by describing these pragmatic situations as the result of crises in judgment, the etymology of the word "crisis" reveals its proximity to the words "criticism" and "critic." The English word "critic" shares similar roots, in *krites*, or "judge," and *krino*, or "to decide." "Crisis" comes from the Greek *krisis* and *krino*, meaning, respectively, "decision" and "to decide." Though "crisis" connotes a problem or time of danger, as a turning point or a time when decisions or judgments must be made, it can also suggest an opportunity for change. With that in mind, I will explore what the difficulties and details of these specific acts of evaluation might teach us about the possibility of changing our pedagogies and our conceptualizations of the work of composition.

EVALUATION AND JUDGMENT

Evaluative acts in composition are discussed using various terms and with multiple purposes. Though the field of composition sometimes employs the terms "evaluation" and "assessment" interchangeably, "assessment" refers predominantly to large-scale testing of writing abilities such as occurs with placement exams and at the department or university level in order to place a student into a course, to advance a student at the end of a course, or to acknowledge the fulfillment of a university requirement.[3] While it might be occasionally considered synonymous with "assessment," "evaluation" more often suggests the multiplicity of responses a teacher might have in response to student writing during, as well as at the end of, a course. As I have suggested above, grading is a kind of evaluation, but not the only kind. Teachers evaluate the writing of individual students at different stages of the writing process for different reasons, or design writing assignments for their class as a result of evaluations made of students as a group.

I have chosen to use the terms "evaluation" and "judgment" rather than "assessment" not only because my interest does not lie primarily in large-scale testing, but also because, as terms, both "evaluation" and "judgment" productively blur the lines between decisions about economic value and decisions about ethical or aesthetic merit, lines that are not as clear-cut as we would sometimes like to imagine.[4]

Although in *Contingencies of Value: Alternative Perspectives for Criti-*

cal Theory Barbara Herrnstein Smith focuses on the evaluation of literary texts (particularly in terms of discourses of aesthetics), her work is useful to my examination of the role of judgment in composition in several ways. First, Herrnstein Smith reminds us that judgments are often made to, or for, some audience. When we evaluate, we are "articulating an estimate of how well that work will serve implicitly defined functions . . . for a specific implicitly defined audience . . . who are conceived of as experiencing the work under certain implicitly defined circumstances" (13). While the context for evaluations can be confined to the composition classroom, where the teacher articulates for the student how his or her writing serves particular functions, in this chapter I am concerned with the kinds of evaluative statements about experimental student writing that are published in scholarly journals and books, as well as what teachers say about how they evaluate experimental student writing. In arguments for the teaching of experimental writing, the audience of composition scholars and teachers implied is often understood as sharing similar values and goals.

For example, underlying many of the arguments for unconventional writing are assumptions about the inadequacy (if not oppressive aspects) of academic writing and the need to liberate students via alternate or experimental forms, as well as assumptions about students' alienation from academic literacies. As these arguments allude to successful student writing (I've yet to find discussions of failed experimental student writing), they suggest not only that these writings are valuable to the particular teacher(s) involved but that they could or should be valuable to other composition teachers and scholars. Furthermore, the judgments or evaluations made of experimental student writing reveal a compositionist's investment in arguing for a certain pedagogy or theory of writing.[5]

Herrnstein Smith also reminds us that analyzing the process of evaluation is no simple matter. It is not easy, or even perhaps possible, to determine everything that has gone into a judgment or evaluation. In a judgment, there can be many "economies" at work, for example, personal, social, literary, pedagogical, institutional, and so on. Yet this does not mean that we cannot analyze evaluative statements or explore their contingencies. Nor does the fact that judgments are often the result of complex and multiple economies doom us to an unproductive or insignificant "subjectivism."[6] Shared judgments, or what Herrnstein Smith calls "constancies," are possible because "our experience of 'the value of the work' is equivalent to *our experience of the work in relation to the total economy of our existence.* And the reason our estimates of its probable value for other people may be quite accurate is that the total economy of their existence may, in fact, be quite similar to that of our own" (16). I am not claiming that the "total economy of our existence" is the same for literary scholars and composition scholars or even the same among composition scholars. For one thing, composition's gatekeeping and remedial functions, along with the mandate to prepare students for academic writing, highlight and emphasize the writing teacher's evaluative role in ways not quite shared by the literary scholar or literature teacher.

EVALUATIVE UNCERTAINTY AND CRISIS MANAGEMENT

One response to unconventional or experimental writings, even when the teacher requests these types of writing, is paralysis of judgment. Such a paralysis prevents a teacher from producing extensive evaluative comments. For example, in her essay "It's Not Mumbo Jumbo: Taking Risks with Academic Writing," Elizabeth Rankin expresses her evaluative uncertainty in the face of unconventional student writing produced as a result of an assignment that suggested the general possibility.[7] Her inability to evaluate her students' writings illustrates the effects of both conflicts in criteria and the lack of criteria: "In several cases, although I liked what the students produced, I found I was uncertain about whether it was "academically sound" or "scholarly" enough. . . . Were these genuine attempts to draw together the work we had read and the things we had said about that work in class? Or were they simply clever evasions of the assignment—unconventional in style but lacking somehow in serious thought and substance?" (Rankin 71). Her taste in writing, her understanding of academic literacy, and her responsibilities as a teacher are in conflict. On the one hand, she "likes" the writing; on the other hand, as a teacher, she knows that it is not enough to just "like" the writing. Her position as a teacher seems to hold her responsible to another set of values expressed by the terms "academically sound," "scholarly," and "serious thought and substance." Additionally, Rankin's different pedagogical tendencies seem to be vying for dominance in her judgment: beginning by thinking about the product—what the students produced—Rankin then switches to trying to evaluate not just the writing as product, but the students, their efforts in their own learning process: were they "genuine attempts" or "simply clever evasions"?

In response to a student named Aaron who wrote a fictional FBI file on Ishmael Reed's *Mumbo Jumbo,* Rankin suggests that it is the utter inapplicability of traditional criteria that results in her evaluative paralysis:

Paging through these imaginary documents, I hardly know what to think, much less how to comment. In fact, looking back at the file now, six months later, I'm embarrassed at how little I wrote in response. There are a few penciled comments in the margins—mostly questions, a few circled typos, but virtually nothing that would give Aaron a sense of how much I admired his work. Why not, I wonder? At the time, perhaps, I was simply stunned. Unable to draw on my usual repertoire of "teacherly" responses ("interesting thesis!" "good point," "transition could be smoother"), I just backed off and admired the effort. And maybe worried a little about what I "should" be saying. (70)

Originally in her assignment, Rankin had suggested an approach to evaluating these student writings: "If I can see, when I read your paper, clear evidence of a mind at work on the page, I'll consider your paper successful" (68). In an attempt that seems designed to encourage students to experiment with their writing, Rankin has generalized her criteria for judgment ("a mind at work") to the extent that, though clearly she admires Aaron's work, she cannot seem to find a way to articulate the specific details or contours of her judgment. In her own words, she is "simply stunned."

Sometimes it is not merely the absence of criteria or the conflicts in criteria that produce crises in judgment for the teacher. Occasionally, the inclusion of unconventional forms and the destabilization of traditional criteria can effectively deny the teacher his or her position as judge. For example, in the process of "freeing" students from the constraints of conventional academic writing by encouraging them to write in unconventional forms, teachers can find themselves unwittingly bereft of their roles as expert readers. Thus, they forfeit their claim to be better judges than students of the writing that students produce.

In "Habits of Opposite and Alcove: Language Poetry in the Composition Classroom," David Starkey recounts his experience teaching language poetry to composition students: "Both Carly and Debra [Stark's students] point to a conspicuous problem: the dilemma faced by any reader, but a writing teacher in particular, when responding to and evaluating work that so consciously flouts conventional ways of making sense. . . . So, if a student claims that her work accomplishes its purpose—no matter how obscure and solipsistic that purpose might be—*what right does an instructor promulgating the values of language poetry have to disparage that work?*" (129; emphasis mine). I find it amusing first of all that the teacher's power to respond to and evaluate student writing is articulated as the "right" to make "disparaging remarks." I suppose this is a nod from Starkey to students' perceptions of the teacher's evaluation, but it does seem to preclude the possibility that, as Rankin suggested above, a teacher might also find himself or herself in the position of wanting to give praise or to articulate positive judgments and be incapable of doing so. Since the composition teacher "promulgating the values of language poetry" has apparently abandoned, however temporarily, his commitment to traditional academic prose and standards, he has also abandoned his position as arbiter and upholder of value. Where has the power of judgment gone? Apparently, the teacher's evaluative authority is usurped by the student, who as "author" now possesses the authority to judge. This conclusion relies on privileging the artist's intention, which is more than a little ironic since, as Starkey claims, the "writing course [is] based entirely on principles of language poetry—that is, one in which writer and reader remain profoundly skeptical of each other, in which meaning is erratic and provisional" (129). In the face of the suggestion by students that it should be enough for a student to claim "that her work accomplishes its purpose," one can almost hear the plaintive tone of the teacher: "So, . . . no matter how obscure and solipsistic that purpose might be?" This is the writing teacher's dilemma, not just "the dilemma faced by any reader." The writing teacher's evaluations are inseparable from his or her institutional obligation to teach and evaluate students' writing; therefore the teacher cannot completely forfeit his or her evaluative authority to the students.

Until now I have been examining some of the kinds of crises in judgment that result from reading experimental writing; yet to say that such unconventional writing always brings about crises in judgment would be to overstate the case. In fact, there are several ways that ease of judgment of unconventional writing can be maintained. For instance, when teachers teach a specific form, know the features of that form, have established reasons for teaching that particular form, and can comprehensibly communicate their criteria for judgment to students, then the process of evaluation can be no more troubled than the evaluation of conventional writing. For example, in "Transforming Connections and Building Bridges: Assigning, Reading, and Evaluating the Collage Essay," Sheryl I. Fontaine and Francine Quaas give some brief background on the collage as form, provide instructions for teachers on how to write a collage assignment, and help teachers anticipate and deal with students' reactions and difficulties, as well as discuss problems of evaluation and ways to deal with them. In addition, Fontaine and Quaas go so far as to suggest that if a given writing program requires a portfolio review, the teacher of the collage will need to inform the writing program director and other teachers.

It is worth noting, however, that Fontaine and Quaas have put unconventional writing in service of a rather traditional goal, that is, helping students to cultivate their synthetic thinking abilities (i.e., to make connections): "To help students understand organization in terms of the structuring power of conventional patterns *and* the structuring power of conceptual relationships" (112). Their essay on the collage is one of the few arguments for unconventional writing that does not situate itself in any discourse of "breaking the rules," or otherwise position itself in opposition in any way to academic discourse. Nor do Fontaine and Quaas claim to be involved in any political or social project, for example, reclaiming the value of personal experience in the face of academic essays or research papers; giving expression to alternate social realities or ideologies; or using the collage form in service of feminist writing (e.g., antilinear, antirational, and so on). The collage in their argument is simply a tool, a means to an end—cultivating students' ability to make connections—and therefore, like any practical task, and given adequate criteria, the success of the collage can be evaluated.

Additionally, they have attempted to preclude the possibility of evaluative uncertainty by combining general composition criteria with criteria specific to the form. A student's collage can be deemed successful if "meaning emerges"; if a writer has "effectively relied on internal relationships rather than external rhetorical conventions to create this text"; and finally, the collage can be evaluated by asking students to turn in reflective writing ("personal 'movies'" of themselves as readers) in order to judge the "success of the writer's intentions" (Fontaine and Quaas 115). The criteria of judgment are established prior to the production of student writing, precluding the possibility that the students' collages might actually challenge the criteria of the teacher. In effect, they have thwarted the radical potential of the collage to challenge traditional evaluative criteria.

Other arguments for experimental student writing avoid or manage crises of judgment not by revising and rearticulating criteria, but by holding fast to traditional criteria, often contiguous with a pedagogy—expressivist pedagogy, for example—which resists challenges posed by experimental writing. For example, in his introduction to *Teaching Writing Creatively*, Starkey gestures to a "polycultural" project of teaching writing. Yet one wonders if such a polycultural project wouldn't need to include a polycultural approach to evaluation. Such a disruption to the methods and criteria of evaluation are denied, however, by the values of expressivist pedagogies, to which Starkey holds allegiance. In his first move, Starkey traces his composition genealogy through Donald Murray and Peter

Elbow and announces a general premise of expressivist pedagogy: "all effective writing is autobiographical" (xiv). In a second move, he links the significance of unconventional writing to values that inform expressivist pedagogies: "They [composition teachers] are likely to share the conviction of contributors to this volume that students should have a stake in the writing they do, and that student and teacher writing problems are often very similar. Teachers like these value playful, passionate writing as much as writing that claims to be objective. They admire innovative forms and alternate style. They cherish honesty" (xv). The majority (if not all) of the examples of good student writing in both *Elements of Alternate Style* (Bishop) and *Teaching Writing Creatively* (Starkey) are written in the first person and as explorations of topics that, at least usually in the teacher's opinion, are important to the student. There are very few attempts to engage topics or issues beyond the purview of personal experience.[8]

Of course, personal experience could be a starting point for students, or personal experience could complement other types of writing or be complemented by the use of other texts and sources. Apparently, however, these students do not critically read other texts or attempt to engage any audience (even if merely hypothetical) beyond the self or the teacher. As we will see below, the student does not try to situate his or her experiences regarding divorce as part of a cultural phenomenon but writes about "my parent's divorce." The student does not attempt to socially or historically situate the concept of friendship, not even by perhaps referring to representations of friendship in literature, television, or other media; instead, the student writes on her "new friendships." Students do not begin with their own religious values or experiences and then expand out to consider histories or accounts of religious values and experiences. Instead, the student of "god revised" writes about experiencing her own religious uncertainty sitting in church (Crissy, in DePeter 33–34). It's hard to see how unconventional writings serve a polycultural project if culture is understood as a commonsensical, unmediated expression of the student's individual experience.

For example, Ronald A. DePeter's "Fractured Narratives: Explorations in Style" suggests that writing fractured narratives is a "technique" that can "be appreciated as a productive way of getting at new, unexplored relationships between writers and their texts and between writers and their readers" (26). This could be, pedagogically, a very interesting project, teaching students about interpretive or discourse communities, the effects of challenging one's reader, or all the work that a writer of narratives might do for a reader (or can refuse to do by fracturing a narrative) and all the work that a reader might do for a writer (by reading a fractured narrative). However, the personal experience narratives that the students produce do not seem to get at new relationships between writers and readers. Below are two examples of student writing DePeter quotes along with his evaluative comments:

Excerpt from Student Writing	DePeter's Evaluative Comments

a. "It's not fair.
    It's not my fault.
    I need to raise my average.
    Just another day at college.
    If only I could have made that
one spare.
        Then I would be doing good."
(Lisa, qtd. in DePeter 29)
	a. Lisa juggles them all together in one narrative, and makes us, as readers, come to some sense of how to react. Suddenly, I begin to see how a person may be preoccupied by (here) three concerns [college, bowling team, her "continuing disillusion with a person's betrayal"], each of varying importance to her. (De Peter 28)

b. Dad, I feel like I can't ever do any thing right . . . I feel like everything I do is wrong, and everything Chris does is perfect.
    One of my friends, Aimee, let me stay at her house for a few days until I decided what I was going to do. I had no car, clothes, or home. I was completely lost.
    Kate: Hey Dad
    Dad: Where are you?
    Kate: Don't worry, I'm okay.
(Kate, qtd. in DePeter 31)
	b. I don't know if Kate's "sampled essay" has impact on you, but it still reminds me how this unusually constructed piece made me look at divorce—through the lens of this particular divorce—in a new way, and how it helped Kate illustrate her own jumbled thoughts in a way she might not have been able to without taking such risks. (DePeter 32).

It seems possible that fractured narratives could indeed get at "new unexplored relationships between writers and readers" and perhaps create realizations not produced by more conventional writing. Yet DePeter has no problems reading, interpreting, reacting to, or valuing his students' writing, and while DePeter says that Lisa juggles all three concerns together and gives her reader some sense of how to react, the only reaction

DePeter seems to have is his rather banal realization: "Suddenly, I begin to see how a person may be preoccupied by (here) three concerns" (28). It's unclear why one needs a fractured narrative to achieve that effect. Similarly, DePeter's response to his student Kate's piece doesn't make clear how the fractured narrative in particular has caused him, as a reader, to have a new relationship to the text. It makes him look at divorce in a new way, but DePeter declines to say what that "new way'" is or how it was effected by the fractured narrative. Finally, the successful unconventional writing merely confirms the teacher's—here DePeter's—presupposition that risk-taking in student writing is important or valuable, since "it helped Kate."

In other words, a pedagogy (here, expressivist) can potentially nullify any specific claims made for the value of a given unconventional form. The students are freed from the burden or constraints of academic rules or conventions, yet the criteria of expressivist pedagogy can remain unaltered, and the students' writing can still be evaluated along the following lines: the student learned something about his or her experience; the student was able to express his or her feelings or experiences in a way significant to the student or teacher, particularly if the teacher is emotionally affected.

Recent arguments for expressivist writing that advocate unconventional writing might see themselves as disturbing the hegemony of rational conventional academic discourse, reclaiming the centrality of the student's experience and capacity for expression in the face of the dehumanizing process of mastering academic conventions, conventions that might alienate a student from his or her other literacies and his or her own experiences. However, what I find remarkable about the expressivist arguments for the teaching of unconventional writing is that they have yet to explore the possibility that unconventional student writing might challenge pedagogies that value "honesty," "self-exploration," and "self-expression" or that such writing might provide alternatives to the limits of expressivist pedagogies, particularly as they may foster solipsism or seem to require disclosure from the student. While savvy students might fake such disclosure, other students might feel more alienated from the request for personal experience than they do from learning the conventions of academic prose, which seems, at least, to have potentially more exchange- and use-value beyond the composition classroom.

As a testimony to how pedagogies and forms taught may change while criteria for evaluation abide, consider that these recent unconventional student writings are evaluated and appreciated in ways very similar to those of the teachers in a collection of conventional student writing: *What*

Makes Writing Good, edited by William Coles and James Vopat. Coles and Vopat's work is a combination anthology and textbook. It offers a collection of student essays and teacher commentary—each student essay is framed by his or her teacher's introduction explaining why the teacher thinks the essay is good, along with Coles and Vopat's questions for analysis and discussion (for those who wish to use *What Makes Writing Good* as a writing textbook). Both Lester Faigley's commentary on and Patricia Bizzell and Bruce Herzberg's review of *What Makes Writing Good* conclude that the teachers in the collection clearly and overwhelmingly prefer descriptions of students' personal experiences. As Faigley points out, "the range of contributors is not matched by a similar range of student writing. By my count, at least thirty of the [forty-eight] examples in the collection are personal experience essays—twenty of them autobiographical narratives—and several of the remaining eighteen include writing about the writer"; "but why is writing about potentially embarrassing and painful aspects of one's life considered more honest than, say, the efforts of Joseph Williams's student, Greg Shaefer, who tries to figure out what Thucydides was up to in writing about the Peloponnesian War?" (Faigley, *Fragments of Rationality* 120).

As Bizzell articulates it, the primary criterion for judging the majority of the student writing in this collection is "whether the student's particular stylistic approach is effective in moving our emotions, the principal criterion for excellence in the personal essay" (245). Bizzell offers several examples of teacher responses in which teachers appreciate the "honesty" of the student's writing or the "tension between flat reporting and personal anguish," or express their appreciation of how the student's writing has "moved" them emotionally (245). Furthermore, Bizzell's criticism of the lack of variety in the types of student writing helps us to understand why unconventional or alternate styles may not require a change in criteria for some composition teachers. Bizzell writes, with irony, "The variety, or lack thereof, in the book's sample writing need not be an issue. Through any good writing, we could arrive at these universal values—but perhaps most easily through personal writing that takes their expression as its particular task" (245). According to Bizzell, the book could "avoid this universalizing tendency" by acknowledging its legacy in nineteenth-century belles lettres, a legacy in which the personal self-reflective essay predominates (244).

The belletristic tradition was in large part an attempt to bring scientific principles to bear on the arts, including rhetoric and literature. In the process, belletristic rhetoricians translated the culturally inflected tastes of aesthetic judgments into empirical and objective principles for good writing. Evaluation of writing in the belletristic tradition, then, is in essence an evaluation of the writer's sensibilities masking as the application of universal principles. The functional complicity between aesthetic judgment in the belletristic tradition and the will-to-power aspects of humanism are revealed as vicious and oppressive when the student fails in presenting, and thus valuing, the right kinds of personal experiences or sensibilities.

This is the coercive aspect of Immanuel Kant's concept of *sensus communis* (common sense), which is responsible for making subjective aesthetic judgments seem universal (i.e., so that what makes writing good for each individual teacher/reader of *What Makes Writing Good* is synonymous with good writing in general). I would suggest, however, that one cannot claim that experimental writings disrupt the status quo of academic writing in composition while at the same time maintaining the commonsense judgments of expressivist pedagogies or belletristic tradition. If unconventional student writing is going to successfully disrupt the status quo of composition, then it must be allowed to disrupt our evaluations of, as well as our pedagogies for, student writing.

An interesting example of the tension between the claim for objective or universal principles and the specificity of unconventional writing that seems to require a revision of these principles or criteria occurs in a book key to the recent movement for alternate or experimental writing in composition: Winston Weathers's *An Alternate Style: Options in Composition*. In the beginning of his book, Weathers acknowledges that good writing is not necessarily a universal or a static category: "We identify our favored 'grammar of style,' our favored game and box, as the 'good' grammar of style, and we identify what it produces as 'good writing'" (7). Since Weathers constantly reassures his readers that alternate styles ("Grammar B") in no way threaten more traditional styles or grammars ("Grammar A"), it seems that he is not critiquing what compositionists might consider "good writing" but merely suggesting that we widen the category to include other kinds of writings. There might be new options for writing students, but there will be no crisis of judgment for teachers since it is still the case that "within alternate style, writers adhere, of course, to certain basic principles of composition" (39).

Weathers's principles can be divided into four rules: writers should be consistent in their use of style; writers should have a rationale for their composition/style; writers should not "bore" their readers (or rather, a writer must maintain the reader's interest); and finally, writers must write conventionally enough to be understood by their readers (39–40). First, Weathers's requirements presuppose that these basic principles of good writing adhere across forms and styles. Second, all of these principles dismiss some of the most radical and interesting aspects of experimental writing: mixed styles that challenge genre and discursive boundaries or boring, irrational writing that calls into question purposes for writing as well as the expectations about the writer-reader relationship. Consider, for example, that boredom might be exactly the effect some experimental writings are aiming for:

> In both the Freudian and Marxist traditions . . . "boredom" is taken not so much as an objective property of things and works but rather as a response to a blockage of energies (whether those be grasped in terms of desire or of praxis). Boredom then becomes interesting as a reaction to situations of paralysis and also, no doubt, as defense mechanism or avoidance behavior. Even taken in the narrower realm of cultural reception, boredom with a particular kind of work or style or content can always be used productively as a precious symptom of our own existential, ideological, and cultural limits, an index of what has to be refused in the way of other people's cultural practices and their threat to our own rationalizations about the nature and value of art. Meanwhile it is no great secret that in some of the most significant works of high modernism, what is boring can often be very interesting indeed, and vice versa. . . . It is a paradox one can get used to: if a boring text can also be good (or interesting, as we now put it), exciting texts, which incorporate diversion, distraction, temporal commodification, can also sometimes be "bad" (or "degraded," to use Frankfurt school language). (Jameson 71–72)

Imagine, in other words, an experimental writing assignment that might ask students to produce a text with the intention of boring each other and their instructor, thus inviting all involved to reflect on "our own existential, ideological, and cultural limits, an index of what has to be refused in the way of other people's cultural practices and their threat to our own rationalizations about the nature and value of art" (Jameson 71–72). How might students and teachers be required to articulate explicitly those limits and cultural practices? But it is just such threats to our own rationalizations and the potential destabilization of tacit criteria for the categories of "interesting" or "boring" that Weathers's principles are meant to prevent. Indeed, though Weathers neglects to elaborate on his fourth principle— writing should be conventional enough to be comprehensible—one might assume that teacher and student would explore the conventions of a given "well-tested" option before the teacher was in a position to evaluate examples of such student writing, thereby preventing again any exploration of the category of "the comprehensible," as well as avoiding any evaluative uncertainty.

Yet how can we use our knowledge about alternate styles and unconventional or experimental writings to change our evaluation practices? And if we change our evaluation practices, do we then need to change our pedagogical theories and practices, as well as our conceptualization of the field of composition? Assuming that we are willing to let unconventional student writing change all of these things, we need to ask what is actually involved in not only renegotiating the criteria but also renegotiating the contingencies of judgment. Below, I will examine several arguments that outline the kind of work involved in attempts to revise our evaluation practices, pedagogies, and conceptualizations of the field of composition as a result of such unconventional writing.

REEVALUATING EVALUATION OF EXPERIMENTAL STUDENT WRITING

Wendy Bishop notes in "Responding to, Evaluating, and Grading Alternate Style" that experimental student writing requires that composition teachers change not only the way they read, but their methods of evaluation: "Experimental writing taxes our reading schemas. . . . I had to set aside my English teacher hyper literacy and stop judging alternate writing against an implicit canon of genres in my head while I investigated the convention making and breaking they [students] were engaged in" (174). If one can set aside the "hyper literacy" of an English teacher and the "implicit canons of genres," then how does the teacher evaluate the student's writing? Where do the criteria come from? One place they come from, apparently, is graduate school: "Those of us who read literature in graduate school know that Joyce's later work and Stein's work of any period are difficult to read, no matter how rewarding" (174). The teacher as qualified judge is apparently greatly helped by having some experience in reading experimental, innovative, or otherwise unconventional literature, though Bishop does not explore the complexities involved in transferring our knowledge of innovative texts and their writers to student texts. But her use of the term "experimental" rather than "alternate" suggests that faced with truly experimental student writing, the teacher might find that even the new canons of Joyce and Stein will fail to provide adequate criteria by which the student's writing can be judged. In other words, if, as Bishop says, experimental writing can tax our reading schemas not only as writing teachers, then I would suggest that perhaps truly experimental writing would depart from imitating other innovative works of literature and so would tax even those reading schemas provided by familiarity with innovative texts such as those by modernists such as Joyce or Stein, not to mention works by much more recent postmodern authors.

Despite her claims to educated expertise, Bishop is hesitant to admit the extent to which experimental student writing might paralyze or disable a teacher's evaluative capacities. In fact, in an attempt to offer some further assistance to the writing teacher looking for help in evaluating alternate styles or experimental writing, Bishop draws on two established pedagogical strategies: first, consult the student writer on his or her intention; and second, ask the student writer to reflect on the experimental piece of writing and use that reflective piece as an aid to evaluation.

One way Bishop suggests that teachers can learn to change their reading schemas is by consulting the student writer's intention. Through a dialogical interaction between teacher and student, where the teacher communicates the effects of the experimental writing on her as a reader, and where the student responds by communicating her intention and self-consciousness, the teacher is able to evaluate not necessarily the success of the student's piece of writing but the student's knowledge and awareness of his or her own intentions as well as the potential effects of his or her writing on a reader. The kinds of questions that Bishop suggests the students ask of their writing, as well as the kinds of questions that teachers ask of students' writing, demonstrate many of the desires, tendencies, and traps of the use of reflective writing in the process of evaluation. Considered positively and generously, these acts of reflection can empower students, making them more autonomous as they learn to evaluate their own writing. Similarly, such reflective writing can be an occasion for the student to see what he or she knows about writing. Considered more skeptically, these reflective writings might be understood as attempts to provide teachers with information that will enable the student's disciplining.

For example, Bishop suggests that students ask themselves about problems they may be ignoring, or, as I would claim, problems that they might be "hiding" from the teacher: "Can I describe why this writing requires this style/format? (*For instance, can I assure a reader that this was an intentional choice, not simply an easy way out?*)"; or, "Are there places in the writing where I covered up, patched, ignored problems I was having understanding my own writing goals or aims? (*Did I find that I couldn't pull two metaphors together in the middle so I simply left white space hoping no one would notice?*)" ("Responding to, Evaluating" 175). These questions seem designed to produce responses from the student in order to reassure the teacher, not the student. Who except for the teacher cares whether or not the unconventional move is an "easy way out" as long as the writing is effective? Additionally, does it matter if the white space in a piece of writing is the result of an inability to pull two metaphors together as long as the effect on the reader is successful? On the one hand, if students want to know how to do these things but are afraid to ask for help, or are apprehensive about appearing inadequate, then their attempt to mask their inability is a problem because they want to learn something and yet can't find a way to ask for help. On the other hand, experienced writers often hide their weaknesses; knowing how to compensate is part of knowing how to write, and it matters little if after producing a piece of effective writing, the writer later admits that those beautifully simple short sentences covered up his or her inability to successfully write more complex sentences.

Though the levels of authority granted to published writers compared to student writers can vary greatly, it seems to me that if the teacher or other readers (e.g., fellow students) don't notice these writing inadequacies, and if the student wants to hide them, then why should there be any pressure on the student to disclose this information? Finally, we should not overlook what Kathleen Blake Yancey calls "the schmooze factor in reflection: the temptation to reward students who tell us what we naturally enough want to hear: that they are learning, that they are taking risks, in the most dramatic case, that they have never experienced such pleasure in learning before, that it is in this class where it has taken place" (100).[9]

Since unconventional writing by its nature can challenge, if not paralyze, a teacher's ability to evaluate, the trend embraced by advocates of writing portfolios to require student reflection seems a particularly attractive way out of the dilemma of evaluative uncertainty. A teacher who might not know how to evaluate a student's experimental writing can put traditional criteria to use in evaluating students' reflection. In effect, grading has been somewhat displaced, or the burden of evaluating experimental writing has at least been shared, if not taken over, by the reflective piece. Yet other possibilities for these ancillary writings are overlooked or remain undeveloped. Of course, reflective writings in general can do more than provide information that contributes to the teacher's evaluation of a student's writing. Many of Bishop's questions are clearly meant to help a student also explore opportunities for revision, in addition to helping a student learn how to articulate what he or she knows about writing, even if he or she can't enact that knowledge in a given piece of writing.

However, particularly as concerns unconventional writing, these reflective pieces of writing could be more than justifications or evidence as proof provided for the teacher in the form of a memo or letter written by the student to the teacher. Instead, a student might produce manifestos, poetics for his or her own texts, or speculative writings. He or she might even theorize, not only about his or her own writing (his or her intentions, his or her problems, etc.), but make observations or comments about his or her own writing in the context of the success (or not) of other unconventional writings in certain historical, social, and rhetorical contexts (e.g., "Me and Gertrude Stein: We Had a Time of It, We Did"). In other words, if, as Bishop suggests, having read Joyce and Stein has helped composition teachers expand and revise their reading schemas, and if we, as composition teachers, need to confront the difficulties in transferring our evaluation of experimental literature to our evaluation of experimental student writing, why not encourage students to participate in that process as part of the work a writer might do?

An interesting example of this kind of work I would like to explore in detail is Min-Zhan Lu's essay "Professing Multiculturalism: The Politics of Style in the Contact Zone." Here, Lu asks several important questions about who gets to experiment, how we evaluate experimental writing as literature compared to how we evaluate it as student writing, what the differences are, and how we might let the respective "contact zones" of "real" writers and student writers inform one another:

> Why is it that in spite of our developing ability to acknowledge the political need and right of "real" writers to experiment with "style," we continue to cling to the belief that such a need and right does not belong to "student writers"? Another way of putting the question would be, why do we assume . . . that until one can prove one's ability to produce "error-free" prose, one has not earned the right to innovative style? . . . It seems to me that one way of helping students to deal with this frustration would be to connect their "difficulties" with the refusal of "real" writers to reproduce the hegemonic conventions of written English. And it seems to me that this will not take place until teachers like myself contest the distinction between "real" and "student" writers and stop treating the idiosyncratic style of the not yet "perfectly educated" solely in terms of error. (Lu 446–47)

As I see it, these moves can help the writing teacher revise her methods of, and criteria for, evaluation in two ways: first, by attending to the "contact" zone of real writers as well as student writers, the writing teacher begins to address the contingencies involved in the evaluative judgments of what Lu calls "experimental style" or, more often, "idiosyncratic" writing; second, the writing teacher resists the power of standards and normative judgments in an attempt to recognize those idiosyncratic or unconventional aspects of student writing that might potentially fulfill the writer's political need (or right) to experiment.

To explore the contingent nature of judgment, Lu begins by comparing the reception and publication process for what she calls the "idiosyncratic" writings of Gertrude Stein and Theodore Dreiser. She notes that when Stein's style was questioned by a publishing clerk—he asked whether she had, as a writer, much experience with the English language—Lu notes that Stein invoked her intention as a writer and relied upon her authority as a well-educated (Radcliffe, Johns Hopkins) American. However, when publishers rejected the work of Theodore Dreiser, Dreiser was unable to authorize himself in such ways. Not only could he not invoke the authority of an excellent education, but his status as an immigrant with "imperfect" English skills limited the extent to which he could claim even his own conscious intention; he couldn't then claim that what a reader might perceive as errors were intentionally unconventional. As Lu describes it, the texts she discusses with her students in writing classes highlight the "politics of stylistic decisions made by 'real' writers, especially those writing from the borderlands by choice or necessity" (445).

Though Dreiser might seem less "oppositional" than Stein, since he sought out friends better educated than himself to help him edit and make his novel more acceptable, Lu is correct in claiming that students of writing find themselves in situations more like Dreiser's than Stein's. In other words, students lack both the authority of a "real" writer and the authority afforded by the certification of a university degree. As novice writers, they cannot yet claim the authority of their intention. Additionally, in their positions as students, they must often defer the authority of judgment to their teacher, who has a better developed sense of what makes certain kinds of writing good, or who is at least institutionally endowed with the power of judgment.

Lu proposes that we take the kinds of insights gained from historical and social contextualization of real writers, such as Stein and Dreiser, and share them with students. By jointly examining with students the details and contours of these examples, we can teach them not to merely dismiss the idiosyncratic aspects of their writing, but to transform those idiosyncrasies into stylistic choices, maintaining parts of their writing that otherwise might have been corrected, or erased, by normative tendencies of teachers or even fellow classmates. In this way, Lu is similar to Weathers, who also thinks that many of the characteristics of student writing need not necessarily be corrected away but that a teacher should help a student move toward an acceptable alternate style. Unlike Weathers, however, Lu is not interested in limiting herself or her students to well-tested models; instead, she emphasizes the political act of the writer in refusing to "reproduce the hegemonic conventions of written English" (446).

The point is that everyone—teacher, student writer, and fellow classmates—should hesitate before immediately correcting the supposed mistake and erasing any traces in a student's writing of "conflicting discourses with unequal socio-political power" (Lu 444). Rather than solving these conflicts by erasing them, Lu suggests that students be made aware of how idiosyncratic aspects of writing come into conflict with conventions of dominant discourses. As Lu acknowledges, she does not assume that students will always want to modify the dominant codes—often, in fact, they "opt for the voices of academic authority" (455)—but she asserts that the decision should be informed and conscious:

> Although the product, their decision to reproduce the code, might remain the same whether it is made with or without a process of negotiation, the activities leading to that decision, and thus its significance, are completely different. . . . If and when this student experiences some difficulty mastering a particular code, she would view it as a sign of her failure as a learner and a writer. On the other hand, if the student's decision to reproduce a code results from a process of negotiation, then she would have examined the conflict between the codes of Standard English and other discourses. And she would have deliberated not only on the social power of these colliding discourses but also on who she was, is, and aspires to be when making this decision. (455)

Instead of immediately correcting the student's writing to make it conform with dominant discourses or to facilitate normative judgments in composition, the teacher and the students ask questions that attempt to make manifest and illuminate the contact zone of the student's writing: What is at stake for the student writer in these discursive conflicts? What are the writer's choices? What are the implications—personal, ideological, social, academic, and the like—of the options available to the writer? Lu calls these "conditions of life": "a definition that includes a whole range of discursive sites, including that of race, ethnicity, gender, sex, economic class, education, religion, recreation, and work" (453). Lu also encourages "each student to think about 'life' in terms of the life she has lived in the past, is living in the present, and envisions for the future" (453).

There are several things I find helpful and important about the kind of work Lu performs and advocates. First of all, it requires thoughtful detailed attention to the particularities of production and reception of idiosyncratic texts, both literary and student texts. This kind of work does not assume that idiosyncratic texts are always the result of intention (e.g., Dreiser and student writing). Intention is not, as it was with Bishop, the basis of evaluation. Idiosyncratic or unconventional texts produced unintentionally can reveal interesting and significant conflicts between discourses, and as a result of attending to those conflicts and their effects, the writer moves toward intention (and self-consciousness), becoming aware of the implications not only for his or her reader, but also for himself or herself as a writer. The value of intention in Lu is not a basis for teacherly evaluation; instead, the importance of intention lies in its ability to "authorize" a student writer in the process of making informed choices about his or her writing. The kind of attention Lu pays to Stein and Dreiser also demonstrates for student writers that writers can find ways to resist dominant discourses if they so choose. Most important to my interests here, Lu considers many levels of evaluation of writing, emphasizing not only the teacher's judgment but also the empowering of the student writer to make his or her own judgments during the process of writing. Lu asks who makes the judgments and how those who make judgments get their authority, as well as how those who apparently have no or little authority can renegotiate the distribution of power and authority by making conscious choices as writers in regard to their relationship to dominant discourses. The authority granted real writers is attained by student writers when they learn how to make their own judgments and decisions about their writing.

What my examination of compositionists' methods of managing evaluative uncertainty—avoiding evaluation, applying traditional criteria, and displacing evaluation onto reflective essays—has shown are the ways in which we limit the potential for experimental writing to effect deep changes in our pedagogies or in the methods and criteria by which we evaluate students' experimental texts. It is my contention that in order for experimental writing to effect significant change in composition, teachers must reflect on the ways in which such writings disturb their pedagogies and unsettle their judgments.

PRUDENT AND IMAGINATIVE JUDGMENTS

One alternative to these methods is to let these *unusual* student writings disrupt the *usual* scenarios of evaluation. I find Lyotard's understanding of the new pragmatic situation produced by experimental writings to be helpful in reimagining the act of judgment for teachers of writing. Simply put, if a student produces a truly experimental piece of writing, then a new pragmatic situation has been created in which the teacher as judge now has to figure out a new way to evaluate that student writing. The situation of evaluating student writing is also pragmatic because a composition teacher, in the context of the institution, must evaluate student writing in some way.

With the specter of Plato's *Republic* hanging heavy over *Just Gaming*, Lyotard and Jean-Loup Thébaud discuss, over the course of seven days, a revision of the concept of "justice" and the problematic of judgment. On day one, Lyotard makes the distinction between innovative and experimental texts. Innovative texts are merely "innovative within fashion" and "complement an already explored field" (14). An experimental text, however, is truly experimental since "it tests hitherto untouched limits of sensibility" (14). Applying these working definitions to composition, much of the student writing I have been discussing here seems to be "innovative within fashion" or "complement[s] an already explored field." In other words, unconventional forms or alternate writings in composition might be understood as both augmenting students' rights to their own language, further strengthening ties between literary studies and composition, and bolstering expressivist or multicultural pedagogies within the field of composition. However, if the possibility exists that students will produce truly experimental writings that not only challenge our "reading schemas," as Bishop claims, but also "test hitherto untouched limits of sensibility," then not only do such writings produce new pragmatic situations, but they also demand that we must produce new methods of, and criteria for, judging that writing.

In *Just Gaming*, Lyotard claims that the judgment of experimental writing does not, and in fact cannot, rely either on the Kantian understanding of common sense or on previously established criteria. In response to this claim, Thébaud asks how judgment is possible:

[Thébaud] JLT: . . . but how do we do it, if there is no *sensus communis*?

JFL: There cannot be a *sensus communis*.

JLT: Yet we do make judgments; there must be a *sensus communis*.

JFL: No, we judge without criteria. We are in the position of Aristotle's prudent individual, who makes judgments about the just and the unjust without the least criterion. (14)

And later:

JFL: I am closest to in this regard Aristotle, insofar as he recognizes—and he does so explicitly in the *Rhetoric*, as well as in the *Nicomachean Ethics*, that a judge worthy of the name has no true model to guide his judgments, and that the true nature of the judge is to pronounce judgments, and therefore prescriptions, without criteria. This is, after all, what Aristotle calls prudence. It consists in dispensing justice without models. (26)

Lyotard goes on to explain how he makes judgment without criteria by claiming that "in each instance, I have a feeling, that's all. It is a matter of feelings, however, in the sense that one can judge without concepts" (15). Thébaud, seeming somewhat astounded, asks Lyotard where the ability to judge without criteria comes from, and Lyotard answers that it comes from the imagination: "The ability to judge does not hang upon the observance of criteria. The form that it will take in the last *Critique* [Kant's *Critique of Judgment*] is that of the imagination. An imagination that is constitutive. It is not only an ability to judge; it is a power to invent criteria" (17).

Lyotard's claim that his judgments are "matters of feeling" and prudence, lacking criteria, continues to trouble Thébaud, and on the second day of their exchange he raises the matter: "To be sure, Aristotle's judge does judge without criteria, does judge without any theoretical purport that permits the fixation of the just, but that is because he has been educated, because there is a habit, because there is a pedagogy of the soul" (26). Lyotard resists this claim by arguing that habits of education or virtue (26) do not cause (nor are they the source of) good judgments; rather, the "ethos" of a judge is based on the fact that he has made good judgments. The dialogue turns to questions of means and opinions, comparing Plato's notion of justice, for which there are objective criteria, and Aristotle's understanding of justice, which, like rhetoric, can operate only at the level of *endoxa*, or commonly held beliefs, that is, without knowledge of the truth provided by objective criteria.

What is most relevant to my discussion of composition teachers as judges, however, is Lyotard's marrying of prudence (*phronesis*)[10] and imagination. Faced with a particular case of experimental student writing (for which there are no prior adequate criteria), the composition teacher as prudent judge must rely on her perceptions, her experience (including her education), and her *imagination* in order to invent new criteria. Clearly, this ability to judge is, as Lyotard suggests in his discussion of Nietzsche, a "will to power" (Lyotard and Thébaud 17). However, I would suggest that it is a different will to power from the kind involved in the otherwise usual normative judgments a composition teacher might make. By attending to the particular case of experimental student writing, the teacher allows the student's text to contribute to her construction as reader and judge rather than applying already existing rubrics or schemas to that writing.

No doubt many composition teachers—recognizing the absence of universal criteria—are already prudent judges. But prudence alone will not do. The evaluation of experimental student writing will require an act of imagination in order to revise old criteria and invent new ones. In the process of revision and invention of new criteria, the composition teacher, prompted by the student's writing, not only attends to the particularity of the student's writing, but also begins the process of reimagining the work of writing in the composition classroom. To put it succinctly, experimental student writing changes the methods and criteria for evaluation, and by extension revises what counts as good writing.

In addition, this kind of judgment, which Lyotard and Samuel Weber, both following Kant, call reflective or indeterminate judgment, is key to the force of experimental writing in composition because it requires teachers not just to reflect on the object of judgment (student writing), but also to reflect on "the effort of judgment itself" (Weber, "Foundering of Aesthetics" 65). Whereas determinate judgment is effected by applying existing laws, concepts, or universals to the given object ("Foundering of Aesthetics" 65), indeterminate or reflective judgment is the result of a different process: "The faculty of judging is said to be 'simply reflective' when 'only the particular is given and the universal has to be found' ([Kant, *Critique of Judgment*] 18, 15). Reflective judgment concerns itself with these objects in their particularity, as they are given. It judges them as if the rules that determined their possibility *a priori* were not sufficient to account for their particularity. It endeavors to 'discover' a generality or a universality in them which is not that of their possibility but of their existence" (Lyotard, *Lessons on the Analytic* 2).

The distinction between indeterminate and determinate judgment is particularly useful to composition if one imagines that many of the kinds of judgments made of student writing are of the determinate kind: either a teacher knows the principles of good writing in general and evaluates a student's work on that basis, or the teacher has designed an assignment that has embedded in it the criteria that will "determine" the teacher's evaluation of the student's writing. Indeterminate or reflective judgment, however, emphasizes the ways in which the judge, in the face of the inadequacy of concepts or principles, reflects on himself in the process of judging:

> In those cases where only the particular is "given" and the universal remains to be found, judgment acts on its own, without the support of existing knowledge. Kant calls this type of judgment reflective, because it represents the effort or the attempt to reach the universal rather than the universal itself. It is reflective because it reflects an effort of judgment itself—Kant calls this the judging subject—rather than cognition of the object. And yet it is only in its reflective form that judgment can be studied as such, since only here does it attempt to "think" its way, as it were, from the particular to the universal. (Weber, "The Foundering of Aesthetics" 65)

Yet the resulting judgments effected by such reflections are not entirely separate from the preexisting universals:

> the particularity of this case, therefore, is defined, not by the absence of universals but by a relationship to those universals that are given but do not suffice to subsume it or determine it. To use de Man's terminology, the condition of reflective judgment is a certain "randomness," since what "follows"—the particular case at hand—is not the logical consequence of what preceded it; it cannot be explained, predicted, or derived from what came before. And yet, this "randomness," this discontinuity, is by no means equivalent to a nonrelationship. It defines itself, to begin with at least, precisely in and through this demarcation from its antecedents. (Weber, "The Foundering of Aesthetics" 67)

The prudent imaginative teacher as judge would need to reflect on his or her own process of judging, ascertaining whenever possible the ways in which the criteria for evaluating student writing fail to apply to a piece of experimental student writing, reflecting on the relationship between those preexisting criteria and the "case" before him or her presented by the student's actual text.

Though the possible rewards of such reflective judgment are rich—deeper understanding of the criteria and methods of evaluation, a more complex approach to discussing evaluation with our students, a more generative attitude about judgment (generating new criteria)—I must acknowledge that this approach to judgment has its obstacles, not the least of which is a deeply ingrained attitude about rhetoric that infuses and informs much of the teaching of writing. For example, while Lyotard invokes Aristotle's prudent judge, one can invoke other ideas Aristotle has about judgment, drawn less from his ethics and more from his work in the *Rhetoric*. In the context of rhetoric, the particular case, the idiosyncratic text, is not to be treated as an occasion for reflection; rather, it is to be ignored or dismissed:

> [A statement] is persuasive because there is somebody whom it persuades. But none of the arts theorize about individual cases. Medicine, for instance, does not theorize about what will help to cure Socrates or Callicles, but only about what will help to cure any or all of a given class of patients: this alone is its business: individual cases are so infinitely various that no systematic knowledge of them is possible. In the same way the theory of rhetoric is concerned not with what seems probable to a given individual like Socrates or Hippias, but with what seems probable to men of a given type. (Aristotle, *Rhetoric* 1.2.135.6b.25–35)

To stay within Aristotle's logic, it is only when an individual case can be linked to or associated with a significant class of people that the arts can theorize about such cases. Consider, for example, that Mina Shaughnessy did not come upon one error-ridden essay and write an entire book (*Errors and Expectations*); rather, she came across many error-ridden essays and an entire "class" (in the broadest sense) of students unprepared for college writing, which caused her to develop a theory of error. Yet experimental writing in composition claims to address not just classes of students but individual students and their individual writings. Indeed, one might suggest that the whole idea of teaching experimental writing is to see what kinds of particular cases it produces, to see significance in what otherwise might appear as idiosyncratic ("idiosyncratic," like "idiom," "idiolect," and even "idiot," shares roots in Greek words such as *idios* [own, private], *idioomai* [make one's own], *idiotes* [private person, layman, ignorant person]) (*OED*). As with "idiosyncratic," so too with many of the other words used to describe experimental writing in composition: "unconventional" (not in accord with agreement), "alternate" (otherwise from the usual or norm), "innovative" (new, previously not known).

The point here is that even if such kinds of indeterminate or reflective judgments are more time-consuming and difficult than determinate or normative judgments, such attempts at reflective judgment are the only adequate way of attending to the kinds of experimental, alternate, innovative writings students produce (and the kinds of writing we, as teachers, invite them to produce). In order for us to imagine that these kinds of student writings can significantly change our pedagogies and evaluations, we must entertain the possibility that one student text, as a particular case, can call into question a pedagogy, or indeed, an entire academic field. By letting experimental student writing truly disrupt the usual business of evaluation; by imagining new criteria for good writing; and by reflecting on acts of judgment—only then can experimental writing change our sense of what it means to teach writing, our goals, our pedagogies, our notion of what it means to do justice to student writing.

COLLAGE

PEDAGOGIES, AESTHETICS, AND
READING STUDENTS' TEXTS

Numerous cases for the teaching of collage in composition have been made, both explicitly (see Elbow, Weathers, Nies, Owens, Fontaine and Quaas, Ulmer) and by example in textbooks (see assignments in both *Text Book* [Scholes, Comley, and Ulmer] and *Ways of Reading* [Bartholomae and Petrosky]). The claims made for the value of the collage form are numerous. Some, such as Peter Elbow, claim that the collage requires no expertise and thus allows student writers to make use of intuition and tap into the unconscious workings of their minds with ease and good results; others claim the collage is an excellent tool for teaching students aspects of the writing process in preparation for writing more conventional essays, such as research papers; or the collage form best represents the fragmented nature of postmodern self; or finally, the collage allows students to explore the dialectic between tradition and innovation in academic writing. How claims for the value of teaching the collage in composition can vary so widely is a testament to the complex history of the collage as a form, but it is also a testimony to the range of pedagogical projects for experimental writing in composition and the complexities of reading and evaluating students' texts.

The dialectical tensions inherent in historical and theoretical debates about the aesthetics of the collage form are inherited by arguments for the collage in composition pedagogy. Compositionists, depending in large part upon their pedagogies, tend to resolve these tensions and oppositions in one direction or another: either collage is intuitive and easy because it requires little knowledge or skill, or collage is difficult because it requires extensive knowledge of the craft of writing and a high degree of self-consciousness and intention; collage is necessarily a process and thus part of the writing process, or collage is a product (epistemological, rhetorical); collage is a form of popular expressivist literacy, or it is the ultimate postmodern genre, or it is a kind of alternative academic writing. By privileging one concept of the collage over another, or one set of values over another, compositionists indicate their understanding of the goals of composition as literacy instruction and the role that experimental or alternative writings might play in composition pedagogies. Thus, collage can serve expressivist or process pedagogies, postmodern pedagogies, or modernist social-constructionist pedagogies (e.g., *Ways of Reading*).

This chapter proceeds with these two strands in mind—the aesthetics and pedagogies of collage—and then revisits issues of judgment that I raised in the previous chapter. Rather than begin with a history of collage, or by defining the textual collage as a form, I start by examining how the various arguments for it in composition begin.[1] Mostly, they do not begin by offering histories or definitions of the collage form. They begin with pedagogical directions for composing collages, or they begin with models and examples of collages. Thus, I address these arguments by beginning with pedagogies of the collage, the directions, the assignments, the models, and the aesthetics of collage that they imply. In the process of examining what we are asking our students to do when we ask them to compose collages, I also investigate why we are asking them to compose collages, what we see as the value in that work, and how our assumptions about the aesthetics of textual collages can be usefully informed by complex histories and theories of the collage.

Arguments abound in composition for why students should write collages, but apparently few seem to think students' collages are worth looking at in detail. Therefore, I read three collages produced by students in one of my first-year writing classes. I present my attempts to read, evaluate, and respond to my students' textual collages as a way to explore, at more length, arguments discussed in earlier chapters about the ways in which experimental writing might or might not change pedagogical practices, such as the evaluation of student writing.[2]

COLLAGE IS EASY OR COLLAGE IS HARD

For Peter Elbow, in "Your Cheatin' Art: A Collage," the best reason to teach the collage in a writing class is that it's "easy," that collages "permit weak writers to produce strong finished texts," and that the collage is one of the "ways to cheat in writing and teaching writing" (310, 304, 312).[3] His four steps to "Directions of writing a collage" might be summarized this way: freewrite or gather as much of your writing on a topic as you can (quickly and in any order); review and choose the best and potentially best bits; revise by cutting, not rewriting; figure out a pleasing order, "perhaps logical, more likely intuitive and associative—even random" (301). After his directions, Elbow adds another option that suggests using "fragments of writing by others" (301). That Elbow seems to add this last option only as an afterthought rather than include it as either a necessary or important part of composing a textual collage reveals the heart of his investment in the collage form. For Elbow, it is not the case that collages are most important for the ways in which they allow a writer to appropriate and work with texts from other contexts (even though in "Your Cheatin' Art" he includes many quotations or found texts by others on the topic of collage). Instead, what are important here are the values typically important to Elbow: freewriting and intuition. Since Elbow claims that the mind, life, and discourse all work like collages, the pedagogical goals of the collage are not primarily or even significantly epistemological or rhetorical; that is, students do not explore how this different way of working with discourses might yield different ways of knowing or produce different rhetorical effects. Although in his list of all the texts that are collages and all the characteristics of collages, he claims that the collage is resistant to dominant academic discourses and that it can produce surprising and sometimes cognitively complex texts, there are no gestures to these goals or effects in his directions to students.[4] Instead, the goals of the collage for Elbow are to explore and enjoy the workings of the mind as they are reflected in texts generated by the collage, to take pleasure in the ease with which one can compose a collage, and to take pleasure in one's sense of "cheating."

The simplicity of Elbow's directions and his valuation of the collage as easy and cheating coincide with his pedagogy, a pedagogy that resists positioning the teacher as master and the student as apprentice. Actually, Elbow's pedagogy resists the whole scene of education. Collage is cheating not only for students but also for teachers because ostensibly teachers have no expertise to offer on the matter. Anyone can do a collage because "everyone can write" (preferably "without teachers"). Yet Elbow recognizes that the scene of teaching and learning writing is infused with the discourses of mastery, craft, even apprenticeship. This is suggested by the following fragment from Elbow's text, wherein he takes on the generalized voice of opposition to the collage: "But damn it, first we've got to teach them to be explicit and clear. *Then* we can give them permission to leave things out. If they are going to use the techniques of the collage, they have to do it from a basis of skill with conscious craft—not just because they are lazy or unskilled. Picasso only made those empty and suggestive line drawings *after* he demonstrated that he could draw bulls the way they really look" ("Your Cheatin' Art" 310). Elbow, of course, rejects this argument, an argument that might be described as the "hierarchy of skills": first one must learn the rules before one can bend the rules; first one must learn the conventions before one breaks them; first one must study the masters, fine-hone one's craft, and then one can play.

What Elbow doesn't acknowledge are the contradictions inherent in other histories of the collage that might actually help him to make his argument for the value of collage as easy and cheating. In histories of the form, the collage is several things: the "invention" of serious and well-trained twentieth-century painters; a popular "folk" practice predating the twentieth century (and not exclusively culturally located in Europe); an avant-garde art technique developed by the Italian futurist F. T. Marinetti and later used by Dadaists and surrealists to take advantage of the element of chance in the artistic process and to represent the subconscious workings of the mind; and the predominant genre of postmodernity.[5] There are, then, several histories one might avail oneself of in order to make the case for the significance of the collage form.

Elbow, however, does not invoke the kinds of arguments about the postmodern or poststructuralist character of the collage that other compositionists will invoke (see my discussion of the work of Scholes, Comley, and Ulmer below). Nor does he, other than by passing references to Picasso or Dadaism ("Your Cheatin' Art" 312), explicitly emphasize modernist legacies or advocate avant-garde collages.

Though Elbow does not theorize the collage, the values that he claims for the collage in his pedagogy resonate with histories and theories of the collage. In bringing these values to the forefront and situating them historically and theoretically, we see the precedents for Elbow's claim as well as the problems with such claims. In particular, the work of Harry Polkinhorn, "Space Craft: Collage Discourse," helps us to explore the ways in which the history of collage as modernist art practice supports Elbow's claim that anyone can do a collage and that collage is a form that rejects the scene of teaching and the master-apprentice relationship it may imply:

> Embedded in collage as a historically conditioned category of discourse we have the gesture of rejection of the process of apprenticeship and all that it is based on—hierarchy, order, the political economy of liberalism. . . . Materiality is introduced into the discourse on art, then, by collage's negativizing or rejecting of craft or the physical acts involved in art marking; inherent in taking objects and pasting them in or on, as indicated above, is a rejection of academy training and the ideology of power which it mediates. Time is not necessary for the collage artist to achieve mastery, itself an ideological token. Rather he or she plugs directly into the instantaneous present of cultural artifacts. Craft becomes equivalent to labor, which is time itself in a material sense. (Polkinhorn 214, 221)

No "academy training," no apprenticeship, no teacher, no years of practicing a craft are necessary. All a student would need, then, is to be "plugged in" and have some time to physically assemble a collage. In these ways, collages can be understood as easy and cheating, cheating the academy, cheating for the student, and cheating for the teacher, who does not need to teach the writing student anything but merely offers the gift of time. Indeed, it's easy to see how compositionists can claim that the collage is subversive because it rejects the ideology of traditional education and pedagogy. Yet, as we will see below, there is something disingenuous about presenting collage this way in the context of the writing classroom.

If one sees parallels between Elbow's simple directions for the collage and the Dadaist Tristan Tzara's recipe for a collage poem, one might argue that Elbow's pedagogy for the collage could be even more subversive in that it denies not only the ideology of schooling generally but also composition pedagogy's presupposition of, and cultivation of, individual agency. Tzara's and Elbow's directions differ, however, on several points. The element of chance is only hinted at in Elbow's directions ("maybe even random") while chance is the guiding principle of collage construction for Tzara in his poem "To Make a Dadaist Poem."

Take a newspaper.

Take some scissors.

Choose from this paper an article of the length you want to make your poem.

Cut out the article.

Next carefully cut out each of the words that makes up this article and put them all in a bag.

Shake gently.

Next take out each cutting one after the other.

Copy conscientiously in the order in which they left the bag.

The poem will resemble you.

And there you are—an infinitely original author of charming sensibility, even though unappreciated by the vulgar herd. (Tzara 39)

Thus, in Tzara's version of collage, the individual writer has minimal agency beyond choosing a newspaper or article, and even that could be more randomized if desired. There is none of the choosing, gathering, self-conscious cutting, figuring out a pleasing order, and so on of Elbow's directions. The element of chance in Tzara's collage poem is meant, as Peter Bürger suggests, to undermine completely the importance of individual creativity to artistic production (*Theory of the Avant-Garde* 53). Furthermore, as with most Dadaist texts, the random collage poem is claimed as art just as any other poetry (e.g., poetry more "craftily" written). Ostensibly, the individual artist's psychology, talent, craft, and the like are beside the point. Furthermore, the artist is merely a vehicle for the collage to be made, and this statement—"the poem will resemble you"—can only disturb Elbow's pedagogy of self-expression as it suggests an identity that is the result of a randomly arranged assortment of others' words. Despite passing references to Dada, Elbow will not highlight these aspects of instructions for Dadaist collages because his pedagogy is more invested in helping students enjoy writing than in language or discourse or the relationship between his students as subjects of/in/to/for discourse. These relationships between students (as subjects) and discourses highlighted by collage will be exactly the point of interest for other compositionists who argue for teaching collage.

Elbow's interest in the workings of the mind as they are evidenced in a collage could also be authorized by a surrealist aesthetics and poetics of collage. Though, like the Dadaists, the surrealists are very much interested in giving the artistic process over to chance, they are also interested in the subconscious: "The spontaneous verbal flow—and later the graphic gesture—which characterized early automatism on the one hand, and the deliberate cutting up and assembling of disparate elements specific to the collage on the other hand, were to be elaborated as the two essential modes of surrealist production, breaking away from traditional codes of mimesis and the aesthetics of coherence, and exploring the language of the irrational and the chance encounter" (Adamowicz 5). Automatic writing is much like Elbow's notion of freewriting, that is, writing produced ostensibly without consciously controlling one's thoughts so that the resulting text can be considered "spoken thoughts" dictated by the mind to the hand even if (or preferably if) the writing appears to be irrational or nonsensical. As I have already discussed in earlier chapters, the value of this kind of work for Elbow and others interested in experimental writing in composition is primarily that it is "fun" for students, and that by introducing creativity and pleasure into the writing classroom, everyone (students and teachers) gets a break from their ongoing boredom and alienation. Though Elbow's claims about the importance of intuition and the subconscious to collage production seem to find their parallels in histories of Dadaist and surrealist collage, for Elbow the result of the students' intuitive process is pleasurable (for both teacher and student) and benign.

As Elza Adamowicz reminds us in *Surrealist Collage in Text and Image*, however, the products of surrealist collages were not often so benign: "collage, as it developed in the 1930s, was linked with an interest in the surrealist object constructed from found materials, which often integrated fetish objects and had strong erotic or sadistic connotations. In collage, the fetishistic appeal of part-bodies and the elliptical erotic narratives of advertising images and slogans are underscored even further by the surrealists' cutting and pasting practice" (11).

One way to look at the ease of Elbow's collage practices is to see him inviting students to tap into the workings of their subconsciousness, temporarily abandoning intention and will. For Elbow this is not only easy but also pleasurable, producing "lively," "surprising" writing for which reading it is like finding "more raisins in the loaf" ("Your Cheatin' Art" 307). The Dadaists and surrealists, however, understood that some of the most significant aspects of the collage form included not just the ways in which it threatened traditional aesthetics (e.g., individual creativity, notions of craft), but the ways in which it aggressively undermined the reign of rationality (or revealed the irrational in the rational order) and offered visions of the subconscious of the human mind (and the subconscious workings of a society one might say) that were scary, violent, erotic, perverse, and even malevolent.

What Elbow embraces, however, is, as I have suggested above, not so much the product of collage (its audience, its rhetorical effects) but the process of collage for the individual writer. The process of producing a collage, for Elbow, is very similar to other processes he advocates, such as freewriting. However, the degree to which freewriting or automatic writing is actually free, or is actually the mind's dictation, is debatable. As Adamowicz suggests, the "immediacy, however illusory, of automatism or 'la pensée parlée . . . as a play of signifiers, appears to contrast radically with the mediated discourse of collage: while the material for the first is the linguistic code (*langue*) or the graphic impulse, collage material involves the recycling of ready-made messages, whether pre-formed linguistic entities (*parole*) or iconographic fragments" (6). Though the surrealists emphasized the lack of conscious agency in the making of collages, the process of making a collage is actually plagued by the presence of a willful conscious writer as agent: "Collage (and by extension frottage), tapping the resources of the unconscious mind, are considered processes parallel if not equivalent to automatic writing, in their capacity to stimulate the hallucinatory powers of the artist and generate a flow of multiple, contradictory images, as in hallucinations or half-sleep. . . . Privileging the mental activity instigated by the collage elements, [Max] Ernst stresses the flow or continuity between the images of the unconscious and their projection onto the page, glossing over the production stage of collage" (Adamowicz 7). Ernst's "glossing over the production stage" is much like Elbow's glossing over all that might be involved in students' acts of choosing, cutting, and arranging elements into a collage. Per Elbow, a student merely writes, gathers, cuts, finds a "pleasing order," pastes, and—voilà, success, a collage, "it works."

Others, both compositionists and art critics, have contested the illusion of immediacy and the ease of the collage process suggested by Ernst's and Elbow's "glossing over the production." The other half of Polkinhorn's story of collage as rejection of apprenticeship, craft, and academy training is that collage can be considered the ultimate manifestation of knowledge of craft and technique. The process of making a collage is not merely "plugging into the perpetual present of cultural artifacts" but also a process requiring a careful and intentional negotiation of reader/writer relationships:

> For collage to be perceived as such, the phases in the composition process
> must be discernable; that is, one must *know* that collaging has occurred
> in the course of art-making. The artist must construct signs whereby the

viewer is told that collaging has occurred. I want to emphasize the present perfect of this signaling, a way of conjoining past and present by blurring their artificial separation. "Collage" as substantive, referring to a process in art-making, has gotten appropriated by criticism which then makes statements about its own linguistic categorizations after the art has reached its final state, thus producing a kind of optical illusion. Beyond the level of sensory appreciation of the materials of art, collage in Western European modernism comes to equal *knowledge of the production of art.* The use of the practice constitutes a historically conditioned gesture which factors in this knowledge as self-consciousness. (Polkinhorn 220–21)

Collage as "knowledge of the production of art" would entail, then, knowing "the preconceptions about how a work should develop," knowing what makes a narrative line or sequence in order to then disrupt it. In terms of composition, a student writer would have to have some knowledge of the production of an essay or a story (or a narrative) in order to know when he or she would have adequately disrupted the "flow" (not only for the writer but for the reader as well).

This tension between competing versions of the role of the artist—collages happen intuitively and subconsciously or collages are thoughtfully and carefully constructed—appears in arguments for the collage in composition. Sometimes the tension or dialectic is resolved away from intention and toward *intuition,* as is the case in Elbow's argument. Other times, the dialectic is resolved away from individual agency and intention but toward the force and *play of language* and *cultural discourse* (not the mind of the individual student), as we will see is the case in more poststructuralist versions of the collage in composition (Scholes, Comley, and Ulmer's assignments in *Text Book*). And sometimes the dialectic is resolved in the direction of *intention, careful craft, attentive reading,* and *knowledge of methods* (Gallagher; Fontaine and Quaas; assignments in Bartholomae and Petrosky).

Like Peter Elbow, Chris Gallagher also wants to legitimize the collage for composition and thus performs his own collage, but for Gallagher, collages are hard. In his "If This Were Not a Collage: A Collage," Gallagher responds to claims Elbow made about collage in an earlier version of "Your Cheatin' Art" published in *Writing on the Edge* (Fall/Winter 1997).[6] There are many ways that Gallagher engages Elbow's arguments: he is more tentative about the value of collage, more self-conscious about the kinds of claims made in the name of collage, less willing to include many things under the umbrella of "collage," and definitely more convinced than Peter

Elbow that collages require knowledge of craft, labor-intensive work, and a high degree of self-consciousness.

In a significant gesture, Gallagher rewrites Elbow's directions for collage under the heading "Invitations (not directions)" (Gallagher 41). By substituting "invitations" for "directions," Gallagher belies his own ambivalence about the significance of collage to composition. Similarly, he manifests his pedagogical attitude, which, since he suggests that students be merely invited (ostensibly students can refuse the invitation without consequence), implies that the collage is not an integral part of the writing classroom.

One difference between Elbow's directions and Gallagher's invitations is that Gallagher asks students to start with texts not their own ("Choose at random ten quotations from *Bartlett's Quotations*"). Whereas with Elbow one freewrites, chooses some bits and pieces, cuts and arranges, with Gallagher one does not freewrite but chooses from "ready-made" texts. A second difference between their directions is that Gallagher emphasizes the composing process. Indeed, most of the steps of his invitation regard the recursive process of selection, arrangement, and revision. After choosing one's texts, one plays with them, orders, reorders, looks for patterns, drops texts, goes back to *Bartlett's,* selects more texts, goes through the whole process of arrangement, selection, cutting, all along consciously avoiding homogenization ("Don't look for quotations that are about the same thing that the others are about; look for those that contribute to them indirectly, unwittingly"). With the addition of new quotations, Gallagher asserts, the arrangement will yet again need to be reconsidered and reworked: "You are using re-vision now: you are seeing again. You are writing between the lines" (41). Finally, Gallagher suggests that the student give the collage to a friend to read, acknowledging that two responses are possible: rejection ("What's *wrong* with you, anyway?") and acceptance and appreciation ("I'll bite . . . I see"). The message Gallagher sends at the end of his directions is a fair summation of his attitude about the collage: "Collages, you see, require patient readers. And patient writers. Both need to learn how to listen and how to form; collages require mutual construction" (42).

If Gallagher rejects the idea that collages are easy, he also rejects Polkinhorn's hypothesis about the role of time as labor (and not craft) in the process of composing a collage. For Gallagher, time is not just time to compose, but also the time it takes to achieve some degree of mastery of collage form, a form he has some doubts about: "Is the form speaking, working, moving us along? Is this more than experiment for its own sake?

More than cuteness, more than cleverness?" (40). With Gallagher, the enthusiastic, cheerful tone of Elbow's piece on collage ("It works. It's a collage," and "Just do it! Things go better with collage" ["Your Cheatin' Art" 300, 307]) is replaced by a deep ambivalence about the collage, an ambivalence that I would suggest haunts all serious scholarship on experimental writing in composition. How this ambivalence gets worked through or advantageously exploited is the subject of my next investigation.

COLLAGE AS TOOL FOR LEARNING THE WRITING PROCESS

One way this ambivalence about the pedagogical value of collage gets resolved, as I have suggested in earlier chapters, is by making collage serve pedagogies for more traditional writing. Fontaine and Quaas argue in "Transforming Connections and Building Bridges: Assigning, Reading, and Evaluating the Collage Essay" that this is, in fact, one of the most important purposes of asking students to compose a collage: to "help students understand organization in terms of the structuring power of conventional patterns and the structuring power of conceptual relationships," as well as to help "focus students' awareness on the relationships and connections that they create whenever they place ideas on the page" (112). In other words, composing a collage helps students think about the concepts of arrangement, organization, and synthesis. The collage is not opposed to the essay as an alternative form but is part of the larger pedagogical process of making students better writers of conventional essays. In service of this project, Fontaine and Quaas offer directions to teachers on "How to Make a Collage Assignment" (113).

As the collage is not usually an isolated assignment in their writing course, nor is it usually presented as an opportunity to reflect on the differences between conventional and alternative forms, Fontaine and Quaas recognize that the writing course must be designed to prepare students to compose collages, especially since in their collage assignment the source of material for students' collages will be primarily or even solely the students' own preexisting writing. Thus, in Fontaine and Quaas's pedagogy, teachers work hard to help prepare students for this final collage by providing them with opportunities to generate a variety of writing (113), offering demonstration collages (models drawn from collages written by other compositionists), and discussing characteristics of successful collages and their criteria for evaluating the collage. In other words, unlike Elbow's directions for collage, students will not produce much, if any, new writing for their collages; and unlike Gallagher's assignment, students' collages will not be composed solely, if at all, of "found texts" (such as those from *Bartlett's Quotations*).

Other than these specific differences, the directions for composing the collage are more or less standard: students select passages from their own writing intuitively ("without analysis" [Fontaine and Quaas 113]) and put the pieces together, looking for "relationships among the segments and the emergent strain of meaning from the whole" and trying to identify a "center of gravity" or realize the "organic nature of text organization" with the ultimate goal of organizing "the reader's movement through the various pieces toward a final grasp of the whole" (113–14). Potentially, Fontaine and Quaas's assignment could present students with an interesting opportunity to "objectify" their own texts in the process of cutting and rearranging, but Fontaine and Quaas are silent on this possibility. Indeed, there is little sense of the content of the students' writing, and there are no examples of their collages.

In another effort to help students gain mastery over conventional forms, Betsy Nies argues, in "Writing History through Collage: Using Crots in the First-Year Research Paper," that the collage form can reinvigorate the traditional research paper for both teachers and students. For Nies, it is not the limits or constraints of the traditional research paper that are necessarily the problem. Rather, it is the fact that as a teacher she finds these research papers deadeningly dull and perfunctory—students' attempts to prove they have mastered the requirements of the form rather than texts that are interesting, lively, or that show any personal investment on the part of the students (Nies 26). What Nies identifies as the problem of traditional research papers is that they are not dialogical enough, that students can't seem to find ways to establish critical distance from their sources or find a place for their own ideas or voices (26). Thus, for Nies, the collage becomes (via her reference to Bakhtin's notion of heteroglossia and Don Bialostosky's use of Bakhtin for composition) a way to objectify the discourses of the resource texts so that students can establish a dialogue with those texts (Nies 28). There is precedence in Nies's linking of heteroglossia and the collage form not just because both are concerned with multiple languages or discourses, but also because as Bakhtin's concept of heteroglossia grows out of and is applied analytically to the novel form, so too is the concept of collage applied to both modernist and postmodernist novels.[7]

The idea that collage as a form can draw special attention to the doubleness of discourse (or the play of signifiers) is indeed claimed by some as the definitive characteristic of the collage form. For example, in *The*

Frame and the Mirror: On Collage and the Postmodern, Thomas Brockelman argues (by quoting from a manifesto on collage) that the collage is
characterized by the presence of irony and double-voicedness: "Each cited
element breaks the continuity or the linearity of the discourse and leads
necessarily to a double reading: that of the fragment perceived into relation to the text of origin; that of the same fragment incorporated into a
new whole, a different totality. The trick of collage consists . . . of never
entirely suppressing the alterity of these elements reunited in a temporary
composition" (2).

The irony and double-voicedness seem to be lost on/in pedagogies
for the collage in composition, or at least I have yet to read a composition
text that advances this particular argument for the value of teaching the
collage form. Even in the work of Nies (or Scholes, Comley, and Ulmer, or
Bartholomae and Petrosky, for that matter), this particular value to the collage—that it might teach students something about the doubleness of language and irony—is not advanced. Perhaps this is because, as Lori Chamberlain argues in "Bombs and Other Exciting Devices, or the Problem
of Teaching Irony," irony is one of the hardest rhetorical devices to teach
(97–98). Yet, she argues, there are reasons for teaching it: "Because it depends on a dissimulation—the pretense of saying one thing and meaning another—irony is associated with the general misuse of rhetoric; but
because of its self-reflexivity, it is also associated with the critical spirit of
self-consciousness, of dialectical inquiry" (100). Ostensibly, the collage is
an ideal form for such dialectical inquiry as it can hold in tension multiple
discourses, multiple significations, multiple contexts for discourses, and
so on.

Yet, Chamberlain's list of reasons why students might have difficulty
with irony helps us to see why these aspects of the collage might be more
often overlooked in the teaching of writing. As Chamberlain argues, it is
not the case that students don't have any experience with irony—"students
. . . speak the language of irony all the time" (102). However, when it comes
to reading texts that make use of irony, students may be stymied for three
reasons: "first, students may lack sufficient contextual information to interpret an ironic text; second, they may apply a limited or inappropriate set
of reading conventions to these texts; and third, they may lack practice at
the sorts of critical reading and thinking skills that irony often requires"
(102). Of the three reasons that Chamberlain offers, the first two are most
relevant to teaching the collage in composition. Given that one of the techniques of collage requires that students extrapolate fragments from other
texts and construct a new text with them, it is a recipe for failure if the stu-

dents don't really either understand or appreciate the fragment's original context; similarly, it is pedagogically (and perhaps rhetorically) ineffective if, in their inability to apply appropriate reading conventions to drafts of their own collages, they don't recognize the doubleness of the fragments they have used to compose a new collage. In these cases, students' collages would not exemplify their ability to manipulate discourses or even dialogue on equal terms with the texts of others. Instead, two things would result. First, students' collages would just be further evidence of the ways in which discourses manipulate them. Second, their collages would unwittingly deny the power of the form by collecting fragments into a new homogeneous totality that erases multiple contexts or significations.

In other words, if the student can't make his or her fragments signify, and has no sense of the original context for the fragment, then the capacity of the collage to exploit doubleness is lost and the collage becomes an example of the worst characteristics of postmodern writing: lack of rhetorical or ideological context, fragments that yield nothing but confusion, meaninglessness, paralysis. So, even as Nies claims that the collage form allows students more authority over their sources and allows them to dialogue their own writing with others' writings, there is nothing inherent in the collage form that suggests her students would succeed or that the collage has such advantages over the research essay. If in the course of writing the research essay, students either subordinate their writing to the writing of their sources or try to subordinate the writing of their sources to their own writing, at least such a process is made obvious by the conventions of the essay form. Nies suggests that the collage—because it works by juxtaposition—allows the source texts and the student texts to share a level playing field. In actuality, however, the illusion of a level playing field could obscure just such hierarchical relationships among discourse in ways that the research essay might manifest.

What I find missing from Nies's (and Fontaine and Quaas's and Elbow's) pedagogical use of the collage is any discussion of how students would need to objectify their own writing in order to treat it as an element on equal ground with their sources. Despite both Fontaine and Quaas's and Nies's valuing of the unity of the collage (indeed, what Fontaine and Quaas call the "organic nature of text organization"), Bürger reminds us that one of the significant differences between organic and nonorganic (avant-gardiste) work is in their relationship to their materials:

> Artists who produce an organic work (in what follows we shall refer to them
> as "classicists" without meaning to introduce a special concept of what the

classical work may be) treat their material as something living. They respect its significance as something that had grown from concrete life situations. For avant-gardistes, on the other hand, material is just that, material. Their activity initially consists in nothing other than in killing the "life" of the material, that is, in tearing it out of its functional context that gives it meaning. Whereas the classicist recognizes and respects in the material the carrier of a meaning, the avant-gardistes see only the empty sign, to which they can impart significance. (70)

I wonder if students could be asked to achieve such distance from their own writing in such ways, commit to destroying the life of their writing in order to redeploy it. Could they be asked to see the "discursive nature" of their own language, to see as well not only the ways in which they manipulate the "discourses of others to their own purposes" but also the ways in which their own discourses are manipulated and changed by their juxtaposition with other texts?

COLLAGE AS POSTMODERN LITERACY GENRE

This very idea of the discursive nature of language—both the language of others and the language of self—is at the heart of what Robert Scholes, Nancy R. Comley, and Gregory Ulmer refer to in *Text Book: Writing Through Literature*[8] as the "mystory": "In this concluding chapter you have an opportunity to bring together all the devices of textual writing that you have learned in the preceding chapters. Traditionally, composition textbooks often include a unit on 'writing the research paper.' *Text Book* conforms to this practice, except that textualist research is conducted somewhat differently. Our name for this new mode of inquiry is *mystory*" (240).

A "mystory" text is not always a collage, but collage is an example of a "mystory," and several of the assignments in *Text Book* invoke the power of collage as a form of research writing. In many ways, Scholes, Comley, and Ulmer's project for the collage as a form of research writing takes up exactly where Nies's project leaves off. *Text Book* is not just interested in helping students learn how to manipulate the writing of others but also invested in helping them see the constructed nature of what is considered to be the students' own languages. As part of their introduction for students to the form of the "mystory," Scholes and colleagues lay out some key terms and concepts, including voice, mood, identification, the personal is political, the writer as actor, recognition, epiphany, popcycle, and pleasure and bliss (240–48). Two key points made in this section (and indeed one could argue in the whole book) are that the individual is an effect of language (243) and that literacy education should be as much about teaching creative, aesthetic modes of writing as it should be about teaching conventions of academic writing. Thus,

> Mystory as research text is partly a text of pleasure and a partly a text of bliss. In both instances, the purpose is to approach literature from the *desire* to know, rather than from the side of knowledge as information. Too often the schools assume this desire and therefore teach the knowledge only as information. The result is a population of students with high verbal scores on the SAT who nonetheless dislike literature or have no idea why it is actually important. Mystory addresses this condition in two respects. First, it constitutes text research as self-knowledge: the inquiry into the library of culture is organized by correspondence, as mapping the match between collective and individual experience. Second, the logic of writing is aesthetic, using literary devices as methods of direct knowledge (metafiction as self-portrait). (247)

Where mystory treats research as self-knowledge (and the process of researching is coming to know one's self), the kind of self-knowledge being proposed shares very little in common with the expressivist pedagogical tradition in composition. The "self" in *Text Book* is understood through the lenses of poststructuralist and cultural studies approaches to discourse:

> The theory [never named] is that human identity—the self—is not a natural essence but is constructed within a specific historical society. The institutions of society maintain discourses (languages, logics, modes of proof, etiquettes) that function to "interpellate" or recruit persons into the dominant belief system or ideology of society. . . . Identification is at the heart of this education in that one becomes who and what one is by internalizing an image of the nurturing authority figures encountered in one's world. According to the theory, this act of identification with parent figures in the family—extended to the authority figures encountered in the other institutions that continue the interpellation process as one matures—is a "misrecognition," a necessary "mistake" that implants alienation at the core of the selfhood as an experience. To be a "self," that is, is to carry internally an image acquired from "outside." Throughout one's life, identity is experi-

enced as a negotiation of this border between the inside and the outside. . . . An individual subject is not autonomous and self-identical, but is dependent upon and an effect of language into which he or she has entered. (242–43)

I quote so much of *Text Book*'s introductory material to the section on mystory because it is key to understanding how the authors figure the work of collage in ways that are significantly different from other uses of collage in writing instruction. Their understanding of the relationship between the individual self (student writer) and discourse has everything to do with why they see the mystory/collage form not only as a viable alternative to traditional research papers (as Nies does), but also as an integral part of students' literacy education. If the self has been effected by discourses, a text which claims to pursue self-knowledge cannot do so unless it includes multiple discourses and examines the ways in which and the degrees to which the student writer "identifies" (or doesn't?) with those discourses: "The principle justifying the mystorical approach to research is that specialized discourses or career fields interpellate subjects in the same way as the other institutions of society. The critical effect is achieved, therefore, not by the denial of this reality and the pretense of objectivity, but through a homeopathic embracing of identification. The critical effect is achieved by composing a mystory in which one juxtaposes the products of different discourses in one composition. The repetitions or correspondences that emerge in the intertext among one's different experiences produce a eureka effect—the epiphany" (Scholes, Comley, and Ulmer 246).

Though *Text Book* doesn't go on to say or even hint at the nature or content of the epiphany (understandably perhaps, since different writers might have different epiphanies), they do hint at the significance of the epiphany in the closing pages of their book:

One assumption of the mystory is that you have to look outside your immediate memory (to history, entertainment, literature, or politics, for example) to discover what may have been assimilated, introjected inside, to become the filter that shapes your awareness. In the case of literary tradition, it is not that you have already assimilated the tradition, but that the tradition is there for you to use, as "equipment for living" (to borrow Kenneth Burke's phrase). The payoff is an experience of "extimacy." The result is not fate but opportunity. Once you discover where you are in language, it is possible to steer any course. (Scholes, Comley, and Ulmer 375–76)

Thus, one suspects that the "eureka" of the student's mystory has to do with discovering something about where one is in language, the nature of one's relationship to discourse, some insight into one's ability to negotiate the "border between the inside and the outside." In other words, the value of composing a collage/mystory is that it enables one to situate oneself in language and thus achieve a certain agency: "Once you discover where you are in language, it is possible to steer any course."

But I have started with the beginning and the conclusion of *Text Book*, and neglected the middle, that is, the pedagogy. Starting with the pedagogical moment—the assignment to write the collage—is harder with *Text Book* than it was with the work of other composition texts for a few reasons. As Scholes, Comley, and Ulmer suggest in their opening to the "mystory" section of their textbook, in writing the mystory, students "have an opportunity to bring together all the devices of textual writing that [they] have learned in the preceding chapters" (240). Thus, as was the case in the work of Fontaine and Quaas and Nies, the collage is the assignment to which a semester-long writing course builds up or for which it prepares, not merely an assignment among other assignments. Where *Text Book* differs significantly from these above-mentioned arguments is in its constant offering of opportunities to students to participate in "the logic of writing" as "aesthetic, using literary devices as methods of direct knowledge" (247). Though *Text Book* includes some familiar and conventional texts, it also includes a substantial amount of literary and cultural theory, as well as a substantial number of examples of experimental or unconventional texts.

In the third edition of *Text Book: Writing through Literature*, experimental texts include images by Man Ray, René Magritte, Edward Hopper, and Giorgio De Chirico and experimental writings from e. e. cummings, André Breton, Jorge Luis Borges, Italo Calvino, John Barth, Raymond Queneau, Roland Barthes, Eunice Lipton, N. Scott Momaday, Susan Griffin, James Joyce, Jacques Derrida, A. C. Evans, John Cage, and Susan Howe. The text by Breton is an example of a surrealist poem that Scholes, Comley, and Ulmer call a "random assemblage" but is paired with excerpts from Freud's *Introductory Lectures on Psychoanalysis* under their section on metaphor (specifically a whole section of the chapter devoted to "surrealist metaphor") in chapter 2, "Texts, Thoughts, and Things." Students are invited to create a cut-up poem of their own and reflect on the ways in which the poem succeeds or doesn't (85).[9] In other words, by the time students get to the end of the textbook (assuming that they have been working through it in order), they have had quite a bit of experience reading difficult and experimental texts; in addition, they have had the opportunity to produce several experimental texts of their own. The kind of reluctance on the part of the students that Fontaine and Quaas caution teachers to recognize would not be a factor for the students of *Text Book* (though one can imagine a different kind of student response—utter weariness of experimentation and a desire to return to reading and writing conventional texts—but I am just speculating here). Scholes, Comley, and Ulmer have not only offered theoretical justifications for their mystory method, and asked students repeatedly to develop their own poetics based on selected readings, they also have asked students to theorize the value of such work.[10] Thus, by the time students get to the final assignment of the textbook, the mystory, students should have a very good idea what they are up against, what kind of work they are being asked to do, and for what reasons.

Under the heading "A Work of Literature/A Play of Text," *Text Book* articulates the actual instructions. Students are to imagine that *Text Book* constitutes a "tradition of writing,"

> a language that speaks you and within which you want to claim your place
> (to pick up the conversation and keep it going). Follow the instructions you
> extracted from Howe (and from other samples in the archive), compose a
> collage composition in which you mine the resources of the book to find
> a voice and style of thought into which you may insert yourself. Include a
> metaphor that expresses your relationship to media and culture, the way
> Howe used the cormorant. The form of the text should emulate Howe's
> essay (supplemented by any of the other sample forms included in the
> archive).
>
> For a more ambitious research project, follow leads in the immediate
> archive wherever they may lead in the library or on the Internet (into history
> or popular culture) to other materials in which you recognize your own
> style and voice. (375)

Where this kind of work differs significantly from the work of a more traditional research paper lies in mystory/collage's unique approach to citation:

> textual approach to research establishes a conduit or interchange between
> simple forms . . . and a more complex practice. . . . The exchange in the
> case of research is between the simple citation and the complex collage.
> The research paper uses citation with an attitude or feeling of proof. The
> researchers subordinate themselves to the voice of authority and document

every claim, although the quotations in an essay are embedded in the framing argument. . . . The mystory however takes a different (nearly opposite)
approach to citation, one that appears to reduce the author to editor or curator, while foregrounding quotation. . . . The attitude of text is aesthetic, and
the effect of the makers' disappearance into the language is the emergence
of their own voice. . . . "Writing" is reduced to the basic operations of selection and combination (or revision and variation)—recycling existing works
into texts. The claim to knowledge or proof is traded in for an experience of
creative invention. (374–75)

A goal of this approach to citation, selection, and arrangement of fragments of other texts is not only to situate oneself in language but also to
discover, represent, or construct an identity:

> Indeed, the effect of recognition or epiphany that often results during the
> composition of a mystory is due not only to the themes of the materials, but
> more often to some repetition of a signifier—a word or shape—across the
> different semantic areas juxtaposed in the composition. The play method of
> miming or citing fragments of the original works is useful in the mystory
> for entering research findings into each part of the figure, without attempt-
> ing to interpret in advance how the different materials cohere. The juxtapo-
> sition often produces some unexpected pattern, and this pattern, elaborated
> into an image, constitutes a kind of identity logo or blazon for the author.
> (374)

Have we returned to the kind of K–12 pedagogical uses of the collage that Derek Owens suggests, a collage of "me"? (The repressed keeps
returning and returning in composition pedagogy.) One could say that
we have, albeit the "me" collage has been framed by some sophisticated
contemporary theory. However, these collages do not represent an autonomous, stable identity; rather, in the tensions created by the collection and
juxtaposition of multiple discourses, students come to realize the irratio-
nality and instability inherent in the ideas of discourse and subjectivity.
They learn that instead of being able to represent themselves, they can
only ever offer interventions into the circulations of discourses (recircu-
lated discourses?). They learn, finally, that knowledge (self-knowledge)
or identity is only and ever the result of the "rhetorical effect of writing"
(Scholes, Comley, and Ulmer 246). One might conclude that these collages are not merely one way to represent an identity (a personal narrative

being another), but that they are *the only way* to accurately reflect the complexity of postmodern subjectivity.

The argument for and against collage as an integral part of literacy instruction in a postmodern context centers on exactly this claim: collage is the postmodern form par excellence. As I suggested earlier in this chapter in my discussion of Elbow, there are many histories of the collage and many ways of theorizing the form, which range from folk practice to high modernist artistic practice, avant-garde strategy to genre reflecting postmodern society. *Text Book* taps into many of these legacies (Dadaists, surrrealists, modernists, etc.) but ultimately aligns itself with a version of postmodern literacy. I pause here to briefly chart how the collage functioned in modernist aesthetics and how it becomes adapted to postmodern contexts.

Critics such as Marjorie Perloff and Thomas Brockelman (following Perloff) argue that the collage as a unique art form was invented in the early twentieth century by cubist[11] painters (e.g., Picasso and Braque): "Collage intends to represent the intersection of multiple discourses. Indeed, it is only this intention that differentiates cubist collage from countless other examples of folk practices using materials (postage stamps, bones, you name it) in pictorial compositions—and thus justifies art's historical talk of its 'invention' at the hands of the cubists" (Brockelman 2).[12] This talk of invention is a little strained for at least two reasons. Ostensibly, there is no reason that one couldn't read a folk collage (of stamps, bones, photos, poems, bits of newspapers, tickets, "you name it") semiotically and thus find in it representations of multiple intersecting discourses (whether "intentional" or not). The kind of play of signifiers that Brockelman reads into Picasso's collages becomes the justification in Brockelman's argument for claiming that the "cubist collage opens the path to postmodernism" (3). Whether or not recognizing the play of signifiers in a text (visual or verbal)—or even recognizing that the artist of the text is obviously and intentionally "playing" with signifiers—allows one to claim the collage as postmodern is debatable. By that logic (logic which has been repeatedly misused) all kinds of texts across all kinds of historical periods would thus be labeled "postmodern."

For Brockelman, the most important aspect of visual collages is that they are read semiotically, and they can be read semiotically because painting and sculpture have been transformed into writing: "Painting and sculpture as writing. . . . Objects are read from a painting, or from a sculpture for that matter, on the basis of what is explicitly for the viewer a language of signs" (Brockelman 4). The conflation of visual and verbal collages is achieved in two broad strokes. First, the painting or collage is read as consisting of "intersecting discourses" and a "language of signs"; in appropriating the discourse of collage from the visual arts, one is appropriating a discourse of the visual that has already been inflected with a discourse of the linguistic so that it is an easy turn to make, subsequently, to read a written text through the discourse of the visual. In other words, we can talk about texts as collages because collages (visual) are already discussed in terms of their textuality. Apparently, very little accommodation needs to be made, in this case, to the differences between visual and written art.[13]

Second, the literal understanding of the word "collage" is transformed into a figurative understanding. Beyond cubism, Picasso and Braque begin modernist collage by gluing materials onto their paintings. Thus, rather than painting the wood grain of a wall, a piece of imitation wood grain wallpaper is glued to the canvas to suggest wood. Within the context of claims made about the avant-garde nature of collage, the wood grain wallpaper is a "real" object of the everyday that disrupts the two-dimensional and hermetic plane of the aesthetic work, thus bringing art and everyday reality into contact (of course, though, the wallpaper is also a simulation of "real" wood).[14] Collage thus begins with a literal "gluing" of something "real" onto an otherwise aesthetic space ("collage" is, after all, from the French word *coller*, to glue). This literal understanding of the collage becomes figurative in the context of visual arts and is then applied figuratively to textual arts.

Ulrich Weisstein attributes the beginning of the transformation of the term from literal to figurative to surrealist collage artists: "Another complication arises as a result of the replacement, on the part of Max Ernst and his fellow Dadaists/Surrealists, of the literal meaning of collage (a form of art in which extraneous objects, such as newspaper cuttings, pieces of paper, string, etc. are glued to a pictorial surface) by a figurative one (an assemblage of diverse fragments drawn from reality and juxtaposed on an essentially flat surface)" (Weisstein 126). For Weisstein, the relationship between the real and the aesthetic is key to the figurative use of the word "collage," so that even when he applies the term to a verbal text, such as John Dos Passos's *Manhattan Transfer* or T. S. Eliot's "The Waste Land," he argues that "non-esthetic" elements and "esthetic elements" are combined in such a way as to preserve the "basic dichotomy between the two realms" (e.g., the realm of the aesthetic and the realm of reality) (135).[15] As we shall see later in discussions of the collage as postmodern form in composition, this modernist definition of collage becomes increasingly problematic in the context of poststructuralist theories that do not maintain this "basic dichotomy," so that even if one is now figuratively "cutting" and "pasting" blocks of texts, one is less sure which is the "non-esthetic," or real, and which is the "esthetic."

As Gregory Ulmer (one of the co-authors of *Text Book*) asks in "The Object of Post-Criticism," "Will the collage/montage revolution in representation be admitted into the academic essay, into the discourse of knowledge, replacing the 'realist' criticism based on notions of 'truth' as correspondence to or correct reproduction of a referent object of study?" (86). Ulmer's essay, and much of his work regarding writing pedagogy, argues that collage/montage *should* be admitted (see "Textshop for Post(e)-pedagogy," *Applied Grammatology*, and especially *Teletheory*). However, it remains debatable the degree to which the collage form—as it reflects the fragmented, diverse, eclectic array of materials and experiences of postmodernity—can also function to critique those materials, discourses, experiences, and so on. Indeed, this debate over the collage, or more generally, fragmented or fractured forms, is at the heart of the disagreement between Georg Lukács and Theodor Adorno (and Ernst Bloch).[16] Broadly speaking, Bloch and Adorno argue that the fragmented and expressionist quality of much contemporary writing is an accurate reflection of its time. Lukács, however, argues that the writing is politically decadent in that, in its failure to grasp and represent social reality in its totality, it prevents people from seeing their historical condition and acting to change it. A version of this debate gets updated by Jean-François Lyotard, who argues that all we have are bits and pieces that we link or that get linked (see Lyotard, *The Differend*), and Fredric Jameson who, deploying the work of Lacan and Deleuze and Guattari, sees in the form of pastiche and collage the symptoms of the paralyzed postmodern schizophrenic, living only in a continual present consisting of discontinuous fragments (Jameson 16–18, 26–31).

Furthermore, whether or not collage should be admitted into the academic essay (replacing "realist criticism" perhaps?) is also debatable. I will not adjudicate these debates because I do not see the debate as either/or—either one replaces realist criticism and the conventional academic essay with the collage or one rejects the collage for the conventional academic essay. Arguments that claim that because the collage represents postmodern society, or that because collage (or) montage is prevalent in media forms (such as television, film, and the Internet), it should be taught as part of students' literacy education are not entirely persuasive. On the one hand, if the collage form is so dominant, then it does seem to behoove us, as writing teachers, to help our students learn to read critically such forms, and to help students learn how to produce such potentially powerful forms of public discourse. This is if you accept our current condition as postmodern and all that goes with it: destabilized subjects, loss of master discourses and grand narratives, predominance of petits récits and local knowledges, and the like. On the other hand, if much public and intellectual discourse is still being done in the form of conventional, rational, coherent forms (or to put it in Habermas's terms, if "the project of modernity remains incomplete"), then it behooves us, as writing teachers, to help students gain access to the conventions necessary to produce such discourse. In that case, the collage is at best beside the point and at worst a perpetuation of certain incapacities. (To return briefly to Elbow—collages might let weak writers produce strong writings, but those students are still "weak" writers).

As is always the case with rhetoric and the teaching of writing, context is significant. I am reluctant to make simplistic claims for the liberatory nature of collage, or claims for the oppressive nature of the academic essay. As my outline above of the theoretical debates regarding such forms suggests, and as my work in previous chapters has shown, one can argue either that experimental writings such as collage are a response to a problem (the limits of academic writing and modernist aesthetics), or that they are an extension and perpetuation of a problem (e.g., endless postmodern play that yields no political project or no course of action, a vast leveling that can yield no critical judgment, an obliteration of historical and social contexts). The dialectical relationship between these two modes of discourse is often obscured, as is the situatedness of students vis-à-vis these different forms of writing. Yet, some arguments for collage in composition not only acknowledge this dialectic but also make it the subject of investigation for students. Such is the case with some of the assignments for collage in the textbook *Ways of Reading*.

COLLAGE IN THE CONTEXT OF SCHOOL WRITING: EXPLORING THE DIALECTIC

I would like to conclude my investigation of the pedagogical uses of collage with examples drawn from Bartholomae and Petrosky's *Ways of Reading*. I don't offer *Ways of Reading* as any kind of solution, or even the culmination of the kind of work collage can do in the writing classroom.

I end with *Ways of Reading* for two reasons. First, *Ways of Reading* offers an approach to teaching the collage that is significantly different from approaches I've already examined. And second, I end with *Ways of Reading* because it is where my experience with collage as a teacher began, and it also provides some context for the readings of my students' collages, which follow.

There have been many texts in various editions of *Ways of Reading* that might be described as collages: Gloria Anzaldúa's "Entering into the Serpent," Paul Auster's "Portrait of an Invisible Man," Robert Schulyer's "A Few Days (Poetry)," Patricia Williams's "And We Are Not Married," and Susan Griffin's "Our Secret."[17] However, it is the framing of and assignments for Susan Griffin's "Our Secret" that I address here, again not just because they are directly related to the work my students did, but because Susan Griffin's "Our Secret" is most clearly and emphatically offered by Bartholomae and Petrosky as a collage.

If *Text Book* and *Ways of Reading* both offer model collages to read and ask students to compose collages of their own, the two textbooks differ markedly in the claims they make for the form, as well as in the claims they make regarding the pedagogical value of asking students to compose collages. One of the things I value about both *Text Book* and *Ways of Reading* is that not only do they offer some introduction to the work of collage, they also offer students the opportunity to generate their own theories (or poetics) of collage. For example, under the "questions for a second reading" of Griffin, Bartholomae and Petrosky give the students an opportunity to name "Griffin's project," her methods, and to discuss "what is at stake in adopting such methods" (*Ways of Reading* 452). Additionally, through questions for a second reading and assignments for writing, students are offered opportunities to work out their readings or interpretations of Griffin's text, either by focusing on a passage from Griffin charting connections or by imagining that they are trying to explain Griffin's collage to someone who hasn't read her work (451–54). If *Text Book* prepared students for the work of composing a mystory through multiple examples and exercises, and with its emphasis on the constant employing of "aesthetic logic" or literary devices in their writing, so too does the apparatus of *Ways of Reading* prepare students to do such interpretive, analytical, and generative work.

Yet, one might argue that both *Text Book* and *Ways of Reading*, through all their mechanisms of introduction and framing, have already determined (at least partially) the kinds of responses students are supposed to have to Griffin's text, what they are supposed to appreciate about her collage. Consider, for example, the language in Bartholomae and Petrosky's headnote to Griffin's "Our Secret":

> *A Chorus of Stones* combines the skills of a *careful* researcher working
> with the documentary records of war, the *imaginative powers* of a novelist
> entering the lives and experiences of those long dead, and a poet's *attention*
> *to language*. . . . As a piece of writing, it proceeds with a design that is not
> concerned to move quickly or efficiently from introduction to conclusion. It
> is, rather, a kind of collage or collection of stories, sketches, anecdotes, frag-
> ments. While the sections in the essay are presented as fragments, the essay
> *is not, however, deeply confusing or disorienting.* The pleasure of the text, in
> fact, is moving from here to there, *feeling a thread of connection* at one point,
> *being surprised* by a new direction at another. The writing is *careful, thought-*
> *ful, controlled,* even if this is not the kind of essay that announces its thesis
> and then collects examples for support. (403; emphasis mine)

With *Ways of Reading,* we arrive at the opposite end of the spectrum from the kinds of claims that Peter Elbow makes about collage as easy and intuitive. Everything about the language that sets up Griffin's text here suggests to students not just that composing such a collage text is a difficult craft, but also that such difficulty and such craft are exactly what is to be admired and appreciated about Griffin's work. In this way, Bartholomae and Petrosky, as did Chris Gallagher ("If This Were Not a Collage"), resolve the easy/hard dialectic in the direction of hard. This resolution, which conceives of the collage as the result of a self-conscious writer in possession of knowledge of craft, also reflects the legacy of modernist aesthetics of the collage rather than the postmodern values (e.g., poststructuralist subject, collapsing of real and aesthetic) that inflect *Text Book.* Not only is Griffin multitalented—with the skills of a researcher, novelist, poet—but what makes her work truly admirable is that her writing is "careful," "imaginative," "attentive to language," "thoughtful, controlled," the result of a "design" (not "deeply confusing"). In this presentation of her work, modernist craft and mastery reign supreme.

If students know they will be asked to write a Griffin-like collage, the message they get is that this work will be hard, might in fact require even more care, thought, attention, and the like than the work for a regular essay. Of course, the presence of these descriptive words has as much to do with the pedagogical project of *Ways of Reading* as the presence of words such as "easy" and "cheating" have to do with Elbow's pedagogical project, or as the presence of words such as "aesthetic logic" and "experience of creative invention" have to do with the pedagogical project of *Text Book*. Indeed, the language of Bartholomae and Petrosky's headnote to Griffin's text repeats much of the language in the introduction to their textbook. The readings in *Ways of Reading* are "difficult," require "strong readers" ("pushing and shoving" with the authors of the readings) (6–12); the assignments "define a problem and the problem will frame the task for you" (14). "The assignments should not be read as a set of directions to be followed literally. In fact, they are written to resist that reading, to forestall a writer's desire to simplify, to be efficient, to settle for the first clear line toward the finish. We want to provide a context to suggest how readers and writers might take time, be thoughtful" (16). Even the assignment to imitate Griffin's methods frames her collage as a "certain kind of intellectual work" and suggests that by enacting her methods, students are presented with "one way to study this, to feel its effects" (453). Here, too, students will need to think about what they are doing, to "think about the stories you might tell, about the stories and texts you might gather (stories and texts not your own). As you think, you will want to think carefully about arrangement and commentary" (453–54).

The value of Griffin's collage in *Ways of Reading* is primarily pedagogical, that is, it offers students another way to do the work of learning to read and write, another occasion to "study" writing, another example of intellectual work to analyze. Compared to the kinds of claims made by other compositionists for the collage, *Ways of Reading* is exceedingly cautious and reticent. Bartholomae and Petrosky will merely mention in passing that Griffin's methods suggest alternatives to "the usual forms and boundaries of academic disciplines" (318). Why these usual forms or boundaries might be limited or why a writer might want to work outside of them, Bartholomae and Petrosky will not say, except to suggest that "there are other ways of thinking about this, she [Griffin] seems to say. There are other ways to do this work" (318). Of course, as I have already suggested, they value certain things about Griffin's work as a writer, but about the value of the form of collage, they decline to speculate. Rather, through their assignments, they ask students to adjudicate the value for themselves. This is apparent in the kinds of assignments I mentioned above where students are asked to reflect on the process of reading Griffin, or name and discuss the value of her methods. However, Bartholomae and Petrosky also offer three other writing assignments which ask students to consider the value of Griffin's methods: as an approach to writing "history," as a kind of "experimental writing," and as an occasion to reflect on the relationship between writing and "education."[18] Where Bartholomae and Petrosky's work with collage, and specifically with Griffin's text, differs from other pedagogical uses of the collage is in the ways in which they call attention to the situatedness of students vis-à-vis this "experimental" form of writing. It is this pedagogical use of the collage which I see as one of the most valuable uses of experimental writing in the classroom and which, as we will see, informs not only my evaluations of student collages but also my class work with students around their writings.

As the assignments in the sequence on experimental writing and in the sequence on education are similar, I will move back and forth between them. In "Sequence One: The Aims of Education," "Assignment 7: The Task of Attention [Griffin]," we see once again all of the cautionary language of the introduction and the headnote (including the striking title of the assignment itself): "Even if the project is not what we usually think of as a 'research' project, Griffin is a careful researcher. Griffin knows what she is doing" (793). Assignment 7 is predicated upon students having written a "Griffin-like" essay and thus asks them to reflect on Griffin's writing as it is a possible example of academic writing: "The point of this assignment is to think about that work—what it is, how she does it, and what it might have to do with schools. . . . What is she doing? What is at stake in adopting such methods? How might they be taught? Where in the curriculum might (should?) such lessons be featured?" (763). Similarly, under "Assignment 6: Writing and Schooling [Griffin, Williams, Schuyler, Anzaldúa]" in the "Experimental Readings and Writings" sequence, Bartholomae and Petrosky ask students to consider how these experimental writings relate to students' education. Interestingly, the language in which this assignment is written echoes much of the language of the arguments for experimental writing in composition, which I discussed in earlier chapters (e.g., breaking the rules, pushing the limits, frustration with usual ways, and so on):

> The selections you took as your models, writing by Griffin, Stevens, Auster, and Anzaldua, certainly did not follow the usual guidelines for school writing. They broke some rules. They pushed the limits. They didn't do what essays or poems are supposed to do, at least by certain standards. They were frustrated by the limits of the usual ways of doing things with words. In a sense, they saw "good" writing as a problem, a problem they could work on as writers. Most likely, the same things could be said about your writing in this sequence. You did things that stood outside of (or that stood against) the forms of writing most often taught in school. (830–31)

Though this language echoes the language of arguments for experimental writing in composition, it also repeats the language of the introduction to *Ways of Reading* in that the above-mentioned writers had "problems" that they tried to solve through altering their styles or methods. Therefore, even as Bartholomae and Petrosky position these experimental writings as outside of, or against, the writings of schooling, they treat the students as writers, albeit writers with more specific problems as they are situated within the context of the university (most likely in a composition class that they are required to take by the university with the aim of improving their writing, or helping them produce "good writing"). Thus, the assignment continues:

> Read over your work. What were you able to do that you wouldn't, or couldn't, have done if you had written in a more conventional style? Be as precise as you can. How and where does this writing differ from the writing you have been taught in school? Again, be as precise as you can—go to old papers, textbooks, or syllabi to look for examples of "good writing" and the standard advice to young writers. Given what you have seen, where and how might more experimental writing be used in the schools (or in schooling)? What role might it play in courses that are not writing courses? What role might it play in a young writer's education?
>
> Write an essay in which you use the example of your work in the sequence to think about writing and the teaching of writing in our schools. (831)

Granted, this assignment seems somewhat leading for several reasons. As the work of experimental writers has been presented as breaking the rules for some undisclosed higher purpose (because they were frustrated or constrained by more conventional writing, they tried to solve their problems in new ways), and because students have imitated these writings in at least four of these assignments, this assignment makes it hard for students to reject the implicit value of these experimental writings (as they have been doubly authorized by their inclusion in the textbook and by their assignment to the students by the teacher) or for students to reject the value of their own work vis-à-vis their education. With all of the authority of the textbook and the teacher and all the work students have done, it's hard (though not entirely impossible) to imagine a student writing an essay about what an enormous waste of time these experimental writings have been, or how completely irrelevant they might be to his or her education. This assignment is also somewhat leading because it asks students to consider only what "you were able to do that you wouldn't, or couldn't, have done if you had written in a more conventional style." Although the assignment goes on to ask how these students' experimental writings might differ from the writing they usually produce in school, it does not ask students to discuss the ways in which these writings might have prevented them from doing certain things. In other words, there is no question in here that asks, "What couldn't you do that you might have been able to do if you had been writing in a more conventional style?" Yet what I value about this assignment is that it asks students to reflect on their own literacy education, on their relationships to school writing, and on their understanding of the function of writing in school ("where and how might experimental writing be used in schooling"—or as the question is somewhat differently phrased in an earlier assignment, "Where in the curriculum might (should?) such lessons be featured?" [763]). The questions of this assignment are in many ways the questions of my project. Indeed, this assignment, somewhat revised, motivates the readings of my students' collages. As I read my students' collages in the next section, I consider not only what my students were able to do with the collage form, but also what they were unable to do.

SUNDAY NIGHT AND MONDAY MORNING: READING STUDENT COLLAGES

"Sunday night" is my extension of Mina Shaughnessy's figurative use of "Monday morning." By "Monday morning," Shaughnessy gestures to the materiality of the writing teacher's predicament: one may have been overwhelmed by stacks of student writing, one may have spent the weekend reading Bakhtin, Lyotard, and so on, but when Monday morning rolls around, a writing teacher has to go in and help her students learn something about writing (Shaughnessy 13). Shaughnessy does not mean to suggest that the research into reading or writing theories that a teacher does is of no help when it comes to the practical matters of teaching. Indeed, she is adamant that the two are related, that one can helpfully bring one's research or theoretical frameworks to bear on the problems of teaching. One might, for example, use one's understanding of linguistics and the history of the English language to read patterns of errors, or one might test out one's ideas about Lyotard's concept of the prudent imaginative judge on a batch of students' collages. Thus, I have titled this section "Sunday Night and Monday Morning" because "Sunday night" stands figuratively for that period when the teacher is reading through her stack of student papers, trying to figure out how to respond, how to translate this latest batch of papers into a lesson plan, and "Monday morning" represents for me what a teacher might do with these collages in the classroom, what kinds of work they might enable.

After my first-year composition class had spent quite a bit of class time reading, mapping, and discussing Susan Griffin's collage "Our Secret," I asked students to try their hand at the form, or as the assignment in *Ways of Reading* had suggested, "to imitate it, to take it as a model . . . to write a Griffin-like essay, one similar in its methods of organization and argument" (Bartholomae and Petrosky 453). Griffin's text combines a variety of discourses and texts, for example, the discourse of science (how cells work), military (how missiles were developed), history (the Holocaust), biography (Heinrich Himmler), psychology and sociology (child-rearing), descriptions of visual art (films and drawings), and personal narratives (autobiographical stories, stories as told to Griffin or as imagined by Griffin). The writing is by turns technical, poetic, factual, and emotional. The pieces are arranged without clear transitions but in juxtapositions and patterns that encourage analogical thinking across fragments.

We had read parts of Griffin's collage together and slowly, talking about how we saw connections between pieces. Students worked with the first question for a second reading (Bartholomae and Petrosky 451–52) on their own, and then in groups in class. We had covered two chalkboards with the result of all our efforts: lists of themes, elaborations on themes, the various sources Griffin uses, perspectives she offers, metaphors she employs, and visual representations of some of the connections we had made as readers (with lots of lines and arrows). Then they had worked in small groups discussing their plans and materials (some plans and materials more prospective than actually physically present in front of them). I circulated, fielding questions, asking questions.

Yet at the end of the class, before they were to go home and write the first drafts of their collages, one student said, amid the chatter of other students getting ready to leave, "So, then, anything goes, right?" I looked around at the chalkboards, densely packed with notes from our class discussions, and began to worry. Another student responded to the first student, "No, not anything goes, you can't just write a regular essay, you have to mess it all up, you have to confuse the reader, make it like a puzzle." "No, it's harder than that, you have to have different points of view and everything." "Well, it's not like you can do everything Griffin does, right? We only have a couple of pages and she had fifty something pages. So, Patricia, can we just pick one or two aspects of Griffin's essay and do it like that?" There is nothing quite like hearing students who have been partici-pating in a thoughtful discussion about the complexities of Griffin's text, faced with the prospect of producing their own collages, suddenly reduce all that work of reading and writing into one very pragmatic and seem-ingly doable suggestion: "You just write a regular essay and then break it up."[19]

Perhaps because the thematic focus of the course had become blurred and the line of inquiry unraveled (were we exploring the issue of educa-tion and "academic" writing, or investigating the power of metaphors, or what?), my students' reactions to their assignment to produce a Griffin-like text that semester startled and unsettled me into questioning my own motives for teaching the collage.[20] What, exactly, was I doing asking them to compose a collage, and for what purpose?

I had tried to help my students all semester (Griffin was the last as-signment) as they revised their ways of reading and writing—took chanc-es, faltered, resisted, forged ahead, fell back on old habits, tried out new approaches. The Griffin assignment, which asked them to compose a col-lage, however, seemed to send them a very clear message: one has got to do something very different; old ways of writing will not help (or at least that is how it might appear). What hadn't yet occurred to me at the time was that while my students would need to figure out new ways of writing, I, as their teacher, might need to figure out new ways of reading. Of course, I had more experience and practice than my students with new and un-conventional forms. As a graduate student in English, I had studied avant-garde and innovative modernist English literature, but also, as a graduate student in a master of fine arts program, I had participated in writing workshops where writers produced experimental texts. But would this experience, along with Griffin as a model, be enough for me in reading students' texts? Would it be merely a matter of evaluating how well they had imitated Griffin's text, or would responsibly engaging with their writ-ing require that I reflect on my own agenda for assigning them to write collages, my expectations, the criteria I assumed I would use in evaluating their work? Could reading their collages produce a new "pragmatic situa-tion" if I let it? As I discussed in my last chapter on evaluation, according to Jean-François Lyotard, "the experimental work will have as one of its effects the constitution of a pragmatic situation that did not exist before" (Lyotard and Thébaud 10). If a student produces a truly experimental piece of writing, then a new pragmatic situation has been created in which the teacher as judge now has to figure out a new way to evaluate that student writing. Why wouldn't I just apply my traditional criteria and move on?

What did I stand to gain by resisting the closure of the circle from pedagogy to evaluation?

The first thing that became apparent to me when I received my stack of student collages was the difficulty students had in resisting the inexorable pull of familiar writing conventions. The Griffin assignment had by its very form—asking students to imitate her collage style and methods—taken what were originally writing goals to work toward and turned them into traps to be avoided. Even with all of our preparation, I realized, those traps couldn't always be avoided; those familiar writing conventions were not always so easily dismissed. As I read some of the most "coherent" essays I had read all semester, my students' interpretations of the writing assignment echoed in my ears. One student wrote about her breakup with her boyfriend in the form of a linear narrative disrupted by descriptions of a roller coaster ride, clearly meant to be a metaphor for relationships. I imagined that all she had heard in the class discussion was the idea that you could write about what you wanted and then break it up a little. Another student's collage was so chaotic that I worked and worked to make connections and finally had to give up. Had she decided that "anything goes," or that the whole idea had been to confuse the reader, to make the writing like a puzzle? And then there were some collages that tried to find a balance, not too coherent, but not too confusing, moving toward the potential of a collage form, yet with traces of essay conventions in them. These were the kinds of collages I focused on in class discussions and the ones that I read here in order to highlight not only the ways in which students were and were not able to take on Griffin's project, but also the ways in which I struggled to learn how to read their attempts.

One of the first collages I read, by my student Cecilia Rodriguez, focuses on the effect on the lives of Chileans under Pinochet and begins this way:

> Chilean Air Force Hawker Hunters fires 18 rockets straight into the 300-year-old presidential palace. By 2:45 p.m. there was total calm. President Allende was found dead at his desk, surrounded by the lifeless bodies of his 14 personal assistants.
>
> General Augusto Pinochet was at the head of this military coup. The General, assisted by the conservative right wing and the North American CIA, that considered Allende's left tendencies a threat to democracy, was able to organize the military and overthrow Allende's government. Despite scattered resistance, the left was crushed. Pinochet became president and the disappearances, tortures and assassinations began. Within 19 days of

the coup 320 people were executed by the military, 13,500 were arrested
and many were rounded up and tortured at Santiago's National Stadium.
(Rodriguez 1)

Another collage by student Anthony Portis begins with definitions
of the word "racist" and "racism," and goes on to discuss how difficult
it is for people to talk about race. As the collage never leaves the topic of
racism, the opening clearly functions as an introduction. Both students
employ two familiar strategies of introductions: offering definitions as
a way to introduce a topic ("racism") and providing necessary exposition
(e.g., Pinochet's military coup). As a class, we had discussed how Griffin's collage differed from more conventional essays, specifically in that it
did not have what we usually thought of as an introduction, middle, and
conclusion. Yes, we decided, it had an opening and an ending, and yes,
there was movement (though not always linear) in the middle, but this
was not the usual essay format. We had also discussed how the collage,
as evidenced by Griffin's "Our Secret," had asked, if not demanded, that
readers do both more and different kinds of work than they were used to
doing. Yet here were some very clear "introductions" in my students' texts.
Were they wary of asking their readers to do too much work or nervous
about losing their readers?

An important question about writing emerged: what might be the difference between an introduction and a beginning? Though we went on as
a class to discuss opening moves for these student collages, when I think
back now, I wonder about not just conventional introductions in terms
of their effects on readers but the role that conventions play in enabling
(or disabling) the writing process: how does one start writing without an
introduction? Could it be that the convention of an introduction actually
helps writing begin, and if that is the case, then how does one decide
where to begin when the requirements of the assignment seem to take
away that enabling device? Or does one write an introduction in order to
get started and then take it away later, or move it, replacing it with something more appropriate to the collage form—a story, an image, a text that
works metaphorically?

Here is an example of an opening from another student, Bernadette
Loftus, whose first draft resists the conventional introduction (or puts it in
the second slot?):

As the corpse of the monstrous entity Chton sinks back into the lava whence it
rose, you grip the Rune of Earth Magic tightly.

> *Now that you have conquered the Dimension of the Doomed, Realm of Earth*
> *Magic, you are ready to complete your task. A Rune of magic power lies at the*
> *head of each haunted land of Quake. Go forth, seek the totality of the four Runes!*

> I don't remember acknowledging or even caring much when I heard about
> the killings in Colorado. Violence in the news does not upset me much.
> Violence just kind of melds into other television programming. "What a
> shame," I remember saying. It was a shame. No one should have to die like
> that, especially kids. Monsters, I thought, tortured every day of their lives.
> They just couldn't take it anymore. (Loftus 1)

When we discussed this opening in class, some students thought the collage was going to be about computer or video games, and though they reported feeling a little disoriented, they said they had been curious to read on and see if they were right. When we discussed the next part—where Loftus relates her response to the news of the Columbine High School shootings in Colorado—students began debating.

One the one hand, the thrill was gone for some students once they realized that the collage was most likely going to focus on the relationship between violent games and youth violence (a topic that had been much in the news at the time). On the other hand, some students argued that the predictability of the connection was mitigated by their surprise at reading about the writer's apparently indifferent attitude: "I don't remember acknowledging or even caring much." Either way, my students recognized that Loftus had found a way to open her collage that was different from yet similar to Griffin's opening. Whereas Griffin had opened with a definition of a "nucleus," Loftus had chosen the discourse of a video game, *Quake,* to pull her reader in before going on to imitate Griffin's next move—the use of a personal narrative (for Griffin, an interview; for Loftus, a personal narrative showing her own reaction).

In some ways, though, the introduction to Loftus's collage begins with her title, "Jocks Are from Earth, Oddballs Are from Venus." Whether intentional or not, there is a play of discourses here that yields multiple significations. The title, of course, alludes to a popular psychology book, John Gray's *Men Are from Mars, Women Are from Venus.* Whether Loftus is aware of it or not, her title recycles some of the detritus of popular culture. By allusion to this book, the "oddballs" in Loftus's collage are associated with Venus and therefore women; thus, oddballs become feminized. Jocks, however, are associated with Earth by Loftus, but by allusion to the title of this popular book, they become simultaneously associated with

Mars and men. There is a lot of irony at work here. Oddballs from Venus are feminine lovers even though the oddballs in question are also representative of teenage killers. Similarly, jocks are masculinized at the same time that Earth is militarized (by allusion to Mars), yet this militarism is naturalized in one more turn toward Earth. I make so much of Loftus's title because the doubleness, irony, and turns permeate and structure her collage. The oddballs are murderers in the media but also sweet, sensitive kids. What Loftus does with her title and her collage is suggest that it is not the oddballs who are the problem but all of society, which is inherently violent and malevolent toward these oddballs. In other words, Earth is a Mars-like place where the jock-men fit in and get along fine as long as they compete, while the feminine, sensitive oddballs transplanted from Venus and struggling to defend themselves are forced to become violent.

Similarly, her use of the discourse of the video game to open her collage maintains the doubleness of such discourse (and the media discourses that surround the role of video games in our society). On the one hand, Loftus knows that these video games can be violent, and that the media links their violence to youth violence. Yet by presenting her reader immediately with the language of the video game, she seems to be reminding us of how unreal these games are, how fictional and fantastical: a "monstrous entity Chthon," "Dimension of the Doomed," "Realm of Earth Magic," "the haunted land of Quake." It's as if Loftus's collage is saying, look at it, it's make-believe, we know it's make-believe.

Through class discussion of the ways Loftus's and Griffin's openings had worked, students reconsidered how they had opened their own collages, seeing that for this new form an introduction might be undesirable. Yet in looking back at Rodriguez's "introduction" to her collage on Chile, I wonder now if advising Rodriguez to take away her introduction and replace it with something else is a piece of advice more easily given than taken. One of the reasons that Loftus's opening seemed to succeed so well, according to my students, was because they recognized the passage as a video game (even if they were not familiar with *Quake*). They were, in other words, able to make this fragment signify and resonate for them, able to establish some context for this fragment. Could Rodriguez rely on her young American readers knowing who Pinochet was or what happened in Chile in the same ways that Griffin might be able to rely on her readers' familiarity with the Holocaust in the same way that Loftus might be able to rely on her fellow students' ability to recognize a video game? In other words, what if the fragment that starts a collage doesn't signify to its readers, what if it doesn't invite them into the collage, invitation being another way to think about introductions? As we will see below, Rodriguez tries to find a way for her reader to enter into her collage. But I wonder now about how helpful some of my generic advice actually was to students when the subject of their collage might pose particular problems for them not answerable by suggesting that they review their notes on "Our Secret," or work harder to imitate Griffin's collage.

The attempts to not only imitate Griffin's moves but adapt them to the specificity of their own work is evident in all three of the collages I include here. For example, though Rodriguez begins her collage with exposition, her next move employs Griffin's use of definition for a different effect:

> Within 19 days of the coup 320 people were executed by the military, 13,500 were arrested and many were rounded up and tortured at Santiago's National Stadium.
>
> *Fear: emotion caused by threat of some form of harm, sometimes manifested in bravado or symptoms of anxiety, and prompting a decision to fight the threat or escape from it (Microsoft Encyclopedia '97).* (Rodriguez 1)

Later, after presenting an excerpt from a personal testimony of a man who watched his wife die as the result of a car bombing, Rodriguez returns to the general idea of fear, this time invoking its physiological manifestation: "It is a strange thing, living in permanent fear. Adrenaline is constantly pumping through your bloodstream. It makes your heart race, strengthens your muscle, raises your blood sugar, and boosts your sugar metabolism. This reaction is often called the 'fight or flight' response; it prepares the body for strenuous activity" (Rodriguez 2). If my class had decided that the scientific definitions and information (particularly of the cell) in Griffin's text could be read metaphorically, Rodriguez's definitions seem to offer something different: a way for the reader—who presumably has felt fear or a fight or flight response at some point in his or her life—to connect to the specific cultural fear of people staying in Chile under Pinochet's rule.

Similarly, when I first read Portis's collage on racism, I noticed how his collage as a whole imitated Griffin's "Our Secret" in that it provided multiple texts, sources, and perspectives: quotations from Malcolm X, job applications, movie reviews, Web sites, excerpts from newspapers and television news, examples drawn from his own experience, and so on. However, one way that Portis apparently makes Griffin's project his own is by inserting statements that look like intertitles into his collage which either name topics for parts of the collage—"Application and Workplace," "The Media," "Let's Go to the Movies," "Web Sites," "My Experience"—or comment on something just discussed or presented—"He Needed a Chance," "Don't Judge Me before You Know Me," "Why Do We Continue to Kill over Color?" "Give Me a Break" (Portis 2–8). Are these titles an instance of revising Griffin's work, or another instance of the conventions of the essay emerging to prevent the different work of the collage as a form? The intertitles seem to have at least two effects: first, as transitions in the service of overall coherence, they work against imitating the kind of abrupt shifts evidenced in Griffin's text; second, the titles seem to be another example of my students' reluctance to risk losing their reader, or their reluctance to risk being misunderstood.

Moreover, I began to see these titles and their accompanying texts as creating mini-essays: a mini-essay on racism in the news media, a mini-essay on racism in the movies, a mini-essay on racism in sports, and so on. In a section titled *"Trading Places,* Eddie Murphy," Portis describes how difficult it was for the white football player Jason Shorn to play cornerback for the New York Giants since all the cornerbacks in the NFL were black at the time. Portis concludes this section with the intertitle "He Needed a Chance," titles the next piece of his collage "Shoe on the Other Foot," and describes playing basketball with his friends in the park: "When we play basketball in the summer at Mellon Park and there are a couple of white guys wanting to play, we pick them up to show them we just want to play basketball. I have a few friends that might say it's us four and 'white boy.' I say to them, 'Hey, he has a name; all you have to do is ask him.' Just think, if the shoe was on the other foot—if it were four whites and the 'nigger' you would be ready to fight" (Portis 4).

These two examples in his collage on racism in sports show how both black and whites, when they are the exceptions (black quarterback, white corenerback or basketball player), "need a chance." Similarly, in a section titled "Let's Go to the Movies!" Portis describes the controversy about the ways in which the character Jar Jar Binks in *Star Wars* is considered a racial stereotype. Immediately following this, in the next section, titled "The Good," Portis offers an example of a movie, *Rosewood,* that shows "how racism is defeated by people of color coming together as one" (Portis 5). Though there is certainly a kind of collage created by all these mini-essays, and though Portis had adopted Griffin's ways of working with juxtapositions (or are they just two opposing examples of the same idea?), his collage lacks the kinds of associative connections present in Griffin's collage. If it doesn't seem to challenge a reader to read and think across parts (since related parts were so often adjacent to one another), could it be that Portis's collage achieves some other effect?

In fact, most of my students had clearly found this work of making associative connections, or asking a reader to think analogically across pieces, the most difficult work. Their collages were often very focused on a specific issue, or a set of clearly related issues, unified thematically. Surely, this was a missed opportunity and something I encouraged them to explore as part of their revision work. But was this absence of associative connections to be considered a failure? Or could it be that their collages were doing other things, going for other effects in an attempt to make Griffin's project their own?

To return to Portis's collage on racism, it had many of the markers of a conventional argumentative essay: an introduction that defined its terms, set forth the problem—"there's something about racism that puts people in denial, and they just don't want to deal with it" (Portis 1)—and a conclusion that acknowledged that racism "is one problem that just won't go away. People of today have to realize it is here and we have to deal with it" (Portis 8). In the end, Portis offers a list of suggestions about how to deal with it, including not prejudging and being respectful of others. One way my students had read Griffin—one path they had taken through her text—was to see her text as making an argument about the necessity of realizing we are all connected. With this in mind, many students thought that the collage form had allowed her to explore and represent the complex and often subtle nature of those interconnections. By providing a varied and critical mass of instances, perspectives, sources, and texts, Portis's collage realizes its argument by disallowing the reader's attempt to deny racism. There is a very real sense of immersion when reading his text, an immersion which challenges the reader to "deal with it," to look directly at instances of racism, rather than think about it as an abstract problem. His collage works, then, less by the power of analogy than by accretion.

Similarly, when my class was discussing Loftus's collage on youth violence, one of my students asked whether or not Loftus's collage was making an argument or had an organizing theme or themes. The collage includes references to a video game, reactions to Columbine from the Internet, statistics, and descriptions of the formation of two different planets (Earth and Venus), as well as Loftus's commentaries and personal narratives. All of the perspectives presented are those of teenagers and young adults describing how ostracized, frustrated, and angry they felt during high school. If discussions in the media had seemed to ask how kids could suddenly murder other kids, Loftus's commentary has a way of putting her reader at ground zero, reminding us that while it might seem that kids just lose it (out of nowhere), in actuality, their actions are often the result of a long struggle:

> For many people school was a breeding ground for pain. Day in and day out, being tortured by peers while other students and administrators turned their back. How much can one person stand before crumbling, before wanting the world to end? It seems you have two choices: you can leave or they can.
>
> But what makes people choose the lives they choose? Hundreds of kids, *millions*, grow up in America tortured. Why do some of them go on rampages. . . .
> Luke Woodham, 16, Pear, Mississippi, 10-1-97
> 2 students killed, 7 wounded, *Mother stabbed to death*
> and how do those who don't prevent themselves acting out their anger and pain? (Loftus 2)

Here Loftus takes advantage of the syntactic flexibility of the collage form in a rather sophisticated manner (I'd like to say that I showed her how to do this, but I didn't). It is as if the statistic literally interrupts Loftus's thoughts because it interrupts her syntax, or that the statistic is offered as evidence to support the preceding phrase "go on rampages." Yet it can also seem that Loftus's question surrounds the statistic, asking us to think not just about the kids who become statistics but about the many other kids who don't resort to murder, who are able to "prevent themselves [from] acting out their anger and pain."

If Loftus's text tries to defend troubled adolescents (or at least generate some compassion), there are also attacks on the adults whose attempts to help or handle troubled teenagers prove inadequate. For example, Loftus includes a long Internet testimony from "Dan in Boise, Idaho," in which he relates how his school advisor suggested students write to express their feelings about what happened in Colorado. However, when Dan wrote an article for the school newspaper arguing that it was wrong to blame "screwed up kids or the Net," that perhaps it was the system that was to blame, and that he felt sympathy for the boys who had done the shooting, his article was "killed" and he was sent home with a letter to his parents: "So this is how they are trying to figure out what happened in Colorado, I guess. By blaming a sub-culture and not thinking about their own roles, about how fucked-up school is. Now, I think the whole thing was a set-up, cause a couple of other kids are being questioned too, about what they wrote. They pretend to want to have a 'dialogue,' but kids should be warned that what they really want to know is who's dangerous to them" (Loftus 4).

Loftus follows this with another statistic and with two pieces: in the first one (since this paragraph is in italics, it's not clear whether it is a quotation or Loftus's writing), she wonders if Columbine had an effect on the "microculture of our own household"; in the second one, she recounts a recent conversation with her father about Columbine:

> *But how many of us actually did anything differently? Spent more time with our children, or someone else's? Came home a little earlier? Skipped a meeting? Turned off the TV? Called other parents, called a teacher, volunteered to help with some after school activity—Girl Scouts, theater, baseball—that will happen only if enough grown ups show up?*

> I sent my father three articles from the other side. He called me up to tell me he refuses to read them; he has made up his mind about the situation. I told him I understand these kids. I play Quake. I was tortured by others for being different. "Did you ever want to hurt them?" he asked. "Sure," I said, "all the time. But I knew better." "Oh, Loftus . . ." he said, his voice heavy with the tone of devastating disappointment. I could almost see him walk away from me like some leprous being. Has he forgotten? Have 54 years washed away the pain of adolescence? (Loftus 4–5)

The story Loftus tells here emphasizes the generation gap and the difficulty that adults and adolescents have talking with each other—the misunderstandings, the fear, the mutual suspicion, the "refusal" to read or listen, the shared disappointments.

But it is the language she uses to open this section that is perhaps most telling and that led my class into a discussion about what perspectives were present and not present in her collage. She writes, "I sent my father three articles *from the other side*" (emphasis mine). What we have here, she seems to be saying, is a matter of sides, one against the other, with a lot of space or static in between. Because at the time of the class discussion, I was still caught up in trying to respond to my students' texts in terms of how well they had imitated Griffin's project, I asked them (rather leadingly, I have to admit) if Loftus's collage needed more and different perspectives (in the spirit of the collage as site of multiple intersecting discourses), for example, texts that quoted what the media were actually saying about the connections between video games and violence, or more texts that let the adults—teachers, administrators, parents—speak. My students were adamant: absolutely not. They argued that those perspectives were already implied by the texts Loftus had chosen as responses and that adding more texts would detract from the forcefulness of the material she had already chosen. I kept pushing, asking them to consider to what good uses multiple perspectives had been put in Griffin's "Our Secret," but to no avail. Apparently there was something more at stake here than students' reluctance to do the work of revision.

Recalling Nies's argument that the collage might allow students some authority over their sources, I think now that Loftus's refusal to include quotations from the parents, school administrators, or media sidesteps the problem of her authority. Of course, one could argue that those other discourses hover in the background and Loftus is responding to them. Yet the authority of Loftus's collage emerges from her understanding that the same discourses can circulate in different ways in different contexts. Thus, the discourses of video games are made to signify differently in her collage (video games are mere entertainment or consolation for her friends after they hear of the suicide of a friend). Similarly, the statistics and the discourses of pain and anger are offered not as evidence of murderous impulses, but as evidence of all the teenagers and young adults who *don't* go on killing sprees.

In my comments on her collage and in conversation with her, I encouraged Loftus to at least experiment with including other perspectives. It would make for a tidy story if I could report here that she acted on my advice, but she didn't. My motives for pushing her seem now rather tangled. I still value the work of revision, particularly exploratory revision. In retrospect, though, I wonder if I hadn't been clinging too much to Griffin's text as a model or to my own notions of what a collage was supposed to do (e.g., how could it be a collage if it represented only one group's perspective?). In many ways, I internalized the values of *Ways of Reading*, wanting to be able to say about my students' collages the kinds of things that Bartholomae and Petrosky say about Griffin's work, examining their collages for evidence of complexity, thoughtfulness, design, and, of course, "carefulness." In some ways, I followed too closely their pedagogical model, the one represented in the language of their assignment: "One way to *study* this, to feel its effect, is to imitate it, to take it as a model" (453; emphasis mine). Perhaps I had been too eager to make a circle, to close the gaps between my pedagogy and what the students produced in their writing, wanting to avoid evaluative uncertainty.

So, I let my evaluation be motivated by the search for evidence in students' collages that they had *studied* Griffin's text. In other words, I felt that Loftus's collage had failed by not imitating more of Griffin's moves. I also felt that I had failed her as a teacher by not convincing her to try to do this work. Yet both she and the class had made strong arguments for excluding those other texts and for respecting the project of the collage form as Loftus had realized it. Perhaps the mistake I had made was in holding on too tightly to the importance of students' taking on Griffin's project or clinging to my own sense of what conventions would make a collage work or make a good collage. Perhaps this looks like a slight mistake, a mere matter of emphasis. Yet, I am beginning to think that shifting one's emphasis might make the difference when asking students to experiment with writing.

Faced with a similar situation in the future, I would want try to give more precedence to the student's writing. I would want, in other words, to let the "tutor text" (as Ulmer might refer to Griffin) help me when possible, but not let it stand in the way of my reading the student's writing for what else it might be doing. I'd want to be able to say, "Let me show how I see your text as not just similar to but also different from Griffin's, and let's talk about how you might use some of her moves, adapt her moves, or create new moves in order to develop your version of the collage."

Maybe my references to Griffin's text would help my students with revision and maybe they wouldn't. Maybe we'd need to collaboratively develop a revised or new poetics (one that builds on or even contradicts the kind of reader-based poetics we developed before they tried their imitations) and thus a specific aesthetics for each student's text, with other students and myself as readers/responders, identifying the features of a given student's collage, articulating appreciation, dismay, confusion. The point here would be to avoid giving too much authority to any one factor—the tutor text, the teacher, the reader, or the writer. I'd want, finally, to be able not only to revise my old criteria, but also to imagine new criteria, not just criteria developed by me in response to the student's writing, but also criteria that the students develop for their own and one another's writing. I see this desire as an attempt not to forfeit my role as judge but rather to extend and share my role as judge.

I suggested in the previous chapter on evaluation that the writing teacher needs to be prudent and imaginative, but I'd like to revise that statement by suggesting that prudence and imagination are not just characteristics of, or possessions of, an individual teacher. Rather, prudence and imagination can exist in the intersections between readers and writers, teachers and students. Of course, I can be (and should be when it comes to experimental writing) a prudent and imaginative judge. But another way to see prudence is to see it as socially shared and constantly renegotiated. In this way, it is not just my prudence (the result of my education, upbringing, experiences, and so on) but the collective prudence developed by me and my students as we work out our responses to experimental texts. Similarly, it is not just my imagination, nor even my students' individual imaginations. Rather, imagination could be understood without a locatable autonomous subjectivity: imagination as the force that is generated by our collective efforts to read one another's collages, and which in turn generates a field of criteria from which we might more consciously select some criteria over others in service of our various commitments to writing: for example, the student who does just want to imitate Griffin; the student who wants to depart from Griffin as a model; the student who doesn't know yet, but is struggling to come up with a text worth working on; the teacher who wants to see evidence of careful composing; and so on.

If when my students tried their hand at this new kind of writing, they sometimes fell back on old ways of writing, I too sometimes fell back on typical ways of reading that prevented me from seeing the nature of the difficulties they were having, or even the nature of their successes. I had to resist my impulse to write quick remarks on their papers like "replace that introduction with a more collage-like fragment," "cut your transitions," "provide more perspectives." Those kinds of comments represent the easier work. The harder work for me is to take the time to reflect, to be able to recognize when students need help revising their ideas about reading and writing, and when they are not necessarily failing but producing (intentionally or not) a text that requires a different kind of reading or evaluation, a text that cracks open my pedagogy and puts my criteria for evaluating their writing on the table for discussion.

POSTSCRIPT

TOWARD A MULTIMODAL COMPOSITION

As with experimental writing, arguments for multimodal composition suggest that especially through the use of new technologies, students may be better allowed to express their individual experiences, articulate marginal or underrepresented social realities, as well as critique the limits of dominant sociopolitical discourses and the institutions that perpetuate these discourses. Additionally, such arguments to expand the composition curriculum include not only print texts generated by the resources of alphabetic literacy but also other media such as digital video, Web pages, social networking applications, mobile applications, audio texts, and even in some cases sculptures and performances. Not surprisingly, arguments in composition for the teaching of the production of multimodal texts, as with arguments for teaching the collage, in writing classrooms have inherited rich (if sometimes problematic) dialectical tensions of avant-garde aesthetics and contemporary composition pedagogies. Some examples of these tensions include the dialectic of the individual and the social, especially vis-à-vis autonomy, alienation, and collective agency; the dialectic of innovation and tradition or convention; the dialectic of knowledge and art, determinate and indeterminate judgment; the dialectic between school (and other institutions) and "the real world." In this chapter, I continue my exploration of the ways in which compositions tend to resolve (or make productive use of) these dialectical tensions. I also revisit the relation of aesthetics and composition pedagogies. As with the pedagogies for the collage and other forms of experimental writing, pedagogies for multimodal composing sometimes articulate explicit aesthetics, often avantgarde, and other times imply or sidestep questions of aesthetics. Thus, many of the questions, issues, and critiques that I raised about pedagogies of experimental writing in previous chapters may also help compositionists to think more critically about the latest claims we are making for the significance of multimodal composition, including the ways in which we might invite students to collaborate with us as teachers and scholars as we reimagine the goals, values, and practices of composition.

The explosion of scholarship and textbooks about teaching new media, multimedia, or multimodal composition in the field (much like the proliferation of texts in the late 1990s and early 2000s with "alternate" or "multi"—as in "multigenre," "multiliteracies") is a testament to the latest attempts to reform and update composition pedagogies, as well as evidence of the latest research and development activity of the corporate university (see chapter 2 for more on this line of argument). There is no way to address or account for the wide range of texts on multimodal composition, but I have chosen to focus on three that I see as indicative of trends: Cynthia Selfe's collection, *Multimodal Composition: Resources for Teachers;* Jeff Rice's *The Rhetoric of Cool: Composition Studies and New Media;* and Anne Wysocki et al.'s *Writing New Media: Theory and Applications for Expanding the Teaching of Composition.*

As one might notice from the titles, composition hasn't yet decided on what to call this relatively new phenomenon. "Multimodal" echoes semiotic approaches but doesn't necessarily connote new media; and "new media" implies a kind of cutting-edge technology but, in reality, often invokes media that have been around for decades. Currently, the terms most in circulation include digital media, electracy, multiliteracies, new media, multimodal, and multimedia. As Claire Lauer demonstrates in "Contending with Terms: 'Multimodal' and 'Multimedia' in the Academic and Public Spheres," "though multimodal has become more commonly used in scholarly literature related to new kinds of texts students are exploring in the composition classroom, it is almost entirely absent from

. . . more public discussions outside of the academy where multimedia is used almost exclusively" (226). Though outside of composition I find myself in conversation with noncompositionists or nonacademics using the more recognizable term, "multimedia," it does seem that composition has more often chosen to work with the different connotations and emphases of "multimodal." I have chosen to use the more expansive term, "multimodal," when referring to any texts that are more than just alphabetical literacy, though occasionally I will discuss as relevant different aspects of multimedia, for example, visual, digital, aural, oral media, new media, modalities, or materialities.[1]

If many of the scholars that I discussed in previous chapters have argued that experimental writing provides the individual student with a way to articulate social or political realities otherwise difficult or impossible to communicate via conventional or academic writing, so too does Selfe situate her commitment to multimodality vis-à-vis a democratic politics. She does this not just as Winston Weathers did in relation to traditional writing styles (what he called "Grammar A"), but in relation to traditional modes of communication, what I would like to call "Mode A," which is what Selfe calls "print literacy" but which might be even more broadly referred to as alphabetic literacy: "I suggest that the almost exclusive dominance of print literacy works against the interests of individuals and cultures and communities that have managed to maintain a value on multiple modalities of expression, multiple and hybrid ways of knowing, communicating, and establishing identity ("The Movement of Air" 617). Selfe's understanding of multimodality is broad and includes digital and other technologies (e.g., photography, film and video, computer and audio and video-recording technology), but she is also interested more generally in orality and aurality, not necessarily digitally mediated.

While Selfe challenges the dominance of print literacy, she does not oppose academic literacies (as, for example, Gregory Ulmer, Geoffrey Sirc, and Jeff Rice do). Indeed, it is part of her argument that multimodal composition is a response to changes in both the academy and society at large. Selfe makes clear how she sees the dependent relation between academic institutions and "culture" in the foreword to *Multimodal Composition*. She posits a kind of belatedness to composition, whereby society and other disciplines have become multimodal, while composition pedagogy lags behind: "But more to the point is that we must recognize that English Departments no longer sustain culture behind impenetrable walls of print. Culture, the product of human relations, now produces texts in multiple, often overlapping forms. . . . And we should also recognize that other disciplines across campus are increasingly moving to multimodal texts in their courses and that our students need to know how to write to learn and write to inform and persuade in these forms as well as they do in print" (xii).

Selfe is not content to claim just the academic value of teaching multimodal composition. Even if, as Gunther Kress suggests, print literacy is still the literacy of the cultural elite,[2] Selfe, like many others, claims that multimodal texts have become dominant: "Thus, while time marches on *outside* of U.S. secondary and college classrooms, while people on the internet are exchanging texts composed of still and moving images, animations, sounds, graphics, words, and colors, *inside* many of these classrooms, students are producing essays that look much the same as those produced by their parents and grandparents" (*Multimodal Composition* 1–2). In many ways, Selfe's argument is pragmatic and commonsensical, and thus very powerful both inside of and outside of the academy, in that it claims to update the teaching of pluralistic composition so that students can participate in the production of texts that are epistemologically (inside the institution) and rhetorically (outside the academy) powerful.

I am laying out, in some detail, the content and gestures of Selfe's argument as representative of many arguments for multimodal composition not just for what it does, but also because of what Selfe's argument doesn't do. It doesn't suggest that new technologies or new media pose any significant challenges to our concepts of rhetoric or to traditional rhetorical principles. Though Selfe and the other authors of *Multimodal Composition: Resources for Teachers* acknowledge that multimodal composition will require the generation and deployment of criteria specific to different modes (e.g., regarding the placement of images, the use of sound), it is also the case that, by and large, rhetorical principles abide:

> Rhetorically based understandings of composition should *drive* and *inform* teachers' approach to assessment in multimodal composition classrooms. . . . Using assessment to teach about the design and production—the composition—of texts seems especially relevant in a multimodal classroom because it is entirely possible that the processes of creating texts that go beyond the alphabetic will be less familiar to many students than the processes involved in creating more conventional word-based texts. In such contexts, we need to teach students not only how to compose in multiple modalities, but also how to connect their understanding with rhetorical principles that guide all language use. (Borton and Huot 99–100)

Selfe's multimodal composition may challenge the dominance of alpha-betical literacy in composition classrooms, but it will not provoke a crisis of judgment in composition pedagogies or institutions. Indeed, much of *Multimodal Composition's* apparatus provides rubrics, worksheets, and ar-guments that help reinforce a sense of the continuity between many crite-ria and pedagogy for writing classes and those that might be used for mul-timodal composition classes. One might even argue that one of the book's most effective (and attractive to some composition teachers) aspects is the way in which it offers the means for avoiding the possible instability that multimodal composition might introduce into more conventional print- and alphabetic literacy–oriented college writing courses.

So while Selfe and colleagues will help teachers and students figure out how to compose and evaluate multimodal texts (vis-à-vis their differ-ent affordances, in particular), it is also true that Selfe and others main-tain some very familiar categories and rhetorical (aesthetics is more or less subsumed under rhetoric) criteria, such as argument, purpose, audience, clear organization, tone, and so on. As with Weathers's well-tested options and application of "certain basic principles of composition" (*Alternate Style* 39), here too in Selfe's book, traditional rhetorical principles, pedagogical structures, and modestly updated criteria abide.

If Selfe represents a moderate approach to expanding the repertoire of composition, other scholars and compositionists, such as Gregory Ulmer, Jeffrey Rice, and Geoffrey Sirc, suggest more radical changes to composi-tion pedagogies and to the field of composition. They argue that teaching students how to produce multimodal or new media texts represents and requires new goals and values for rhetorical education, as well as new ways of thinking about writing, communication, and rhetoric. For example, in "Box Logic," Sirc continues the project he articulated in *English Composi-tion as Happening* with a new media compositional project modeled after the box collages of Joseph Cornell. The general import of his argument for the significance of collage as a conceptual, generic, formal category for composition echoes arguments I have already discussed in my previous chapter on collage. Here he repeats his self-proclaimed avant-gardist proj-ects of uniting art and the everyday lives of students (117); of striving for noninstitutional spaces ("We still have not learned from the work done by our field's historical avant-garde about the failure to see our composition classes in the larger world" [127]); of advancing a neoexpressivist move-ment in composition, choosing, with Peter Elbow and Ken Macrorie, to teach life over college (*English Composition as Happening* 113, 127); of choos-ing to teach the "associational logic of linkages . . . [in order] to help foster a personal aesthetic among our students" (123); and arguing that, in the end, "the expressive, substantially refined now, returned to prominence in our curriculum, end[s] the long reign of the strictly analytic" (124).

Additionally, if in his arguments in "What Is Composition . . . ? After Duchamp" he railed against the curatorial impulse in composition, as represented by Bartholomae and *Ways of Reading*, here he embraces the "cyber-flaneur" and claims for the composition instructor the role of curator: "We are, indeed, curators, but we need to do our job well" (126). In sum, unlike Selfe, Sirc sees new media as an opportunity to thwart the academic aspects of composition: "it's the key tension in all fields throughout modernity with the idea of composition at their center: the tension between the academic and the avant-garde" ("What Is Composition" 128). He goes on to quote Hal Foster, who differentiates the avant-garde's attack on artistic and social conventions from the neo–avant-garde's attack on the institutional (128). That Sirc can so easily and unproblematically import his arguments about avant-garde aesthetics and the low-tech (high craft) techniques of Cornell's box collages into the context of "new media" composition is one of many examples of how aesthetics may be used to try to override (or elide or exploit) technological issues by appearing to have prophesized paradigmatic shifts in forms, genres, and criteria. New media, in the case of Sirc's essay on box logic, is enlisted to serve (or serve alongside) avant-garde aesthetics in the project of destroying (or attempting to destroy) the institution (and institutional drive) of composition pedagogies.

If Sirc represents one of the more radical desires in composition to destroy its many institutions, then the work of Jeff Rice in *The Rhetoric of Cool: Composition Studies and New Media* offers a more (seemingly) modest challenge to traditional composition goals and values, though still in many ways embracing an avant-garde aesthetic. Rice has two broad and related goals in his book. First, he aims to write an alternative (sub-versive) history of composition studies in order to challenge the grand narratives of modernist composition (Rice 15–18).[3] Second, he aims to construct new goals, values, and pedagogies for composition that engage the production of new media texts: "I recognize that rhetoric and rhetorical invention emerge out of a number of influences: art, film, literature, music, record covers, cultural studies, imagery, technology, and, of course, writing" (Rice 10). Against the old goals and values and conventions—topic sentences, paragraph-based structuring, interpretation over production, logical reasoning and ordering, referential-based argumentation, purpose, audience recognition, Rice offers the new media practices and values of chora, appropriation, juxtaposition, commutation, nonlinearity, and imagery (Rice 8).

Many of these new practices and values continue the work of Gregory Ulmer. Rice particularly makes use of Ulmer's arguments and methods in *Heuretics,* a book in which Ulmer claims that electronic and digital technologies, in critical mode, require an avant-garde aesthetic: "As an 'experimental' humanities, heuretics appropriates the history of the avant-garde as a liberal arts mode of research and experimentation" (Ulmer, *Heuretics* xii). I have already discussed the limits of Ulmer's project of appropriating the history of the avant-garde in previous chapters and so will not repeat it here, especially as I would suggest that *Heuretics* does not significantly differ much from arguments he has made in *Applied Grammatology,* "Textshop for Post(e)pedagogy," and *Text Book,* even if, for example the tutor text of Blake is replaced by the tutor method of surrealist—Breton—manifestos. Rice, unlike Selfe, will not uphold traditional rhetorical values and principles, but neither will he, like Sirc, try to escape judgment altogether in the name of art. Instead, Rice continues the experimentalist attitude of much of Ulmer's work, an approach that attempts to embrace the aesthetics of the collage or cut-up at the same time it tries, as Sirc's work does, to postpone judgments. Rice asks, "How do you measure the funkengine scientifically? How do you assess it? I ask these questions not to find answers but to note the limitations they can pose when new media practices are being invented. . . . The time has come to perform and not only to explain or assess" (Rice 91).

But if my comparison of Selfe's work to Weathers is meant to help us see a certain kind of pluralistic presentation of alternatives, Rice not only explicitly invokes his debt to Ulmer, but aligns himself with what he sees as a sub-versive strain in the work of Winston Weathers. "My argument, therefore, resembles (even if only slightly) Winston Weathers's call in *Alternate Style: Options in Composition* for a 'Grammar B.' . . . Cool belongs in this tradition of alternatives, a tradition, Weathers notes, that emerges out of digital culture" (Rice 26). More specifically, Rice emphasizes the ways in which Weathers addressed the importance of electronic influences—radio, television, and movies—on writing, particularly literature (e.g., the work of William Burroughs). Rice concludes, however, by saying, "I want to push Weathers's interest in the rhetoric of literature even further so that we draw on a variety of media forms for rhetorical instruction and not just novels and poetry. But like Weathers, I want it to be understood that this rhetoric—even as it comes from literature, film, music, and elsewhere—is the result of electronic culture" (26–27). Whereas Sirc will reference primarily avant-garde painters and plastic artists (Duchamp, Cornell), and Ulmer will avail himself of a mixture of avant-garde artists (e.g., Beuys) and writers (e.g., Breton) with some French theory (mostly Derrida), Rice will continue Ulmer's emphasis on Derrida but will choose French and American theorists (Barthes, Marshall McLuhan) and artists primarily from 1960s America (e.g., Amiri Baraka, William Burroughs, Jack Kerouac). He seems to do this as a way of retelling the history of composition (circa 1963). Like Sirc, Rice is interested in telling alternative histories, especially histories that highlight anti-institutional aesthetics.

As my discussion in chapter 2 of the institutionalization of avant-garde art and the formation of the field of composition shows, there is much to be gained from studying these parallels between avant-garde anti-institutional aesthetics and composition's institutionality. Indeed, while Rice makes more of the influence of electronic technologies on literature in Weathers than Weathers actually does (it is one rather minor factor among many factors Weathers discusses), and Rice also attempts to move beyond the strong literary bent of Weathers, Rice's interest in popular culture (sometimes in the name of cultural studies) suggests an even more overt connection to some of the thinking of Andreas Huyssen about the avant-garde and its relation to technology, which I merely hint at in my discussions.

In *After the Great Divide*, Huyssen suggests that the hidden dialectic is between the avant-garde and mass culture, and that technology made mass culture possible and transformed art: "Mass culture as we know it in the West is unthinkable without twentieth-century technology—media techniques as well as technologies of transportation (public and private), the household, and leisure. . . . It is much less widely acknowledged that technology and the experience of an increasingly technologized life world have also radically transformed art. Indeed, technology played a crucial, if not *the* crucial, role in the avantgarde's attempt to overcome the art/life dichotomy and make art productive in the transformation of everyday life" (Huyssen 9). Huyssen discusses various examples of the avant-garde's use of technology, in terms of both techniques (e.g., montage) and content (e.g., "art objects in which humans are presented as machines and automatons") (9, 11). Furthermore, he acknowledges that "by incorporating technology into art, the avantgarde liberated technology from its instrumental aspects and thus undermined both bourgeois notions of technology as progress and arts as 'natural,' 'autonomous,' and 'organic'" (11). What Huyssen also suggests, however, is that the avant-garde was not entirely able to escape the instrumental functions of technology, nor was it able to quite ignore the bourgeois notion of technology as progress. It was not always able to make these two moves, nor did it always want to.

Indeed, it is the avant-garde's ambivalence about technology, its hope for technology and art, paired with its critique of bourgeois ideology and institutions that I see present in arguments for new media or multimedia composition. On the one hand, for example, Selfe in *Multimodal Composition* represents the bourgeois concern with progress, with keeping up with the new technologies of business and entertainment. On the other hand, compositionists such as Ulmer and Rice want to challenge not only the instrumental functions of technology but also the instrumental functions of writing.[4] While Selfe and others will maintain composition and rhetoric's language of argument and other rhetorical principles, such as purpose, audience, clear organization, tone, and focus (see also Borton and Huot), perhaps adding new criteria that address sound or images or color, or the like, Ulmer and Rice go right to the core of the instrumentalism of writing technology and writing instruction. For Ulmer, there are no more linear cause-and-effect logic (*Heuretics* 34) or five-paragraph themes (35), no conventional topoi (48).

Rice similarly dismisses these values and strategies, but is even more adamant about doing away with thesis statements (78–79), as well as predetermined organization and authorial purpose (83) and authorial control (23–24). Both Ulmer and Rice advocate associational writing, linking, and intuition, among other compositional strategies and values. Both also, in the avant-garde spirit, avail themselves (or say they are willing to avail themselves) of any materials that are available, academic, artistic, scientific, popular, old, new, trash, found, made, and so on. Similarly, the work of Sirc, in its advocacy of avant-garde aesthetics, appears to embrace mass culture, though Sirc's preference for certain types of culture (e.g., rap music) belies blind spots vis-à-vis the relative relations of mass culture, popular culture, commodity culture, and "art," a category Sirc upholds despite its apparent instability.

Indeed, much of multimedia composition relies on, or engages, texts and objects of mass culture made possible by technology. How do we think about the effect of these technologies on the teaching of writing when writing, following Selfe and Kress, is more representative of a historical and cultural elite (despite its democratic pretensions) and is now increasingly and intensely competing with mass culture and other technologies? When publishing changes from a printed, bound classroom anthology that may or may not be placed in a college library to a public Web site that showcases student work (or for which students write from the beginning of a course), how do we consider the role of mass culture in relation to that student writing (mass culture as catalyst, as resource, as model)? What will be the role of writing in relation to YouTube, where students post and share videos as part of academic projects, but which also leaves students and instructors sometimes stuck watching commercials or ads or finding their videos or texts in contexts they hadn't anticipated or desired?

In other words, there are unanswered questions about the effects of mass culture (not just popular culture) on writing and the complex inter-relationships among technology, mass culture, and economic interests. It is no longer possible (if it ever was) to consider student writing apart from questions of aesthetics, technology, and mass culture. One way (oversimplified, but shorthand) might be to put the question in the following terms: if writing/print-page culture becomes elitist (Kress), then does writing plus technology become mass culture? And if so, what are the roles and relationship of writing, technology, and mass culture vis-à-vis education and democracy in a posthumanist global context?

I raise these questions about the affordances of modes and art/technology/mass culture not because I have answers but because I think that many of the issues that I have addressed in this book are already being repeated in discussions of multimodal (multimedia, new media) composition. Questions that I raise in chapter 1 about autonomy and expression and alienation will not be solved by encouraging students to post videos of themselves any more than they were by suggesting students write personal collage essays. Technology will not solve what are philosophical, political, and experiential tensions. Similarly, as I have already hinted, multimedia composition is torn between an academic/institutional understanding of rhetoric and a cultural (out there) societal version of rhetoric. Here are some more questions I am left with: cultural studies composition has addressed popular culture in the composition classroom, but how might the work that has already been done help us to better understand the ways in which cultural studies pedagogies and scholarship, including recent arguments for multimodal composition, rest on or invoke troubling notions of progress and mass culture? What is the relationship between the notions of mass culture embedded in new media approaches to teaching composition and the recent "public turn" in composition? For Huyssen (and I find him persuasive on this point), "the legitimate place of a cultural avantgarde which once carried with it the utopian hope for an emancipatory mass culture under socialism has been preempted by the rise of mass mediated culture and its supporting industries and institutions. . . . It was the culture industry, not the avantgarde, which succeeded in transforming everyday life in the 20th century" (15). But Ulmer and Rice and Sirc still seem to think the cultural avant-garde is possible, want to bring art back together with everyday life, but maybe that's not possible; or maybe that's not an issue for our students, maybe art and everyday life are already entwined for them, just not in ways that Ulmer or Rice or Sirc or I recognize or appreciate; or maybe students are not (rightly) interested in art (an old-fashioned idea if there ever was one). Maybe students recognize that the culture industry and mass culture are more powerful than anything that anyone might try to call "art."

I think the work that needs to be done is more like the work that Anne Wysocki starts both in her introduction to *Writing New Media: Theory and Applications for Expanding the Teaching of Composition* and in her essay in that collection, "The Sticky Embrace of Beauty: On Some Formal Problems in the Teaching of Writing." In both texts, I value the work that she does to contextualize writing practices, to think cautiously (rather than idealistically and naïvely) about new media and new technologies, and to identify the limits of our inherited aesthetics in a self-conscious way, as she works collaboratively with her students to try and imagine new aesthetics for new designs.

Wysocki suggests in her introduction that the collection is more interested in the materiality of writing. To me, this means that she is (and we should be) less interested per se in how technologies have produced an experimentalist paradigm (Ulmer) or seem to require an avant-garde attitude toward compositions and institutions (though Sirc's "Box Logic" is part of this collection):

> I think we should call "new media texts" those that have been made by composers who are aware of the range of materialities of texts and who then highlight the materiality: such composers design texts that help readers/consumers/viewers stay alert to how any text—like its composers and readers—doesn't function independently of how it is made and in what contexts. Such composers design texts that make as overtly visible as possible the values they embody. Considering new media texts in this way, I think and hope, helps us see where openings for agency are within new media texts we compose.
>
> Under this definition, new media texts do not have to be digital; instead, any text that has been designed so that its materiality is not effaced can count as new media. (Wysocki 15)

Unlike Selfe's project, which maintains rhetorical principles, Wysocki articulates a project that asks teachers and students to problematize agency and writing and to take into account new media and how it affects the materiality of texts (their production, circulation, reception). This materiality, however, does not require experimental texts or an avant-garde sensibility, that is, the argument that Sirc makes and that Rice, following and extending the work of Ulmer, also makes. Yet, if we take Wysocki's contribution to the *Writing New Media* collection as an example, this project requires (or benefits strongly from) thinking critically about the role that aesthetics has played in composition pedagogies.

In "The Sticky Embrace of Beauty," Wysocki demonstrates the powerful contribution that reflecting self-consciously on inherited aesthetics can make to composition pedagogy. Unlike many of the texts I have examined in previous chapters, Wysocki is not arguing for the power of writing as art; instead, she argues that students need to examine how they read graphic designs (in her case an advertisement in an issue of the *New Yorker*) and consider what they value in certain designs and reflect on how aesthetic legacies (in Wysocki's argument, the Kantian legacy of an abstracted idealized formalized beauty) can contribute to what we can and can't see or can or can't value in particular designs. Ultimately, such awareness may lead students to construct texts of their own that are rhetorically and ethically reciprocal (Wysocki 173). Here, she doesn't borrow what she sees as the power of previous examples from some artist or writer. She doesn't claim to know the answer, unlike Ulmer and Rice and Sirc, who ironically perpetuate a particular avant-garde (mostly male, mostly European-Anglo-Saxon-American) tradition. Wysocki, looking at an advertisement, examines the aesthetic traditions she brings to her understanding of design, and this prompts her to help students come to such an awareness, but inductively, by collecting examples and then reading theory and theorizing their own aesthetics and rhetorics.

Reflecting on these attempts—by Wysocki and others—to invite students into a multimodal composition, I'm left with the following questions at the end of this book. What if teachers worried less about what they don't know about the techniques of certain modes and media and thought more about the role that inherited aesthetics are playing in our sense of the possibilities and limits of certain designs, genres, texts, media, and modes? And what if instead of "new" composition theories fashioned from old aesthetics, we articulated new aesthetics and new theories and practices of agency? Maybe we need to stop wishing that technology were inherently progressive or that art was a locus of freedom, personal expression, or liberal politics for our students. How might composition be different if we examined our inherited aesthetics and rhetorical values, and then developed new aesthetics and rhetorics, new understandings of agency and new practices of composing, not *for* our students, but *with* our students?

NOTES

INTRODUCTION

1. While I will explore the theoretical and methodological limits of structuring my discussions in terms of dialectics throughout the book, especially in my discussion of postmodern pedagogies, I would like to pause here to acknowledge both Byron Hawk's reference to *dissoi logoi* and his rejection of dialectics in *A Counter-History of Composition*. On the one hand, Hawk rejects various versions of dialectics throughout his book, most particularly in response to the work of James Berlin, and argues for a postdialectical composition (perhaps a contradiction in terms?). Yet, in his introduction to his book, he argues, "At its core, this book seeks nothing more than to enact the ancient principle of *dissoi logoi*, making the weaker argument stronger. Once a way of thinking becomes so ingrained that no one bothers to question it, the most effective way to make it show up is to attempt the opposite argument that no one would even consider investigating. Such a strategy reopens the question and provokes renewed consideration" (Hawk 10). In many ways, my project is similar in its intent; however, such a project of "investi-

gating opposite arguments" depends on understanding the dialectics underlying *dissoi logoi*, and thus a postdialectical scholarship and version of composition will not yield the same kinds of "renewed consideration" of assumptions of the field. In other words, there is a closer relationship between the strategy of *dissoi logoi* as exploring opposing arguments and various broader understandings of dialectics than Hawk seems willing to acknowledge.

2. What "academic prose" actually means is less obvious or less important than the functions it serves or what it stands for: it represents the idea or set of values to which innovative or experimental writing is the alternative. Academic prose or discourse is not a monolithic category. In fact, it is so variously described and construed that any potential critiques leveled at its dominance are difficult to sustain. While "academic discourse" gestures toward the academic community, and "academic prose" emphasizes the formal aspects of writing, I often use them interchangeably (with noted exceptions) as the formalist emphasis in arguments for innovative or experimental writings tends to conflate the two terms. For a longer discussion, please see chapter 2. Increasingly, proponents of teaching the production of experimental multimedia texts in composition classrooms position themselves less in relation to academic discourse per se than in relation to print or alphabetic literacy.

3. See my discussion in chapter 2 of Bizzell's and Dobrin's reflections on the implications of different word choices, including "hybrid," "mixed" or "alternative" discourses.

4. See also *College English* 71.3 (Jan. 2009), which is devoted entirely to the role that creative writing studies plays or might play in English studies.

5. Heller's piece captures effectively the chaos of conflicting concepts of aesthetics—beauty, pleasure, value, judgment—as well as a sense of hope and ambivalence about what a return to aesthetics might mean for literary studies:

> Scholars like Mr. [Emory] Elliott do not wish to turn back the clock, but to nudge the pendulum just a little. They want attention to aesthetic criteria, but not just a new New Criticism, which held that literary texts should be read for formal properties, divorced from the social and cultural forces that affected their creation. "If aesthetics comes back, which I think it will, I want the best people in the profession to be in charge of taking it to new places," says Mr. Elliott. In the canon wars, cultural conservatives have been the only ones arguing for aesthetic criticism, he notes. "I want my guys to be leading this direction," he says. (A15)

6. See, for example, the work of Robert Scholes and Richard Lanham.

7. See, for example, Rice on the rebirth of rhetoric in 1963 *College Composition and Communication* and the relation of writing to rhetoric and communication more broadly (*Rhetoric of Cool* 21–27) and Shipka's *Toward a Composition Made Whole*.

8. Critics who differentiate between modernism, the avant-garde, and post-

modernism by emphasizing formal differences (e.g., organic texts versus fractured or fragmented texts) or political differences (e.g., modernism is politically conservative, whereas the avant-garde is politically progressive) seem to select their examples rather arbitrarily and to suit their arguments. See, for example, my allusion later in the introduction to the different representations of Eliot's writing as either modernist or avant-garde.

1. EXPERIMENTAL EXPRESSIVISM: AUTONOMY AND ALIENATION

1. See Crowley: "During the late 1960s, students began to express dissatisfaction with business as usual in the freshman writing class. Sometimes this dissatisfaction was expressed quite compellingly: at the University of Iowa, for example, the rhetoric building was burned down" (205).

2. Two very different recent works that explore the role of experimental writing in 1960s and 1970s pedagogy include Sirc's *English Composition as Happening* and Warnick's "Student Writing, Politics, and Style." Sirc reads key moments, texts, and compositionists (e.g., William E. Coles, Ken Macrorie, Charles Deemer, William Lutz) usually represented and understood as expressivist in composition histories of the time through the lens of avant-garde happenings, thus turning expressivists into avant-garde artists. Warnick reads student writings within their specific institutional and historical contexts to argue that what composition history understands as (or dismisses as) a merely rather homogeneous expressivist genre is, in fact, better understood as a range of active heterogeneous generic approaches of students not only engaged in personal expression, narrowly conceived, but engaged in social, political, and epistemic negotiations through experimentation with genre.

3. That Weathers's book didn't immediately spawn a revolution of experimental writing in composition in the 1980s is interesting. It seems it could have, but speculations about why it didn't change the character of composition might provide some insights. First, as the 1980s dawned, critiques of expressivism and the writing process approach were beginning in earnest, and Weathers's book, with its emphasis on the uniqueness of the individual, smacked of old-school expressivism, with its equation of unique styles with unique individual students. Second, the canon was exploding, and Weathers's preferences for European modernists and white American modernists and writers of the new journalism did not speak strongly enough to the arguments in literary and composition studies for more representation of social diversity. Third, theory was on the rise in composition (imported mostly from literary and cultural studies), and Weathers did not speak the language of high theory, nor did his text hold up particularly well under such theoretical pressure. It was not until the second wave of expressivists of the mid- to late 1990s, still fighting for the individual against dominant academic structures (whether the new emphasis was on the employment of cultural studies theories and rhetorically oriented academic prose in the classroom or on the

dominance of theory in the field of composition), that Weathers was dramatically reclaimed and his project redeployed.

4. Competent writers, according to Weathers, include Walt Whitman, D. H. Lawrence, Gertrude Stein, John Barth, Donald Bartheleme, Richard Brautigan, William Burroughs, William Blake, Emily Dickinson, E. M. Forster, Marianne Moore, John Dos Passos, and Tillie Olsen, to name just a few.

5. Starkey's essay on teaching language poetry to composition students, "Habits of Opposite and Alcove," even argues that expressivist values are evident in "language" poets (127). This position is highly contestable, not least by reference to the work of Charles Bernstein.

6. See, for example, Newkirk, Gradin, and essays by Elbow. Gradin's argument in *Romancing Rhetorics* is representative as she retells histories in order to recover the social and political dimension of romantic rhetorics at the same time that she argues for what she calls "social-expressivism" in composition.

7. Of course, the rise of the personal in writing pedagogy (and not just expressivism per se) has been variously attributed to any or some of the following: the decline of oral rhetoric and its agonistic/antagonistic traditions of public debate; the increase in women attending colleges and universities in the nineteenth century and the formation of more coeducational institutions; the rise of literary studies and the replacement of the study of rhetoric (and logic) by the study of literature, especially in the vernacular; the increase in student population and democratization of universities (e.g., returning G.I.s of the 1950s or open admissions of the 1970s, that is, an increase in underprepared—albeit in different ways—college students); a response to the political and social unrest of the 1960s and 1970s; feminist and multicultural pedagogies that politicize the personal; and a return to the personal through autoethnographies in the context of postmodern pedagogies.

8. Crowley argues that while expressivism and the writing process movement opposed explicitly or tacitly the current-traditionalist approach, current-traditional rhetoric was easily able to accommodate certain process-approach strategies (e.g., multidrafting) since both the writing process approach and current-traditional rhetoric share a conception of the student as humanist subject. Thus, current-traditional rhetoric, affected (perhaps improved) by process approaches and updated through more contemporary theories of social-epistemic pedagogies, continued its dominance in writing instruction (211–13).

9. "A possible technique: students move through an interesting collection of materials (rather than, as usual, a collection of essays)—the course pack then becomes, say, a miscellany of quotations, pictures, poems, advertisements, brief advertisements, brief excerpts from novels, cartoons, crossword puzzles, and many other things—then watching the textual progression that happens (even joining in, as I respond to those *e-pensées* I'm sent)" (Sirc, *English Composition as Happening* 165).

10. "The very distinction between academic writing and expressivist writing is

bogus because both obey the same logic of structure and function; the texts and students in these courses are always in *service to* empty, boring uses—discoveries of authentic voices or (equally mystic) patterns of discursive power" (ibid., 200).

11. "The development of the art market (both of the old 'commission' market and the new market where individual works are bought and sold) furnishes a kind of 'fact' from which it is difficult to infer anything about the developing autonomy of the aesthetic. The process of the growth of the social sphere that we call art, which extended over centuries and was fitful because it was inhibited time and again by counter movements, can hardly be derived from any single cause, even though that cause be of such central importance for society as the market mechanism" (Bürger 38).

12. "For Shelley, the poet is not a relic of the past but a harbinger of the future. In the concluding part of 'The Defence of Poetry,' poets are specifically termed 'heralds,' and their minds are called 'mirrors of futurity.' 'The Poet,' Shelley writes, making a memorable statement, "is the unacknowledged legislator of the world'" (Calinescu 105). Russell (47, 43) is quoting Williams's assessment of romanticism from *Culture and Society*.

2. EXPERIMENTAL WRITING AND THE POLITICS OF ACADEMIC DISCOURSE: COMPOSITION'S INSTITUTIONS

1. "It has been argued that if we could peel away the many layers of discourse manufactured in the academy, we would discover almost all of it to have in common a shared structural foundation: the form of the essay" (Owens, *Resisting Writings* 29).

2. Richard Lanham, construing the teaching of writing in humanist terms, has repeatedly argued against the dominance of orderly rational writing in the teaching of composition, favoring teaching students the play and pleasure of language (see, for example, *Style: Literacy and the Survival of Humanism;* and *The Electronic Word*). More apparently posthumanist arguments against reason can be seen in the work of Gregory Ulmer.

3. See, for example, Bizzell's *Academic Discourse and Critical Consciousness* (125, 139, 145). Though Bizzell has recently expressed some skepticism about the dominance of academic discourse in composition in both her introduction to *Academic Discourse* and in her essays on "mixed" forms of academic discourses (Schroeder, Fox, and Bizzell, *Alt Dis*), these earlier essays about academic discourse represent major lines of argument for proponents of teaching academic discourse in composition.

4. This politics of form is echoed by Bizzell, who revised her earlier arguments about academic discourse (discussed above) in favor of teaching alternative discourses in "The Intellectual Work of 'Mixed' Forms of Academic Discourse." Here, she makes three broad arguments: (1) diversity in discourses is being practiced more frequently by academics and therefore it is important to value and promul-

gate that diversity (a point echoed by Thaiss and Zawacki's study of academics); (2) alternative discourses help teachers of writing to fulfill the 1974 Conference on College Composition and Communication Resolution on Students' Right to Their Own Language; (3) similar to Bridwell-Bowles and others, Bizzell argues that alternative academic discourses allow for a different kind of intellectual work than more traditional academic discourses. Many if not most of the essays in the *Alt Dis* collection, edited by Schroeder, Fox, and Bizzell, argue for alternative discourses that either mix the personal with the academic (this is predominantly what is meant by "mixed" or "hybrid"), or take a more sociolinguistic approach, advocating the use of dialects and cultural knowledges and traditions. Few texts invoke or imitate literary experimentation, usually in the form of collage or meta-texts. Thus, unlike previous arguments for experiments and alternatives, *Alt Dis* maintains its commitment to academic discourse as the production of knowledge, even if what counts as knowledge has been expanded to include emotional or experiential narratives. It does not, by and large, make explicit claims for the role of art or aesthetic experiences or values.

5. One might even argue, as Richard Lanham did back in 1974, that innovative art is most alive in advertising: "We might even find in the full sacramental speech of America—advertising—signs of the play-Spirit. . . . Advertising causes people to mistrust language, but might it not also be teaching people to enjoy it?" (*Style* 129).

6. See, for example, Richard Miller, "Fault Lines in the Contact Zone," which makes many interesting points, among them that writing teachers, while seeing their classrooms as "contact zones," are not particularly prepared to handle the texts students might actually produce: "how little professional training in English Studies prepares teachers to read and respond to the kinds of parodic, critical, oppositional, dismissive, resistant, transgressive, and regressive writing that gets produced by students writing in the contact zone of the classroom" (394). Such a fact might provide some insight into Owens's and others' hesitancy to explore the ideological challenges of teaching experimental writing.

7. There is some argument as to whether or not this quote is attributed to Saint-Simon or Olinde Rodrigues; see, for example, Calinescu, who attributes this work to Rodrigues (101).

8. See Russell's discussion (91) of F. T. Marinetti's "The Founding and Manifesto of Futurism."

9. Russell's extended discussion of the case of Vladimir Mayakovsky is particularly enlightening and representative. Throughout his career, Mayakovsky vacillated between arguing for the freedom of the artist and willingly writing slogans and poems for the Communist Party. With the assertion of social realism as the official aesthetic of the Communist Party, Mayakovsky came under increasing criticism and censorship even though he still wanted his poetry to serve the goals of the party. Interestingly enough, five years after Mayakovsky committed suicide, Stalin designated him a great Russian poet (Russell 183).

10. This may be why Peter Bürger, who focuses on Dadaism throughout his *Theory of the Avant-Garde,* downplays the futuristic tendencies of much avant-garde art.

11. One suspects that the "discipline" referred to here is literary criticism (and not the discipline of composition) because of the effort Ulmer makes to exchange moves of literary criticism (e.g., interpreting Blake's "Tyger") for more creative relationships to literary texts (transforming Blake's "Tyger" by antonymy). Similarly, Robert Scholes, Nancy R. Comley, and Gregory Ulmer will extend this blurring of disciplines in their pedagogical project, *Text Book,* which teaches literature not as criticism but as production through the imitation of experimental texts. I discuss *Text Book* in more detail in chapter 4, and *Heuretics* and *Internet Invention* in chapter 5.

12. Ulmer's figuration of the role of pleasure in writing education is significantly different than that of Richard Lanham, who also advocates a writing pedagogy of play and pleasure. Lanham's project, particularly in *Literacy and the Survival of Humanism* and in *The Electronic Word,* attempted to restore play and pleasure as categories of the human and argued for a version of rhetorical education in which students, through playful and pleasurable writing, could find wholeness and balance in a society fragmented by the division of labor and overdetermined by Aristotelian rationalist discourse. In other words, Lanham's position is comparable to that of Friedrich Schiller in *The Aesthetic Education of Man.*

13. "The function that Walter Ong once attributed to the avant-garde arts— 'a vacation from oppressive rationalism'—may be extended by post(e)pedagogy to the humanities in general in order to meet the needs of students working in the postmodern condition of information overload" (Ulmer, "Textshop for Post(e)-pedagogy" 61).

14. "Avant-garde and experimentalist art (as distinct from modernism) has demystified the artist and dematerialized the art object as part of working through the separation of 'art' from 'craft' or 'skill.' The point of this development is that anyone *can* 'do' art in this experimental sense, in which the only requirement is to actively make something" (Ulmer, "Textshop for Post(e)pedagogy" 57). Ulmer's primary examples of avant-garde artists in this article are Joseph Beuys, Jacques Derrida, and Marcel Duchamp.

15. See, for example, "Never Mind the Tagmemics: Where's the Sex Pistols?" "English Composition as Happening II, Part One," and "What Is Composition . . . ?" After Duchamp (Notes toward a General Teleintertext)," versions of which are included in Sirc's book *English Composition as Happening.*

16. "Our pedagogy is the curatorial, we teach connoisseurship. . . . As instructors, our classroom activities combine the docent's tour (explaining how the great masterpieces are put together) with the hands-on workshop of family day (now that gallery-goers understand how the masterpieces work, they get to try to make one)" (*English Composition as Happening* 267).

17. "Popular culture was accepted uncritically (Leslie Fiedler) and postmodern-

ist experimentation had lost the avantgardist consciousness that social change and the transformation of everyday life were at stake in the every artistic experiment. Rather than aiming at a mediation between art and life, postmodernist experiments soon came to be valued for typically modernist features such as self-reflexivity, immanence, and indeterminacy (Ihab Hassan)" (Huyssen 170).

18. For a brief overview of abolitionist movements in composition, see Connors, "The Abolition Debate in Composition." Connors describes some of the reasons that typify arguments for abolishing composition: "basic literacy should be a prerequisite for college; freshman composition in a semester or a year tries to accomplish the impossible and does not really 'take'; students are ill-motivated; the course is a financial drain on colleges; English teachers would be happier teaching other courses" (55). However, he also briefly acknowledges ideological arguments for abolishing composition such as those articulated by Sharon Crowley in "A Personal Essay on Freshman English." Crowley argues, much as Louis Kampf did in his 1970 address to the Conference on College Composition and Communication, that attempts to reform composition have been and will continue to be unsuccessful as long as composition is still a required undergraduate writing course: "I . . . entertain hope that the cultural and institutional roles played by Freshman English might be interfered with; . . . we might be able to alter the functions of Freshman English by altering its institutional status. In this spirit, I offer a modest proposal. Let's abolish the universal requirement" (170). For a similar take, with a slightly more radical 1970s tone, see Kampf: "Composition courses should be eliminated, not improved: eliminated, because they help support an oppressive system. . . . The skills we teach (and many studies show that it is doubtful whether they are ever learned) serve the needs not of our students, but of the institutions which oppress them. . . . Thus, the most meaningful question is not how we might improve freshmen composition courses, but whether we can change the social context within which they are taught" (248).

19. For example, the sequence found in the fifth edition of *Ways of Reading* includes Susan Griffin's "Our Secret"; Carolyn Steedman, "Exiles"; Paul Auster, "Portrait of an Invisible Man"; and Gloria Anzaldúa, "Entering into the Serpent: How to Tame a Wild Tongue" (Bartholomae and Petrosky 825–31). The sequence offers students the opportunities to write critically and to imitate texts that mix personal and academic writings, collages, writing in fragments, a "mosaic" or "montage" text representing multiple voices and social positions, and so on. The eighth edition renames the sequence "Experiments in Reading and Writing" and moves it out of *Ways of Reading* and into the *Resources for Teaching "Ways of Reading."* In this eighth edition, the sequence includes Susan Griffin, "Our Secret"; Edward Said, "States"; John Edgar Wideman, "Our Time"; Gloria Anzaldúa, "Entering the Serpent: How to Tame a Wild Tongue"; W. G. Sebald, "Rings of Saturn"; and Cornelius Eady, "Brutal Imagination."

3. THE CRISIS OF JUDGMENT IN COMPOSITION: EVALUATING EXPERIMENTAL STUDENT WRITING

1. Chris Anson, "Reflective Reading: Developing Thoughtful Ways to Respond to Students' Writing," identifies some of the factors that might influence a teacher's evaluation of student writing, such as "Institutional Standards," "Personal Belief," "Rhetorical and Situational Goals," and "Reader's Circumstances" (308–16).

2. In perhaps one of the most pointed arguments, Richard Ohmann discusses the ideological limits of emphasizing concrete and specific language in his "Use Definite, Specific, Concrete Language": "the injunctions to use detail, be specific, be concrete . . . push the student writer always toward the language that most nearly reproduces the immediate experience and away from language that might be used to understand it, transform it, and relate it to everything else" (250). Additionally, much of the work by feminists in composition argues that certain principles of good writing, particularly academic writing, are predicated on masculine discourses, for example, aspects of writing described as forceful, direct, powerful, rational.

3. See Lynne, *Coming to Terms;* Huot, *(Re)Articulating Writing Assessment;* and Speck and Jones, "Direction in the Grading of Writing?" for commentary on the confusion over, and conflation of, various terms such as "evaluation," "assessment," "commenting," "responding," and "feedback."

4. See, for example, the opening of chapter 3, "Contingencies of Value," in Herrnstein Smith, *Contingencies of Value* 31–36.

5. Given the number of arguments for experimental or alternative writings in composition, there are very few essays that engage the problem of evaluation by actually quoting from or looking at samples of student writing. In the spirit of addressing this deficiency, I offer readings of three of my students' collages in the next chapter.

6. Speck and Jones conclude that "the literature [on the grading of writing] seems to be saying that grading is subjective, so subjective, in fact, that the same teacher cannot be relied upon to use his or her grading 'standards' uniformly" (18). Notice here how the desire for the uniformity of standards for evaluation (by a department, a university, a field) is paralleled by the desire for "consistency" at the level of the individual. The problem of evaluation can thus be rephrased as a rhetorical question: How can departments or universities hope to maintain evaluative consistency when an individual teacher cannot even be consistent?

7. Rankin admits that her assignment was "a little looser" than usual. The relevant part of her assignment reads as follows: "But it might be that your paper looks very *un*conventional: incomplete, unpolished (at least in terms of thought or argument), full of questions and contradictions. As far as I'm concerned, that's okay too. In fact, it might be preferable in a course like this, in which there is no set material to convey and we're raising more questions than we're answering" (67).

8. Some exceptions include Rankin's student Aaron, who creates a fictional

FBI file on Reed's *Mumbo Jumbo,* and several of Flagg's students who write, variously, a guide for students traveling to Europe on a budget, a guide to getting into medical school, a piece on affirmative action, and a piece on the Crazy Horse memorial (see Flagg, "Why Writers Relish Research"). However, as Flagg admits, much of this writing is actually rather conventional in form, the experiment supposedly having been to allow students to be more flexible regarding their research methods.

9. I'm not sure what can be done about the "schmooze" factor, and sometimes I think that if a teacher asks for these kinds of reflective essays, and a student knows that it contributes significantly to his or her grade, then let the schmoozing begin and may the most savvy schmoozer win. In some ways, though, it does seem a little unfair since we don't explicitly teach schmoozing techniques, and the most accomplished students tend to succeed (because schmoozing has allowed them to succeed in the past, perhaps), while many other students can't schmooze with such sophistication or panache and can find themselves producing clumsy, awkward, forced, and therefore hard to believe testimonials.

10. As Aristotle discusses it in *Nicomachean Ethics,* prudence (also translated as "practical thought" or "practical understanding" or "practical wisdom") is necessary in the face of particulars (6.1143a.25–36). As Terence Irwin summarizes, "For particular circumstances, perception and experience are needed, though some general rules will also help [1109a30, 1126b2, 1164b27, 1165a34]" (327).

4. COLLAGE: PEDAGOGIES, AESTHETICS, AND READING STUDENTS' TEXTS

1. I use the term "textual collages" to differentiate the objects under investigation from visual collages (or multimedia collages that employ both images and written texts) and from electronic collages (hypertexts). Though recent arguments have been made for the use of both types of collage in composition (see, for example, Christopher Schroeder's work with multimedia collages in *ReInventing the University* and Joseph Jarangelo's argument for a poetics of collage for student hypertexts in "Joseph Cornell and the Artistry of Composing Persuasive Hypertext"). It is beyond the scope of this chapter to address at length multimedia collages. The role of avant-garde aesthetics in arguments for new media in composition will be addressed in the following chapter.

2. Since I am commenting on what I'm doing and not doing, I should acknowledge that many of the arguments for collage in composition are written *as* collages (e.g., Elbow, Owens, Gallagher, Nies). I understand this performance as part of the compositionist's attempt to persuade his or her audience that the collage is an intellectually and academically worthy form. However, since the goal of this chapter is not to persuade my reader to teach the collage, I did not write this text in the form of a collage.

3. Peter Elbow's essay is the most recent solidification of his long-standing interest in collage writing techniques. As Elbow explains (authorizes himself) in a

footnote: "I've been writing about the collage for a long time, but I've never made it the center of an essay or chapter till now" ("Your Cheatin' Art" 300).

4. Things Elbow claims are collages or work like collages: some television documentaries (300), television ads (307), call waiting (307), hypertext (307), medieval stained glass windows (303), symphonies, concertos, and suites (303), poetry (303), the Bible (or at least it's paratactic if not a collage; see "Your Cheatin' Art" 305), *Roland Barthes on Roland Barthes* (309), modernist texts, which if not exactly collages are at least discontinuous in a collagelike way and thus lend credence to Elbow's claims for the value of the collage form (308). And if that list isn't diverse and exhaustive enough, Elbow claims that the *mind works like a collage* (308); that life is a collage: "*They told us life was a connected narrative but it feels more like a collage*" (307); and that "*the collage is the universal paradigm for discourse*" (313; emphases mine). Characteristics of collage, besides "cheating": "hodgepodge—completely 'disorganized'—no connectives" (303); consists of "fragments" (301) also called "crots," "blips," "notes," "blocks," and "boxes" (301–3); the order of texts in a collage is more likely "intuitive and associative—maybe even random" (301); collages are built by "the simplest but most effective aesthetic principle: put things together if they 'sort of go'" (307); a good collage has the following characteristics: "some friction, resistance, difference . . . a sense of craft—of an intentional and shaping consciousness . . . resonance across gaps" (307); collages are more dramatic because of the gaps and jumps (309); collages are built on the principle of association—the mind's gift for thinking of things that are *different* and yet *linked*" (311); collages are surprising (both for writers and readers) (311); the collage "is just a bundle of fragments that don't *say* what they are saying . . . it just *presents* material (313)."

5. The attitudes of Marinetti, the Dadaists, and the surrealists toward collage techniques vary. Of the three, the Dadaists embrace the element of chance the most. Both Marinetti and the surrealists have certain "rules" or "guidelines" regarding the construction of verbal collages. In his "Technical Manifesto for Futurism," Marinetti offers all kinds of guidelines including using verbs only in the infinitive form, advocating writing composed primarily of comparisons and analogies (without the use of conjunctions such as "like" "as," and so on) and ultimately destroying syntax and merely scattering nouns (Rainey 123). Similarly, Breton's guidelines for collage suggest that texts may be chosen at random but that syntax must be maintained (Adamowicz 49).

6. "If this were not a collage, I would announce my intention here: to speak back to Elbow's "Collage: Your Cheatin' Art'" (Gallagher 33).

7. Thus the concept of collage (and/or montage) has been invoked, for example, in criticism of Virginia Woolf's *The Waves* and *Mrs. Dalloway,* John Dos Passos's *Manhattan Transfer,* Ishmael Reed's *Mumbo Jumbo,* William Burroughs's *Naked Lunch,* Kathy Acker's *Don Quixote,* and Donald Barthelme's *Snow White.*

8. The subtitle of *Text Book* has undergone a change from the first and second editions to the third. Originally, *Text Book* was subtitled "An Introduction to Literary Language." The subtitle of the third edition is "Writing through Literature."

Though the authors do not remark on the change, one could conjecture that the change is not only a marketing strategy that packages the book for literature classes, literature-composition classes, and first-year composition classes (competing with other reading-based composition textbooks), but also a stronger assertion of the theoretical position of the authors (Scholes, Comley, Ulmer), who are committed to blurring the boundaries between composition and literature and who, by adopting a poststructuralist stance, encourage students to see all writing as texts and all texts as the occasion to produce (analytically and creatively) texts in response.

9. This cut-up poem is not in the Dadaist spirit but in the surrealist spirit: "but remember, this is not a merely random enterprise. You must tease the reader with near approaches to normal syntax and meaning, and surprise the reader by strange deviations from the normal" (Scholes, Comley, and Ulmer 85).

10. See, for example, their assignment for an excerpt from Susan Griffin's "Chorus of Stones" that asks the students to "compose a set of directions that generalizes Griffin's method from her specific materials, that could be used by writers interested in working with their own histories and interests" (Scholes, Comely, and Ulmer 313); or one of their last assignments of the textbook, entitled "Generating a Poetics of Knowledge," which similarly asks students to write generalized instructions (373–74).

11. Cubism ostensibly broke up an image in order to convey multiple perspectives from which that image might be seen, perspectives that could not be realistically simultaneously sustained in time and space (i.e., one cannot see under, behind, in front of, and around an object all at once). The fragments of the image were then assembled into a distorted representation of the object or landscape or person, often so abstract as to be unrecognizable. Beyond the fracturing of an image, Picasso and Braque began modernist collage by gluing materials onto their paintings.

12. As more recent scholarship done by feminists and theorists of popular literacy has shown, the idea and practices of collage were evident in domestic, folk, and popular literacy practices such as quilting, scrapbooking, handcrafting books, keeping albums and commonplace books, and the like. Indeed, in "Recasting the Culture of Ephemera," Todd S. Gernes claims that such prior practices *yielded* modernist collages (109). I have not come across any allusion to this longer folk tradition of collage in arguments for collage in composition.

13. The relationship between visual and verbal arts has a long history in both aesthetic theory and art and literary criticism and is most clearly evidenced in debates around the relationship between poetry and painting. Additionally, critics and theorists of modern literature continue to debate the role of the temporal and the spatial in written texts. Thus, references to texts as collages problematize the temporality of language as well as the spatiality and materiality of text. In practice, both literary and art critics have occasion to contest the easy conflation of the visual and verbal, arguing that such conflation tends to ignore material differences between the two media. It is beyond the scope of this project to mediate these

theoretical debates. However, it is worth noting that the term "collage" in composition studies is predominantly employed figuratively and expansively, including not just the visual and verbal but the sculptural as well. For example, in Joseph Jarangelo's "Joseph Cornell and the Artistry of Composing Persuasive Hypertexts," Jarangelo employs the term "collage" to cover the assemblages of Joseph Cornell (boxes with pictures, texts, and objects glued into them) in order to apply collage principles to the composition of hypertexts.

14. In most stories of the "invention" of the collage, *Fruit Dish and Glass* (1912) by Georges Braque, which pastes the above-mentioned wood grain wallpaper onto a charcoal sketch, is a seminal point of reference.

15. "Thus the basic dichotomy between the two realms is preserved in novels like John Dos Passos' *Manhattan Transfer* . . . where news reports, advertisements, slogans and the legends on billboard signs freely intersect with the narrative. Similarly, in poems written in the 'high' style (Eliot's "Waste Land," for example) the introjection of random bits of colloquial talk and perhaps even snatches of popular ditties . . . might be taken to fall under the heading [of collage]" (Weisstein 135–36).

16. See Taylor, *Aesthetics and Politics*. The debate that is most relevant here is between Lukács and Bloch over the merits of expressionism: "But what if Lukács's reality—a coherent, infinitely mediated totality—is not so objective after all? . . . What if authentic reality is also discontinuity? . . . Any art which strives to exploit the *real* fissures in surface inter-relations and to discover the new in their crevices, appears in his eyes merely as a willful act of destruction. He thereby equates experiment in demolition with a condition of decadence" (Bloch in Taylor 22).

17. This list spans the fourth through sixth editions of *Ways of Reading;* not all readings are in all editions. All quotations are drawn from the fifth edition of *Ways of Reading* (1999), unless otherwise noted.

18. These three approaches to Griffin's text are embedded in assignment sequences in the back of *Ways of Reading*, respectively, "Sequence Eleven: Working with the Past (II)," "Sequence Thirteen: Writing History (II)," "Sequence Five: Experimental Readings and Writings," and "Sequence One: The Aims of Education." The writing assignments, which ask students to read Griffin's methods as history, inform students that Griffin's text is not just writing about the past, but making an argument about the past through "the way she writes" (837). Thus, students are asked to reflect on her methods as argument. Unlike Nies or Scholes, Comley, and Ulmer, Bartholomae and Petrosky do not claim to know the value of Griffin's methods but instead ask students to work that out for themselves.

19. Obviously, like many teaching narratives that are told after the fact, this is not a social scientific account, or even a very journalistic account, of what happened. I did take some rough notes after the classes on Griffin and have endeavored to recall conscientiously what students said and did. It is not the accuracy of detail I am concerned with here, but the spirit of the class and the conversations we had about Griffin and the students' own collages that I am trying to convey in narrative form.

20. The theme of the course to which I refer above had started out as an exploration of the relationship between metaphors and education but had fallen apart by the time we got to Griffin.

5. ART AND TECHNOLOGY: MULTIMODAL COMPOSITION

1. For further discussion of the different connotations of various terms, especially "multimodal" compared to "multimedia," see Lauer's excellent essay. An older, but also extremely helpful, set of essays regarding terminology includes the two introductions (one by Janet Murray and one by Lev Manovich) to *The New Media Reader.*

2. "One might say the following with some confidence. Language-as-speech will remain the major mode of communication; language-as-writing will increasingly be displaced by image in many domains of public communication, though writing will remain the preferred mode of the political and cultural elites. The combined effects on writing of the dominance of the mode of image and of the medium of the screen will produce deep changes in the forms and functions of writing. This in turn will have profound effects on human, cognitive/affective, cultural and bodily engagement with the world, and on the forms and shapes of knowledge. The world told is different to the world shown. . . . It is already clear that the effects of the two changes taken together will have the widest imaginable political, economic, social, cultural, conceptual/cognitive and epistemological consequences" (Kress 1).

3. "I want to foreground a heterogeneous composition studies history, one that sheds light on how cool's impact on communication, or what Diane George and John Trimbur have named the missing 'Fourth C' in composition, needs to be recognized for its rhetorical influence and, specifically, for how it generates a new kind of electronic rhetoric" (Rice 16). Recent arguments in composition about new media or multimodal composition represent a mix of theoretical differences and turf wars. Jeff Rice situates himself in relation to reclamation projects for the fourth C (communication), though the title of his book manages to work "composition," "rhetoric," and "media" into it. Pushed by Douglas Hesse to choose writing or composition, Cynthia Selfe chooses rhetoric as her key term. This exchange begins with Cynthia Selfe's essay, "The Movement of Air." Hesse's response appears in *CCC* 61.3 (February 2010): 602–5, along with Selfe's response to Hesse in the same issue, pages 606–10.

4. I don't want to make an artificial dichotomy between writing and technology, especially as writing is a kind of technology, which has laid claims historically to instrumentalism, art, and progress, among other values. I am, however, aware, as Selfe is, of the specific historicity and materialities of writing as a technology compared to other modes (e.g., speaking, graphic design) or technology (e.g., film, video).

WORKS CITED

Adamowicz, Elza. *Surrealist Collage in Text and Image: Dissecting the Exquisite Corpse*. New York: Cambridge University Press, 1998.

Anson, Chris M. "Reflective Reading: Developing Thoughtful Ways to Respond to Students' Writing." *Evaluating Writing: The Role of Teachers' Knowledge about Text, Learning, and Culture*. Ed. Charles R. Cooper and Lee Odell. Urbana, IL: National Council of Teachers of English, 1999.

Aristotle. *Nicomachean Ethics*. Trans. Terence Irwin. Indianapolis, IN: Hackett, 1985.

———. *The Rhetoric and the Poetics of Aristotle*. Trans. W. Rhys Roberts [*The Rhetoric*] and Ingram Bywater [*The Poetics*]. Intro. Friedrich Solmsen. New York: Modern Library, 1954.

Bartholomae, David. "What Is Composition and (If You Know What that Is) Why Do We Teach It?" *Composition for the Twenty-First Century*. Ed. Lynn Z. Bloom, Donald A. Daiker, and Edward M. White. Carbondale, IL: Southern Illinois University Press, 1996. 47–63.

Bartholomae, David, and Anthony Petrosky. *Ways of Reading: An Anthology for Writers*. 5th ed. New York: Bedford/St. Martin's, 1999.

Berlin, James. *Rhetoric and Reality: Writing Instruction in American Colleges, 1900–1985*. Carbondale: Southern Illinois University Press, 1987.

Bernstein, Charles. *A Poetics*. Cambridge, MA: Harvard University Press, 1992.

Bishop, Wendy. "Alternate Styles for Who, What, Why? Some Introductions to *Elements of Alternate Style: Essays on Writing and Revision*. *Elements of Alternate Style: Essays on Writing and Revision*. Ed. Wendy Bishop. Portsmouth, NH: Boynton/Cook, 1997.

———, ed. *Elements of Alternate Style: Essays on Writing and Revision*. Portsmouth, NH: Boynton/Cook, 1997.

———. "Responding to, Evaluating, and Grading Alternate Style." *Elements of Alternate Style: Essays on Writing and Revision*. Ed. Wendy Bishop. Portsmouth, NH: Boynton/Cook, 1997.

Bizzell, Patricia. *Academic Discourse and Critical Consciousness*. Pittsburgh: University of Pittsburgh Press, 1992.

———. "The Intellectual Work of 'Mixed' Forms of Academic Discourse." *Alt Dis: Alternative Discourses and the Academy*. Ed. Christopher Schroeder, Helen Fox, and Patricia Bizzell. Portsmouth, NH: Boynton/Cook/Heinemann, 2002. 1–10.

Bizzell, Patricia, Peter Elbow, Jacqueline Jones-Royster, and Victor Villanueva. "The Future of College Composition: Impacts of Alternative Discourses on Standard English." Conference on College Composition and Communication, Denver, 2001.

Bizzell, Patricia, and Bruce Herzberg. Review of *What Makes Writing Good*. Ed. William Coles Jr. and James Vopat. *College Composition and Communication* 37 (1986): 244–47.

Bloom, Lynn. *Composition Studies as a Creative Art: Teaching, Writing, Scholarship, Administration*. Logan: Utah State University Press, 1998.

Borton, Sonya C., and Brian Huot. "Responding and Assessing." *Multimodal Composition: Resources for Teachers*. Ed. Cynthia Selfe. Cresskill, NJ: Hampton Press, 2007.

Bridwell-Bowles, Lillian. "Discourse and Diversity: Experimental Writing within the Academy." *College Composition and Communication* 43.3 (Oct. 1992): 349–68.

———. "Freedom, Form, Function: Varieties of Academic Prose." *College Composition and Communication* 46.1 (Feb. 1995): 46–61.

Brockelman, Thomas. *The Frame and the Mirror: On Collage and the Postmodern*. Evanston, IL: Northwestern University Press, 2001.

Brodkey, Linda. "Making a Federal Case Out of Difference: The Politics of Pedagogy, Publicity, and Postponement." *Writing Theory and Critical Theory*. Ed. John Clifford and John Schilb. New York: MLA, 1994.

Bürger, Peter. *Theory of the Avant-Garde*. Trans. Michael Shaw. Foreword by Jochen Schulte-Sasse. Minneapolis: University of Minnesota Press, 1984.

Burnham, Christopher. "Expressive Pedagogy: Practice/Theory, Theory/Practice." *A Guide to Composition Pedagogies*. Ed. Gary Tate, Amy Rupiper, and Kurt Schick. New York: Oxford University Press, 2001.

Butler, Paul. *Out of Style: Reanimating Stylistic Study in Composition and Rhetoric*. Logan: Utah State University Press, 2008.

Calinescu, Matei. *Five Faces of Modernity: Modernism, Avant-Garde, Decadence, Kitsch, Postmodernism*. Durham, NC: Duke University Press, 1987.

Chamberlain, Lori. "Bombs and Other Exciting Devices, or the Problem of Teaching Irony." In *Reclaiming Pedagogy: The Rhetoric of the Classroom*. Ed. Patricia Donahue and Ellen Quandahl. Carbondale: Southern Illinois University Press, 1989.

Clifford, John. "The Subject of Discourse." *Contending with Words: Composition and Rhetoric in a Postmodern Age*. Ed. Patricia Harkin and John Schilb. New York: Modern Language Association of America, 1991. 38–51.

Coles, William E., Jr. *The Plural I—and After*. Portsmouth, NH: Boynton/Cook/ Heineman, 1988.

Coles, William E., Jr., and James Vopat, eds. *What Makes Writing Good: A Multiperspective*. Lexington, MA: D. C. Heath, 1985.

Connors, Robert. "The Abolition Debate in Composition: A Short History." *Composition in the Twenty-First Century: Crisis and Change*. Ed. Lynn Z. Bloom, Donald A. Daiker, and Edward M. White. Carbondale: Southern Illinois University Press, 1996. 47–63.

Crowley, Sharon. *Composition in the University: Historical and Polemical Essays*. Pittsburgh: University of Pittsburgh Press, 1998.

DePeter, Ronald D. "Fractured Narratives: Explorations in Style." *Elements of Alternate Style: Essays on Writing and Revision*. Ed. Wendy Bishop. Portsmouth, NH: Boynton/Cook, 1997.

Dobrin, Sydney I. "A Problem with Writing (about) 'Alternative' Discourse." *Alt Dis: Alternative Discourses and the Academy*. Ed. Christopher Schroeder, Helen Fox, and Patricia Bizzell. Portsmouth, NH: Boynton/Cook/Heinemann, 2002. 45–56.

Elbow, Peter. "Ranking, Evaluating, and Liking: Sorting Out Three Forms of Judgment." *College English* 55.2 (Feb. 1993).

———. "Your Cheatin' Art: A Collage." *Everyone Can Write: Essays Toward a Hopeful Theory of Writing and Teaching Writing*. New York: Oxford University Press, 2000.

Elliott, Emory, Louis Freitas Caton, and Jeffrey Rhyne. *Aesthetics in a Multicultural Age*. New York: Oxford University Press, 2002.

Enzensberger, Hans Magnus. "The Aporias of the Avant-Garde." *The Consciousness Industry: On Literature, Politics, and the Media*. New York: Seabury Press, 1974.

Faigley, Lester. *Fragments of Rationality: Postmodernity and the Subject of Composition*. Pittsburgh: University of Pittsburgh Press, 1992.

Fike, Darrell, and Devan Cook. "'Would You Like Fries with That?': Ordering Up

Some Writing: Fast Food for Thought." *Elements of Alternate Style: Essays on Writing and Revision.* Ed. Wendy Bishop. Portsmouth, NH: Boynton/Cook, 1997.

Flagg, Amy Cushette. "Why Writers Relish Research: Alternative Writing Projects." *Elements of Alternate Style: Essays on Writing and Revision.* Ed. Wendy Bishop. Portsmouth, NH: Boynton/Cook, 1997.

Flannery, Kathryn. *The Emperor's New Clothes: Literature, Literacy, and the Ideology of Style.* Pittsburgh: University of Pittsburgh Press, 1996.

Fontaine, Sheryl I., and Francine Quaas. "Transforming Connections and Building Bridges: Assigning, Reading, and Evaluating the Collage Essay." *Teaching Writing Creatively.* Ed. David Starkey. Portsmouth, NH: Boynton/Cook, 1998.

Gallagher, Chris. "If This Were Not a Collage: A Collage." *Writing on the Edge* 11.2: 33–42.

Gernes, Todd S. "Recasting the Culture of Ephemera." *Popular Literacy: Studies in Cultural Practices and Poetics.* Ed. John Trimbur. Pittsburgh: University of Pittsburgh Press, 2001. 107–27.

Gradin, Sherrie L. *Romancing Rhetorics: Social Expressivist Perspectives on the Teaching of Writing.* Portsmouth, NH: Boynton/Cook/Heinemann, 1995.

Greenberg, Clement. "Avant-Garde and Kitsch." *Art and Culture: Critical Essays.* Boston: Beacon Press, 1961.

Griffin, Susan. *A Chorus of Stones: The Private Life of War.* London: Women's Press, 1994.

Guillory, John. *Cultural Capital: The Problem of Literary Canon Formation.* Chicago: University of Chicago Press, 1993.

Haake, Katherine. "Teaching Creative Writing, If the Shoe Fits." *Colors of a Different Horse: Rethinking Creative Writing Theory and Pedagogy.* Ed. Wendy Bishop and Hans Ostrom. Urbana, IL: National Council of Teachers of English, 1994.

Habermas, Jürgen. "Modernity—An Incomplete Project." *The Anti-Aesthetic: Essays on Postmodern Culture.* Ed. Hal Foster. Seattle: Bay Press, 1983.

Hadjinicolaou, Nicos. "On the Ideology of Avant-Gardism." *Praxis* 6 (1982): 39–70.

Hardin, Joe Marshall. *Opening Spaces: Critical Pedagogy and Resistance Theory in Composition.* Albany, NY: State University of New York Press, 2001.

Hawk, Byron. *A Counter-History of Composition: Toward Methodolgies of Complexity.* Pittsburgh: University of Pittsburgh Press, 2007.

Heller, Scott. "Wearying of Cultural Studies, Some Scholars Rediscover Beauty." *Chronicle of Higher Education* 45.15 (Dec. 4, 1998): A15.

Herrnstein Smith, Barbara. *Contingencies of Value: Alternative Perspectives for Critical Theory.* Cambridge, MA: Harvard University Press, 1988.

Hesse, Doug. "Response to Cynthia L. Selfe's 'The Movement of Air, the Breath of Meaning': Aurality and Multimodal Composing." *College Composition and Communication* 61.3 (2010): 602–5.

Hewitt, Andrew. *Fascist Modernism: Aesthetics, Politics, and the Avant-Garde.* Stanford, CA: Stanford University Press, 1993.

Horner, Bruce. *Terms for Work in Composition: A Materialist Critique.* Albany: State University of New York Press, 2000.

Huot, Brian. *(Re)Articulating Writing Assessment.* Logan: Utah State University Press, 2002.

Huyssen, Andreas. *After the Great Divide: Modernism, Mass Culture, Postmodernism.* Bloomington: Indiana University Press, 1968.

Jameson, Fredric. *Postmodernism, or, the Cultural Logic of Late Capitalism.* Durham, NC: Duke University Press, 1997.

Jarangelo, Joseph. "Joseph Cornell and the Artistry of Composing Persuasive Hypertexts." *College Composition and Communication* 49.1 (Feb. 1998): 24–44.

Kampf, Louis. "Must We Have a Cultural Revolution?" *College Composition and Communication* 21.3 (Oct. 1970): 245–49.

Kant, Immanuel. *The Critique of Judgment.* Trans. James Creed Meredith. New York: Clarendon Press/Oxford University Press, 1952.

Kress, Gunther. *Literacy in the New Media Age.* New York: Routledge, 2003.

Lanham, Richard. *The Electronic Word: Democracy, Technology and the Arts.* Chicago: University of Chicago Press, 1993.

———. *Literacy and the Survival of Humanism.* New Haven: Yale University Press, 1983.

———. *Style: An Anti-Textbook.* New Haven: Yale University Press, 1974.

Lauer, Claire. "Contending with Terms: 'Multimodal' and 'Multimedia' in the Academic and Public Spheres." *Computers and Composition* 26.4 (Dec. 2009): 225–39.

Levine, George. *Aesthetics and Ideology.* New Brunswick, NJ: Rutgers University Press, 1994.

Lindemann, Erika. "Freshman Composition: No Place for Literature." *College English* 55.3 (Mar. 1993): 311–16.

Loftus, Bernadette. "Jocks Are from Earth, Oddballs Are from Venus." Unpublished, University of Pittsburgh, 1999 (used with permission).

Lu, Min-Zhan. "Professing Multiculturalism: The Politics of Style in the Contact Zone." *College Composition and Communication* 45.4 (Dec.1994): 442–58.

Lynne, Patricia. *Coming to Terms.* Logan: Utah University Press, 2004.

Lyotard, Jean-François. *The Differend: Phrases in Dispute.* Minneapolis: University of Minnesota Press, 1988.

———. *Lessons on the Analytic of the Sublime.* Trans. Elizabeth Rottenberg. Stanford, CA: Stanford University Press, 1994.

———. "The Sublime and the Avant-Garde." *The Inhuman: Reflections on Time.* Trans. Geoffrey Bennington and Rachel Bowlby. Cambridge: Polity Press/ Blackwell, 1988.

Lyotard, Jean-François, and Jean-Loup Thébaud. *Just Gaming.* Trans. Wlad Godzich. Minneapolis: University of Minnesota Press, 1985.

Macrorie, Ken. *Telling Writing.* New York: Hayden Book Co., 1970.

Mann, Paul. *The Theory-Death of the Avant-Garde.* Bloomington: Indiana University Press, 1991.

Manovich, Lev. "New Media from Borges to HTML." *The New Media Reader.* Ed. Noah Wardrip-Fruin and Nick Montfort. Cambridge, MA: MIT Press, 2003.

Marcuse, Herbert. "The Affirmative Character of Culture." *Negation: Essays in Critical Theory.* Trans. J. Shapiro. Boston: Beacon, 1968. 88–133.

Mayers, Tim. *(Re)Writing Craft: Composition, Creative Writing, and the Future of English Studies.* Pittsburgh: University of Pittsburgh Press, 2005.

Miller, Richard E. "Fault Lines in the Contact Zone." *College English* 56.4 (Apr. 1994): 389–408.

Mirtz, Ruth. "'You Want Us to Do *What?*' How to Get the Most Out of Unexpected Writing Assignments." *Elements of Alternate Style: Essays on Writing and Revision.* Ed. Wendy Bishop. Portsmouth, NH: Boynton/Cook, 1997.

Monroe, Jonathan. "Poetry, the University, and the Culture of Distraction." *Diacritics* 26.3–4 (Fall–Winter 1996): 3–30.

Murphy, Richard. *Theorizing the Avant-Garde: Modernism, Expressionism, and the Problem of Postmodernity.* New York: Cambridge University Press, 1999.

Murray, Janet. "Inventing the Medium." *The New Media Reader.* Ed. Noah Wardrip-Fruin and Nick Montfort. Cambridge, MA: MIT Press, 2003.

Newkirk, Thomas. *The Performance of Self in Student Writing.* Portsmouth, NH: Boynton/Cook/Heinemann, 1997.

Nies, Betsy. "Writing History through Collage: Using Crots in the First-Year Research Paper." *Dialogue: A Journal for Writing Specialists* 7.1 (2000): 22–35.

Ohmann, Richard. "Use Definite, Specific, Concrete Language." *Poetics of Letters.* Middletown, CT: Wesleyan University Press, 1987.

Owens, Derek. "The Aggregate Eye/A Rhetoric of Collage." *Readerly/Writerly Texts* 4.1 (Fall/Winter 1996): 9–30.

———. *Resisting Writings (and the Boundaries of Composition).* Dallas: Southern Methodist University Press, 1994.

Oxford Concise English Dictionary of Current English. Ed. J. B. Sykes. New York: Oxford University Press, 1976.

Perloff, Marjorie. "The Invention of Collage." *Collage.* Ed. Jeanine Parisier Plottel. New York: New York Literary Forum, 1983

———. *Radical Artifice: Writing Poetry in the Age of Media.* Chicago: University of Chicago Press, 1991.

———. *21st-Century Modernism: The 'New' Poetics.* Malden, MA: Blackwell, 2002.

Polkinhorn, Harry. "Space Craft: Collage Discourse." *Collage: Critical Views.* Ed. Katherine Hoffman. Ann Arbor, MI: UMI Research Press, 1989.

Portis, Anthony. "Racism." Unpublished, University of Pittsburgh, 1999 (used with permission).

Raaberg, Gwen. "Beyond Fragmentation: Collage as Feminist Strategy in the Arts." *Mosaic* 31.3 (Sept. 1998): 153–71.

Rainey, Lawrence. "Taking Dictation: Collage Poetics, Pathology, and Politics." *Modernism/Modernity* 5.2 (1998): 123–53.

Rankin, Elizabeth. "It's Not Mumbo Jumbo: Taking Risks with Academic Writing." *Elements of Alternate Style: Essays on Writing and Revision.* Ed. Wendy Bishop. Portsmouth, NH: Boynton/Cook, 1997.

Rice, Jeff. *The Rhetoric of Cool: Composition Studies and New Media.* Carbondale: Southern Illinois University Press, 2007.

Rodriguez, Cecilia. "Truth and Reconciliation." Unpublished, University of Pittsburgh, 1999 (used with permission).

Rose, Mike. "Remedial Writing Courses: A Critique and a Proposal." *The Writing Teacher's Sourcebook.* Ed. Edward P. J. Corbett, Nancy Myers, and Gary Tate. New York: Oxford University Press, 2000. 193–215.

Russell, Charles. *Poets, Prophets, and Revolutionaries: The Literary Avant-Garde from Rimbaud through Postmodernism.* New York: Oxford University Press, 1985.

Sayre, Henry M. *The Object of Performance: The American Avant-Garde since 1970.* Chicago: University of Chicago Press, 1989.

Schapiro, Miriam. "Femmage." *Collage: Critical Views.* Ed. Katherine Hoffman. Ann Arbor: UMI Research Press, 1989. 295–315.

Schiller, Friedrich. *On the Aesthetic Education of Man in a Series of Letters.* Ed., trans., with an introduction, commentary, and glossary of terms by Elizabeth M. Wilkinson and L. A. Willoughby. Oxford: Clarendon Press, 1968.

Scholes, Robert. *Textual Power: Literary Theory and the Teaching of English.* New Haven, CT: Yale University Press, 1986.

Scholes, Robert, Nancy R. Comley, and Gregory L. Ulmer. *Text Book: Writing through Literature.* 3rd ed. New York: Bedford/St. Martin's Press, 2002.

Schroeder, Christopher. *ReInventing the University: Literacies and Legitimacy in the University.* Logan, UT: Utah University Press, 2001.

Schroeder, Christopher, Helen Fox, and Patricia Bizzell. *Alt Dis: Alternative Discourses and the Academy.* Portsmouth, NH: Boynton/Cook/Heinemann, 2002.

Schulte-Sasse, Jochen. "Foreword: Theory of Modernism versus Theory of the Avant-Garde." In Peter Bürger, *Theory of the Avant-Garde.* Trans. Michael Shaw. Minneapolis: University of Minnesota Press, 1984. vii–lv.

Selfe, Cynthia. "The Movement of Air, the Breath of Meaning: Aurality and Multimodal Composition." *College Composition and Communication* 60.4 (June 2009): 616–63.

———, ed. *Multimodal Composition: Resources for Teachers.* Cresskill, NJ: Hampton Press, 2007.

Shaughnessy, Mina P. *Errors and Expectations: A Guide for the Teacher of Basic Writing.* New York: Oxford University Press, 1977.

Shipka, Jody. *Toward a Composition Made Whole.* Pittsburgh: University of Pittsburgh Press, 2011.

Sirc, Geoffrey. *English Composition as Happening.* Logan: Utah State University Press, 2002.

———. "English Composition as Happening II, Part One." *Pre/Text* 15.3–4 (1994): 264–93.

———. "Never Mind the Tagmemics, Where's the Sex Pistols?" *College Composition and Communication* 48.1 (1997): 9–29.

———. "What Is Composition . . . ? After Duchamp (Notes toward a General Teleintertext)." *Passions, Pedagogies, and Twenty-First Century Technologies.* Ed. Gail Hawisher and Cynthia Self. Urbana, IL: NCTE, 1999.

Speck, Bruce W., and Tammy R. Jones. "Direction in the Grading of Writing? What the Literature on the Grading of Writing Does and Doesn't Tell Us." *The Theory and Practice of Grading Writing: Problems and Possibilities.* Ed. Frances Zak and Christopher C. Weaver. Albany: State University of New York Press, 1998.

Starkey, David, ed. *Teaching Writing Creatively.* Portsmouth, NH: Boynton/Cook, 1998.

"Students' Right to Their Own Language." *College Composition and Communication* 25.3 (Sept. 1974): 1–18.

Tate, Gary. "A Place for Literature in Freshman Composition." *College English* 55.3 (Mar. 1993): 317–21.

Taylor, Ronald, ed. and trans. *Aesthetics and Politics: Debates between Ernst Bloch, Georg Lukács, Bertolt Brecht, Walter Benjamin, and Theodor Adorno.* London: New Left Books, 1977.

Thaiss, Chris, and Terry Myers Zawacki. *Engaged Writers, Dynamic Disciplines: Research on the Academic Writing Life.* Portsmouth, NH: Boynton/Cook, 2006.

Tobin, Lad. "The Case for Double-Voiced Discourse." *Elements of Alternate Style: Essays on Writing and Revision.* Ed. Wendy Bishop. Portsmouth, NH: Boynton/Cook, 1997.

———. *Taking Stock: The Writing Process Movement in the 90s.* Ed. Lad Tobin and Thomas Newkirk. Portsmouth, NH: Boynton/Cook, 1994.

Tzara, Tristan. *Seven Dada Manifestos and Lampisteries.* Trans. Barbara Wright. London: Calder, 1977.

Ulmer, Gregory. *Applied Grammatology: Post(e)-Pedagogy from Jacques Derrida to Joseph Beuys.* Baltimore: Johns Hopkins University Press, 1985.

———. *Heuretics: The Logic of Invention.* Baltimore: Johns Hopkins University Press, 1994.

———. *Internet Invention: From Literacy to Electracy.* New York: Longman, 2003.

———. "The Object of Post-Criticism." *The Anti-Aesthetic: Essays on Postmodern Culture.* Ed. Hal Foster. Seattle, WA: Bay Press, 1983.

———. *Teletheory.* New York: Routledge, 1989.

———. "Textshop for Post(e)pedagogy." *Writing and Reading Differently: Deconstruction and the Teaching of Composition and Literature.* Ed. Douglas G. Atkins and Michael L. Johnson. Lawrence: University Press of Kansas, 1985.

Warnick, Chris. "Student Writing, Politics, and Style, 1962–1979." Dissertation, University of Pittsburgh, 2006.

Weathers, Winston. *An Alternate Style: Options in Composition.* Rochelle Park, NJ: Hayden, 1980.

———. "Teaching Style: A Possible Anatomy." *The Writing Teacher's Sourcebook.* Ed. Edward P. J. Corbett, Nancy Myers, and Gary Tate. New York: Oxford University Press, 2000.

Weber, Samuel. "The Foundering of Aesthetics: Thoughts on the Current State of Comparative Literature." *The Comparative Perspective in Literature.* Ed. Clayton Koelb and Susan Noakes. Ithaca, NY: Cornell University Press, 1988.

———. "The Unraveling of Form." *Mass Mediuras: Form, Technics, Media.* Ed. Alan Cholodenko. Stanford, CA: Stanford University Press, 1996.

Weisstein, Ulrich. "Collage, Montage, and Related Terms: Their Literal and Figurative Use in and Application to Techniques and Forms in Various Arts." *Comparative Literature Studies* 5.15.1 (Mar. 1978): 124–39.

Wysocki, Anne, et al. *Writing New Media: Theory and Applications for Expanding the Teaching of Composition.* Logan: Utah State University Press, 2004.

Yancey, Kathleen Blake. "Dialogue, Interplay, and Discovery: Mapping the Role and the Rhetoric of Reflection in Portfolio Assessment." *Writing Portfolios in the Classroom: Policy and Practice, Promise and Peril.* Ed. Robert Calfee and Pam Perfumo. Mahwah, NJ: Lawrence Erlbaum, 1996.

INDEX